MORAL EDUCATION
IN ARISTOTLE

Gerard Verbeke

MORAL EDUCATION
IN ARISTOTLE

The Catholic University of America Press
Washington, D.C.

Copyright © 1990
The Catholic University of America Press
All rights reserved
Printed in the United States of America

LIBRARY OF CONGRESS CATALOGING-IN-PUBLICATION DATA
Verbeke, Gerard.
 Moral education in Aristotle / Gerard Verbeke.
  p.   cm.
 Includes bibliographical references.
 ISBN 0-8132-0717-7 (alk. paper)
 1. Moral education. 2. Aristotle—Ethics. I. Title.
LC283.V48 1990   89-38380
370.11'4—dc20

CONTENTS

PREFACE

In his drama *Troilus and Cressida* Shakespeare refers to Aristotle's teaching on moral education. In a discussion with Paris and Troilus, his brothers, Hector states that he cannot fully agree with their viewpoint: in his opinion it is contrary to moral laws to keep Helen at Troy instead of returning her to her husband, the king of Sparta. Hector declares the considerations of his brothers to be superficial and influenced by passion:

> Paris and Troilus, you have both said well;
> And in the cause and question now in hand
> Have gloz'd but superficially; not much
> Unlike young men, whom Aristotle thought
> Unfit to hear moral philosophy.

The moral judgment of Hector is more balanced and does not yield to irrational movements and emotional inclinations:

> For pleasure and revenge
> Have ears more deaf than adders to the voice
> Of any true decision.

Finally, however, Hector is willing to keep Helen at Troy and to defend her against the Greeks for reasons of dignity:

> For 't is a cause that hath no mean dependance
> Upon our joint and several dignities.[1]

If Aristotle had to assess Hector's judgment he probably would agree on the first part, but not on the second: it is not likely that he would accept that important moral laws be infringed in order to preserve what is regarded as personal dignity. Hector does not

---

1. *Troilus and Cressida*, II, 2, v. 163–193.

approve of the rape of Helen, yet he believes that it would be dishonoring for the royal family to acknowledge the fault of Paris and to return Helen to Sparta.

In any case, the reference of Shakespeare to Aristotle is right: at the beginning of the *Nicomachean Ethics,* the Greek Master declares that young people are unfit to attend lectures on moral philosophy, because in their case the intended knowledge will be useless.[2] They are in the same condition as incontinent people: assimilation of moral knowledge will not change their conduct. Incontinent individuals know what is right, and yet they do not do it: there is a gap between their knowledge and their behavior. With respect to agents whose inclinations conform to reason and who act accordingly, it is very fruitful to be taught on moral issues. But why are youths so unfit to attend ethical lectures? The author mainly indicates two reasons. Young people have no experience of moral conduct in the various circumstances of life.[3] They are not responsible for this lack: because of their age they cannot possess the experience that is needed. In Aristotle's view this factor is indispensable: in ethical matters arguments are not merely theoretical and speculative; they largely proceed from a concrete insight into human behavior.[4] Moreover, young people predominantly follow their emotional inclinations and are still dominated by their passions: in their case moral teaching cannot be fruitful, since the goal that is intended is not knowledge but action. In fact, it makes no difference whether somebody be young in age or in character. What matters is that people who live according to their passions are unsuited to attend lectures on moral philosophy.[5]

At first glance this viewpoint is paradoxical: young people who have little experience of ethical practice and who generally live under the impact of emotional propensities badly need moral education. How could they ever become virtuous individuals without an adequate preparation and training? Aristotle would certainly agree on the necessity of moral education; what he actually wants to stress is the insufficiency of learning, particularly in the case of young people.

2. *Nicomachean Ethics (Eth. Nic.),* I, 3, 1095a2–3.
3. *Eth. Nic.,* I, 3, 1095a3–4.
4. *Eth. Nic.,* I, 3, 1095a3–4: arguments in moral philosophy not only deal with practical matters (περὶ τούτων) but proceed from experience of ethical behavior (ἐκ τούτων).
5. *Eth. Nic.,* I, 3, 1095a4–8.

Of course, one could object that people who already have experience of moral conduct and who are not dominated by their passions do not need more ethical education. Yet what is at issue in Aristotle is to specify who are appropriate hearers of lectures on ethical subjects. Since this matter is not merely theoretical and speculative, it is indispensable to have some experience of moral conduct and some control over irrational tendencies, if one wants to receive such teaching fruitfully. This viewpoint of Aristotle's is closely connected with his interpretation of ethical wisdom and his criticism of Socrates' intellectualism.[6]

The occasion giving rise to this book, *Moral Education in Aristotle,* was a series of lectures I delivered in Italy (Catania) in 1987. I decided to treat this topic because it is a central issue in Aristotelian ethics, still relevant in the present time, but also because most of the students attending my lectures were interested in education problems. In Aristotle's view humans are by nature moral beings: they are endowed with a spontaneous sense of ethical values; they are naturally inclined to meet each other and to live together in smaller or larger communities; they establish political societies governed by laws that are the expression of common moral intuitions. Nevertheless the Greek Master is also persuaded that ethical education is indispensable. The natural equipment of human beings is to be developed and promoted through learning and training. When Aristotle describes the actual moral situation of average people in his time, his picture is rather negative and pessimistic. In spite of the natural inclination of humans toward ethical life, people ought to be educated in order to reach moral harmony and happiness.

As to the problems of our own time, one may wonder whether the teaching of a philosopher who lived in the fourth century B.C. is still relevant. It is true the social and cultural context in which Aristotle lived was different from our own situation, yet basic moral issues are not linked to a particular period: they are always to be

6. In a recent book entitled *Aristote aujourd'hui* and published by UNESCO, Charles Hummel points to the central place of education in Aristotle's life: "Pourtant, Aristote s'est consacré autant à l'enseignement qu'à la recherche. Il est le prototype du "professor." La partie de son oeuvre qui nous est transmise à travers vingt-trois siècles est son oeuvre enseignée, ce sont ses cours. Le souci pédagogique, la dimension éducative y sont partout présents" (*Aristote aujourd'hui,* sous la direction de M. A. Sinaceur à l'occasion du 2300ᵉ anniversaire de la mort du philosophe, Paris, 1988, p.136).

faced; they have a perennial character. Moreover, Aristotle is one of the most influential ancestors of Western thought, especially in the field of science and philosophy. His works have been translated into Latin and Arabic: they were carefully studied in medieval Western universities as they were in Alexandria and Byzantium. It is always beneficial to return to the roots of Western philosophy and to question an outstanding Master such as Aristotle on a topic with which he was deeply concerned during his whole life, moral education.

I hope that the following reflections will contribute to clarifying Aristotle's views on this matter and also help in promoting an appropriate moral education in our time.

MORAL EDUCATION
IN ARISTOTLE

[1]

EDUCATION IN ARISTOTLE

I N A little essay, *The Education of Children,* attributed to Plutarch and rather popular in the Renaissance period,[1] the
author writes: "Of all things that are in us, education only is
immortal and divine."[2] The exceptional value of education could
hardly be emphasized more strongly, yet the meaning of this statement must be carefully examined. What is obviously intended is not
the training of the body, nor the acquisition of some particular
skills, but the education of the mind, the highest component of a
human being: this constituent is considered to be immortal and
divine.[3]

The author agrees that at least some training in the liberal arts is
advisable; it may be achieved through hearing and observation,
through attendance at lectures and through personal experience.
This pattern of education, however, is considered to be less impor-

1. The *De liberis educandis* is no longer considered to be an authentic work of
Plutarch; cf. K. Ziegler, *Plutarchos von Chaironeia.* Stuttgart, 1949, p.174: the author
mainly relies on research done by Wyttenbach, who points not only to the content
of the work but also to some stylistic and grammatical-linguistic characteristics. The
author believes that nobody who is acquainted with Plutarch could question the
inauthentic character of this writing.

2. *De liberis educandis,* 5, p.5c. It is not easy to translate adequately: τῶν ἐν ἡμῖν.
I cannot agree with the version given by F. Cole Babbitt: "of all things in this world"
(*Plutarch's Moralia,* vol. I, London-Cambridge, 1960, p.25). What Plutarch has in
mind is the various constituents of human beings. Of all the components mind is
the most worthy, and since education aims at the development of the mind, it ought
to be put on the same level.

3. The author mentions two elements regarded as supreme: mind (νοῦς) and
reason (λόγος); the mind is invested with authority over reason, whereas reason is
the servant of the mind. This hierarchy corresponds to the teaching of both Plato
and Aristotle. (Plato, *Phaedo* 97c; *Philebus* 28c: the mind is maker and king of
everything; in Aristotle's view the νοῦς deals with the basic principles of our knowledge; cf. *Eth. Nic.,* VI,6,1151a7).

tant. It should not be pursued too far; some taste of this kind of knowing is believed to be sufficient; it is not yet true education, but only a preparatory stage.[4]

The program of the liberal arts gradually developed from the teaching of the Sophists to the medieval trivium and quadrivium.[5] It concentrated on the one hand on writing, arguing, and speaking; on the other, it dealt with some mathematical branches of learning (arithmetic, geometry, astronomy, and music). Such a program is actually very limited: in the area of humanities there is no formal study of history, no geography, no interest in foreign languages, whereas in the field of sciences, no time is dedicated to the study of physics, chemistry, or biology.[6] The horizon of the program was rather narrow; it was intended to educate people in order that they might play some part in political life; therefore, they had to possess the capacity of developing arguments in public meetings and the art of persuading their fellow-citizens. Moreover, they needed some deeper understanding of the world in which they lived; the key to this insight was believed to be mathematical knowledge. Pythagoras had taught that numbers are the essence of everything.[7] This idea

4. The author deals with what is called general education: τῶν καλουμένων ἐγκυκλίων παιδευμάτων. A freeborn child should have some knowledge of the branches included in this program: however, the child should not devote too much time to them. He should learn them only incidentally, to get some taste of them; this restriction is motivated by the rule that as much time as possible should be dedicated to the study of philosophy. The other branches have no special value (*De liberis educandis*, 10, p.7c–d).

5. Cf. L. M. de Rijk, Ἐγκύκλιος παιδεία: *A study of Its Original Meaning*, in: *Vivarium*, III,1 (1965), p.24–93. The author writes (p.92): "From the first century, B.C. onwards the term ἐγκύκλιος παιδεία re-introduced by Neopythagoreanism, is used in order to denote the new ideal of *all-round* education preparatory to any specialistic training (especially to that of the future orator). From then on the ἐγκύκλια μαθήματα are the constitutive parts of ἐγκύκλιος παιδεία which is the whole circuit (κύκλος) of both the arts of literary culture and the mathematical sciences."

6. As far as Aristotle is concerned, he was undeniably very interested in physics and biology; being the son of an outstanding physician, he frequently dealt with questions of anatomy and physiology, not only of humans but of many other living beings. In his view, however, this kind of research belongs to philosophy; it is not considered an autonomous branch of learning; cf. T. Tracy, *Physiological Theory and the Doctrine of the Mean in Plato and Aristotle*, Chicago, 1969, p.18–19.

7. Numbers are considered to be the οὐσία of all things. The term *ousia* derives from the participium of εἶναι (to be): it refers to the very beingness of beings. In Pythagoras' view the beingness of everything must be numerical. It can be expressed in numbers. There is, for example, a correspondence between the length of a cord and the tone that it produces; both can be reduced to numerical proportions.

penetrated into the Greek system of education and was adopted even by Plato.[8] According to Pseudo-Plutarch this learning is only marginal: it may be important in order to be influential in a political community or to reach some understanding of the sensible universe, but what is more essential is man himself, and how he ought to behave in daily life to attain perfection and happiness.

Some disciplines deal with the illnesses of the body: medical science and gymnastic training both intend to promote the harmonious development of the body.[9] With respect to the illnesses of the mind philosophy is the only remedy.[10] As a matter of fact, not only may the body be ill, but also the mind, when under the influence of irrational affections it makes erroneous judgments. For that reason philosophy is the top and summary of all education: in order to support his viewpoint the author especially stresses the practical function of philosophy in human life. Presumably under the influence of Stoic ideas, which were widely spread at the beginning of our era, the main duty attributed to philosophy is to guide man's conduct in everyday life[11]: philosophy teaches man to worship the gods, who according to Stoicism are a mythological expression of the one divine Reason; it tells humans to obey the laws, which embody the moral feeling of a political society. It asks men to honor their parents and to pay respect to elderly persons; to be subordinate to those who are invested with authority, to love friends, to be chaste in contacts with women, to be affectionate with children and not overdominant with slaves. According to the Stoics all humans are equal: not only barbarians and Greeks, but also women and men, free citizens and slaves.[12] With respect to the love of boys,

8. In Plato's view mathematical objects occupy an intermediary level between the transcendent Forms and sensible reality. Hence somebody who wants to reach the contemplation of Ideas should be trained in geometry as a preparatory stage.

9. *De liberis educandis*, 10, p.7d. The purpose of medical science is to promote the health of the body, whereas gymnastic training aims at implanting vigor ($\varepsilon \dot{v}\varepsilon \xi \acute{\iota} \alpha$).

10. *De liberis educandis*, 10, p.7d.

11. *De liberis educandis*, 10, p.7d. Through philosophy man becomes able to frame right moral judgments: he is able to grasp what is just and what is unjust, what is to be chosen and what is to be avoided. According to Aristotle, ethics is a philosophical discipline: it teaches one how to behave in view of reaching human perfection and happiness. As to the Stoics, they mainly concentrated their philosophical reflection on ethical subjects.

12. *De liberis educandis*, 10, p.7d: $\delta o \acute{v} \lambda o v \varsigma \mu \grave{\eta} \pi \varepsilon \rho \iota v \beta \rho \acute{\iota} \zeta \varepsilon \iota v$. This recommendation corresponds to the Stoic doctrine. According to these philosophers there are no slaves by nature. Yet slavery was not suppressed. The attitude toward slaves evolved

the author is cautious[13]: he knows that some fathers repudiate it decidedly, but on the other hand he does not ignore that some outstanding individuals were lovers of boys; he mentions examples such as Socrates, Plato, Xenophon, Aeschines, and Cebes.[14] In this respect the author makes a capital distinction between love of external beauty and love of the true self: this latter will be beneficial, whereas the former may be very harmful.[15] The distinction had already been introduced by Socrates in the *First Alcibiades* of Plato: Socrates came to the conclusion that he was the only lover of Alcibiades; all others loved his body, not his true self.[16] The author also strongly recommends marriage—it is the most secure bond for young people—but he warns them not to marry girls who belong to a much higher condition in birth or wealth.[17]

In our author's view philosophy is not devoted to scientific research nor to abstract speculation: it is a practical wisdom, a school of life, which deals with human behavior in society. It aims at an attitude of moderation in all circumstances of life, which teaches man to dominate his emotions and passions: man should not be too joyful when he succeeds in his initiatives, nor too distressed when he falls victim of some misfortune.[18] As an ideal way of life the author suggests a combination of speculative philosophy and political activity[19]: in his view contemplative activity without practice is useless, but practice without philosophical contemplation is devoid of culture and harmony.[20]

---

gradually: it became more and more mild and humane (cf. Seneca, *Epistolae ad Lucilium*, 5,4;95,52–53).

13. *De liberis educandis*, 15, p.11d: the author even hesitates to deal with the subject. He calls himself ἀμφίδοξος and διχογνώμων; he has, in fact, two contrary opinions and two conflicting views.

14. *De liberis educandis*, 15, p.11e.

15. *De liberis educandis*, 15, p.11f. In this context the author speaks of lovers of the soul, τοὺς δὲ τῆς ψυχῆς ἐραστάς. Those are to be admitted unreservedly. In his ethical treatise Aristotle also stresses the importance of friendship. It is a virtue or at least it is connected with virtue, because friendship is oriented toward the true self of another person and this true self is primarily the mind (*Eth. Nic.*, IX, 4, 1166a17; X, 7, 1178a2).

16. *Alcibiades*, 131c.

17. *De liberis educandis*, 19, p.13f. The recommendation with respect to marriage is shaded: it is intended for young people who are unable to dominate their desires.

18. *De liberis educandis*, 10, p.7e.

19. *De liberis educandis*, 10, p.7f.

20. *De liberis educandis*, 10, p.8a. The author's viewpoint does not truly correspond to Aristotle's doctrine. According to this teaching contemplative life represents the highest degree of human perfection and is only possible on the basis of moral conduct.

Quite in agreement with Aristotle's teaching Pseudo-Plutarch declares that three factors contribute to the moral education of young people: nature, reason, and training.[21] According to Aristotle nature is the basic element of all moral conduct; man is by nature a moral being. Nature always tends toward the good: according to his natural equipment man also is inserted into this universal orientation; moreover he is gifted with rational knowledge and the capacity of free choice. Reason is a fundamental factor in moral life, although ethical conduct cannot be reduced to mere knowledge: man may deviate from what he knows to be good, at least when this knowledge is only universal or potential. He cannot, however, accomplish a particular act that he actually knows to be wrong. For this reason ethical conduct is also a result of some training: each virtue is an abiding habit comparable to a technical skill, which is gradually acquired by repeating similar actions.[22] From the beginning of their life children and young people are gifted with a natural ability of becoming temperate, wise, brave, and just, but it is only by means of an enduring and perseverant training that they effectively acquire these habits as steady moral dispositions.[23] Many ideas in this little treatise about the education of children correspond to the teaching of Aristotle, whereas others are rather Platonic or Stoic. In a sense the whole life of Aristotle was concerned with education: at the age of seventeen he traveled to the Academy of Plato in Athens and became a member of the school. The choice he made was a decisive one and it already indicated the further development of his career; as a matter of fact, the Academy was not the only school of higher education in Athens. Aristotle had to choose between two institutions, that of Plato and that of Isocrates, which represented two systems of education.[24] The latter was oriented toward immediate practical results: young people were prepared to become good citizens, to take part in various activities of political life, and to play

21. *De liberis educandis*, 3, p.2a.

22. Virtues are like technical skills: one can only acquire them by repeating the same acts; by frequently accomplishing acts of justice or temperance, an individual becomes just or temperate (*Eth. Nic.*, II, 1, 1103a31–b2).

23. Man is by nature a moral being. This, however, does not imply that man by nature is equipped with all ethical virtues. Virtues are the outcome of intense training.

24. J. Düring, *Aristoteles: Darstellung und Interpretation seines Denkens*. Heidelberg, 1966, p.3: "Die beiden Schulen repräsentierten zwei verschiedene Erziehungsprogramme, die noch heute gegeneinander ausgespielt werden. Kurz gesagt, vertrat Isokrates eine Zweckpädagogik."

some influential part in society. There was no major concern with investigating the true nature and the real end of a political community: it was rather taken as it was, without discussing its deeper roots and finality; the training was above all technical and practical in view of attaining an influential position in society.[25] Hence the emphasis put on the study of dialectics and rhetoric: Isocrates was firmly convinced of the persuasive power of speech; what young citizens had to learn was above all the art of communicating their opinion to other people. They had to be trained in order to become skillful speakers.[26] In the school of Plato the orientation was different: the deepest meaning of human life and society was put into question. The main interest of Plato was a political one but at a profound level: he had been heavily injured by the trial and death of Socrates. He could never forget these tragic events; they had left his soul with an incurable trauma. Socrates was a deeply religious and wise man: he had been condemned by a corrupt society on behalf of some mythological beliefs and superficial traditions. Plato wanted a radically new society, in which a man like Socrates could never be killed: hence his constant craving for an ideal republic, a utopia that would be grounded on a philosophical doctrine. Instead of being killed by his fellow-citizens, a philosopher should be the king of future society.

Entering into the Academy, Aristotle found an institution in which the main concerns of the director were political philosophy and moral education. When he first went to Athens Plato was at Syracuse and the school was temporarily directed by Eudoxos of Cnidos[27]: this travel to Sicily was also intended as a contribution to

---

25. H. J. Marrou, *Histoire de l'éducation dans l'antiquité*, Paris, 1948, p.126. The program proposed by Isocrates included not only reading and interpretation of literary works but also the study of mathematics. Concerning the influence of Isocrates Marrou writes: "c'est Isocrate, beaucoup plus qu'aucun autre, qui porte l'honneur et la responsabilité d'avoir inspiré l'éducation à dominante littéraire de notre tradition occidentale" (p.122).

26. J. Marrou, *Histoire de l'éducation*, p.127. Isocrates was not indifferent to moral values and political ideas: "Certainement préoccupé de répondre au défi porté, depuis Socrate et le *Gorgias*, par la philosophie, Isocrate a voulu lester son art d'un contenu de valeurs: son éloquence n'est pas indifférente au point de vue moral; elle a, en particulier, une portée civique et patriotique" (p.129).

27. J. Düring, *Aristoteles*, p.5. The presence of Eudoxos in the Academy was a very important factor in the development of the school: "Die Ankunft des Eudoxos und seiner Schüler gab der Akademie einen neuen Charakter als Treffpunkt für Gelehrte aus allen Teilen der griechischsprechenden Welt. Mit Eudoxos begann die wirkliche Blütezeit der Akademie."

Plato's political activity; the author wanted to put into practice the results of his philosophical speculation.[28] Aristotle could not have ignored the fact that the repeated efforts of his master were not successful. In any case, when he himself in a later period endeavored to describe an ideal republic, he was very cautious and started by studying 158 existing constitutions.[29] As always his point of departure was experience of the real world. At the Academy Aristotle was introduced immediately to the most famous tradition of Greek education. Plato had been the disciple of Socrates, who effected a deep change in his way of life, a kind of conversion to philosophy: Socrates was, as it were, the embodiment of philosophy; he never abandoned his pursuit of wisdom; he regarded this dedication as a divine vocation and was not willing to resign it, even when he had to choose saving his life or continuing in what he believed to be his duty. It was not the intention of Socrates to proclaim some firm convictions of his own and to attempt to persuade other people: he hardly professed firm views and always wanted to learn from other people. In a sense he was persuaded that people bear within themselves a treasure of hidden truth and yet are ignorant, because they are not conscious of what they possess. Socrates' method of education was one of contributing to the self-discovery of truth: a pupil should not receive his knowledge from a master; he has to find it within himself. By asking questions the master gradually induces the pupil to look within his own mind and to disclose the knowledge that is already there. A typical example of this procedure is found in the *Meno:* this example shows that the pupil does not immediately provide the right answer when a question is asked but needs to be guided in order to discover

28. J. Düring, *Aristoteles*, p.6: "Platon gründete seine Schule, um die junge Generation für sein Ideal zu gewinnen, nicht eigentlich um wissenschaftliche Forschung zu betreiben. Er wollte die jungen Leute für das politische Leben erziehen: es war seine Absicht, dass sie alles was sie in der Akademie gelernt hatten auch in die Tat umsetzen sollten."

29. *Eth. Nic.*, X, 9, 1181b17: Aristotle refers to a collection of constitutions (Diogenes Laertius, V, 27,143). The author wants to discover which factors generally save or destroy cities; he also endeavors to answer the same question with respect to the various kinds of constitutions. Some cities are well ruled; others are not. Aristotle wants to uncover the causes of these situations. Only the constitution of Athens has been preserved; some unimportant fragments of sixty-two other constitutions are also available (cf. J. Düring, *Aristoteles*, p.477).

the knowledge he is looking for.[30] True knowledge, although it
is always present in the mind, in various ways may be prevented
from being uncovered: the status of sensible knowledge is ambiguous.
It can be a starting point that allows the mind to be lifted
to higher levels of contemplation, but it may also be an obstacle
that ties the soul to what is immediately given. Plato followed
the method of his Master: his work is a philosophical dialogue
in which Socrates is the central character, the man who never
stops his search for truth and who is never satisfied with the
result already attained. We may reasonably accept that the same
method was practiced in the Academy. Even if formal lectures
were given, there must have been plenty of opportunity for
discussion, criticism, and questioning.[31] The aporematic method
in Aristotle presumably derives from these oral discussions: a
whole book (B) of the *Metaphysics* is devoted to such inquiry
concerning being. Before entering into the study of a subject one
has to know exactly which problems are to be solved. A mind
without questions cannot be eager to find answers.[32] A philosophical
dialogue stimulates further questioning and in this way allows
a more profound penetration into the subject at stake. An old
anecdote tells us that at the entrance of the Academy people were
warned that knowledge of geometry was required of all those
who wanted to participate in the activity of the school.[33] Whether
this information is true or not, great importance was attributed
to the study of mathematics: students had to spend ten years

30. *Meno*, 81d: Socrates declares that inquiry and learning are in fact a process of
reminiscence. Yet the slave questioned by Socrates does not immediately discover
the solution of the proposed problem. Some of his answers are erroneous. The
knowledge that is wanted is not ready at hand; it is to be recovered gradually, since
it had never been exercised (82a–85b).

31. Plato was not in favor of writing philosophical works. In this respect also he
was a faithful disciple of Socrates. In his view an oral explanation is more flexible, less
liable to all kinds of misunderstanding, and able to defend itself against objections,
criticisms, and attacks. Through the testimony of Aristotle we know that the whole
philosophy of Plato is not contained in his written works; some doctrines belong to
what is called the *agrapha dogmata*, or unwritten theories. As a result of Plato's
viewpoint concerning written philosophical teaching, it is quite understandable that
at least some of his doctrines remained unwritten (*Phaedrus*, 278d; *Letters*, VII, 341c)
Cf. G. Reale, *Per una nuova interpretazione di Platone*, Milan, 1986, p.21–24; J.
Krämer, *La nuova immagine di Platone*, Naples, 1986, p.39ff.

32. *Metaphysica*, III, 1, 995a24–b4.

33. ἀγεωμέτρητος μηδεὶς εἰσίτω (Elias, *In Categorias*, 118, 18; Philoponus, *In de
anima*, 117, 29).

studying mathematical subjects before being permitted to devote themselves for five years to dialectics.[34] If the study of mathematics is recommended by Plato it is not primarily as a training of the mind; the true reason is to be found in the ontological structure of reality. It is impossible when starting from sensible things to pass immediately to the transcendent level of ideas; there is an intermediary level, that of mathematical objects. According to Aristotle human mind with the help of an intellective active principle is able to grasp universal forms in particular sensible objects. In Plato the creative power of the mind is less emphasized: the intellectual faculty contemplates its objects; it does not produce them. But why ten years devoted to the study of mathematics and only five to dialectics? This difference must be regarded as an expression of the relative difficulty of both steps: it is very hard to pass from the sensible level to the mathematical one, whereas it is much easier to move from mathematics to dialectics, since mathematical objects already belong to a higher area of being.[35]

Did Aristotle ever accept Plato's teaching on subsisting mathematical objects and separate forms? Since he entered the Academy when he was only seventeen years of age, it is most likely that at least at the beginning of his stay he accepted the theory of his Master. Moreover there are some indications in his early writings that he did not reject the separate subsistence of forms.[36] There seems to be a close relation between Aristotle's criticism of transcendent ideas and his own theory of knowledge; insofar as we are informed this theory does not appear in his early writings. During his stay in the Academy Aristotle had already written some of his own works, only fragments of which have been preserved; they show a striking similarity between Plato and Aristotle with respect to composition, style, and doctrinal content. In his concept of

34. *Respublica*, VII, 536d; *Leges*, VII, 817e–822c: in this later work the author emphasizes even more strongly the importance of mathematical preparation.

35. In the School of Isocrates mathematics was also considered to be a significant component of the educational program (cf. H. J. Marrou, *Histoire de l'éducation*, p.126–127).

36. One of the most relevant passages in this respect is a fragment of the *Protrepticus* (*Aristotelis dialogorum fragmenta*, ed. R. Walzer, Florence, 1934, fr. 13). In this text the author declares that only philosophers contemplate what is truly intelligible; all other people deal with imitations or likenesses. This viewpoint clearly corresponds to the doctrine of Plato that the sensible world is only a shadow of true reality.

man, the young Aristotle seemingly has maintained an outspoken spiritualistic dualism.[37] During this early period Aristotle also wrote a work on the question of education, entitled *Protrepticus*. In this writing the author strongly insists on the value of philosophical learning. In his view there is a close connection between the worth of knowing activity and the level of the object known: if the level of the object is very high, the activity of the knowing subject belongs to the same rank. The basis of this argument is, of course, that there must be some similarity or kinship between the knowing principle and its object: such an argument is used by Plato in the *Phaedo* in order to demonstrate the immortality of the human soul.[38] Philosophical contemplation represents the most perfect knowledge, since it is related to the highest level of reality: only a philosopher contemplates the eternal and immutable patterns of sensible things. This intuition is important also in view of moral behavior, since ethical values belong to this transcendent world.[39] In this respect Aristotle sides with Plato and Socrates against the relativism of the Sophists. Being the highest activity of which man is capable, philosophical contemplation guarantees happiness: in Aristotle's view this activity provides the noblest kind of pleasure, as it corresponds to the most worthy power in man, the mind.[40]

In his recommendation of philosophical education, Aristotle points to the fact that the study of philosophy is easy: everybody feels at home in philosophy; man is by nature a philosophical animal, asking ultimate questions about human existence, moral behavior,

37. *Aristotelis dialogorum fragmenta, Eudemus*, fr. 8. In this period Aristotle believed human soul to be a kind of idea (εἶδός τι). This teaching conforms to the psychological doctrine of Plato, particularly as it is expressed in the *Sophistes*: "In fact the *Sophistes* ranks soul more definitely as included in the truly real than the *Phaedo* does, which only describes it as akin to the truly real." (Cf. W. D. Ross, *Plato's Theory of Ideas*, Oxford, 1951, p.107).

38. *Phaedo*, 78b–80e, especially 79d–e.

39. *Aristotelis dialogorum fragmenta, Protrepticus*, fr. 13. The life and behavior of a philosopher fully conform to true nature and divine reality. He is the only person who grasps the eternal and immutable patterns and organizes his life in conformity with them. The knowledge of the transcendent Forms is a theoretical one, but it gives us the capacity of arranging everything in accordance with it (τὸ δημιουργεῖν κατ᾽ αὐτὴν ἅπαντα).

40. *Aristotelis dialogorum fragmenta, Protrepticus*, fr. 6. The author writes that wisdom (φρόνησις) is part of virtue and of happiness, for happiness either springs from wisdom or coincides with it. The reason is that the very center of a human individual is the mind (ὡς ἤτοι μόνον ἢ μάλιστα ἡμεῖς ἐσμεν τὸ μόριον τοῦτο).

political society, past and future of the universe. Philosophical questions are not imposed on man from without, they are not artificial, they correspond to the deepest cravings of human beings.[41] Moreover people who dedicate themselves to the study of philosophy are able to make much progress in a short time, more than in any other branch of learning: other disciplines are more directly linked to observation and experience, whereas philosophy, without being detached from sensible perception, involves a higher level of intelligible objects.[42] Finally, philosophers do not need special tools nor particular places for their work; a philosopher is able to reflect everywhere. Wherever he may happen to be he will find himself "surrounded on all sides by the presence of truth."[43] Even the study of the highest level of reality is not difficult in Aristotle's view: man has to turn within himself, and he will gradually disclose the richness of truth, without compulsion and without special effort.[44] Philosophy has made tremendous progress in a short period of time, precisely because it corresponds to the deepest nature of human beings. Philosophical education is not the acquisition of some strange knowledge; man has to become aware of the truth he bears within himself. Aristotle left Athens in 347: after a short stay in the Near East (Atarneus, Assos, Mytilene) he was invited to Micra by King Philip of Macedonia and was entrusted with the education of Prince Alexander, who at that time was thirteen years of age. We know very little about the way in which Aristotle fulfilled this duty: in his essay on Alexander's fortune Plutarch declares that the young prince was more deeply influenced by his master than he was by his father.[45]

41. At the outset of his *Metaphysics* (I,1, 980a1) Aristotle declares that everybody is longing for knowledge: man is constantly in search of truth. And as metaphysics represents the highest level of human knowing, each individual either consciously or unconsciously aspires to grasp the most intelligible objects, the ultimate principles of whatever exists. In Aristotle's view metaphysical inquiry is both easy and difficult: it is easy because everyman is able to take part in it; it is also difficult, not because of its object but because of the human subject, who is blinded by the light of what is contemplated, as the eyes of bats are blinded by daylight (*Metaph.*, II, 1, 993a30–b11).

42. *Aristotelis dialogorum fragmenta, Protrepticus*, 5a (p.30).

43. *Aristotelis dialogorum fragmenta, Protrepticus*, 5a, (p.30).

44. *Aristotelis dialogorum fragmenta, Protrepticus*, 6 (p.36): to think and to contemplate are for humans the most desirable activities (αἱρετώτατον τοῖς ἀνθρώποις).

45. *De fortitudine Alexandri (De fort. Alex.)*, I, 4, 327d. According to Plutarch Alexander was a true thinker; he is even called an outstanding philosopher (φιλοσοφώτατος, *De fort. Alex.*, I, 5, 329a). Yet Alexander did not devote his life to

Yet his great project of gathering all humans into one single community, a well-ordered and philosophic commonwealth in which all members would behave in agreement with the same rules of justice and adopt the same way of life, did not correspond to the teaching of Aristotle.[46] This thinker did not accept the equality of all humans: he certainly rejected the equality of barbarians from Asia with the Greeks; in a sense he was more mild in his judgment of Europeans. With respect to the Asian peoples he blamed them for being homosexuals and on a low level of mental development; he compared them to epileptics or the mentally ill.[47] These were precisely the peoples whom Alexander united with the Greeks: in Plutarch's view he was an incomparable educator, far superior to Socrates and Plato, since he was able to civilize Asia. He founded more than seventy cities and radically transformed the savage and primitive character of innumerable tribes. It was their good fortune to be conquered by Alexander: in this way they became civilized.[48] Unfortunately Alexander died much too early: some parts of the world never knew him and remained in darkness; an area of the world was deprived of sunlight, because it didn't know this exceptional man.[49] According to Plutarch Alexander was a great philosopher; this idea clearly appears in his words, his acts, and the instructions he gave. He was an educator of mankind.[50]

To what extent was Alexander's activity in conformity with Aristotle's political doctrine? As I already mentioned, it deviated from it in some important aspects: Aristotle did not accept the equality of barbarians and Greeks, nor did he want to suppress the city-states and to replace them by a single republic, in which all peoples would be incorporated. This idea is clearly of Stoic origin. Nevertheless some characteristics of Alexander's conquest are in agreement with the Stagirite's teaching on the nature and role of political society: in Aristotle's view all humans are by

---

speculative thought, but, he had a really philosophical soul, he loved wisdom, and he was full of admiration for wise men (*op cit.*, I, 10, 331e). What Alexander achieved manifestly proved that he was an eminent representative of practical philosophy and an exceptional educator.

46. *De fort. Alex.*, I, 8, 330d.
47. *Politica*, III, 14, 1285a19–22.
48. *De fort. Alex.*, I, 5, 328a–329a.
49. *De fort. Alex.*, I, 8, 330d.
50. *De fort. Alex.*, I, 4, 328b.

nature political animals.[51] If humans are not equal, they are still gifted with the capacity of speech and with an inborn sense of right and wrong; in this respect Aristotle does not mention any exceptions: barbarians, slaves, and women may be on a lower level of rationality, but they are not totally deprived of rational insight.[52] The main duty of a political society is to guarantee the moral education of the members: in this perspective laws are necessary; they are a permanent expression of the moral sense of a community. From childhood members of a republic have to make their behavior conform to the laws.[53] If Alexander founded many cities and contributed in this way to the civilization of Asian tribes, this activity is entirely in agreement with Aristotle's view, according to which it is impossible, outside a political community, to behave morally and to reach human perfection.[54] The role of the state and of laws has been strongly emphasized by the Stagirite: in this respect Alexander behaved in conformity with his Master's teaching.

In 335–334 Aristotle returned to Athens and devoted all his time and energy to research and teaching in his own school, the Lyceum. He carefully prepared his lectures, and the works that have been preserved and edited in the *Corpus Aristotelicum* were not intended to be published: they are mostly lecture notes, composed to be used by the Master in his teaching.[55] In one of these works (*Politics*) Aristotle handles the question of education in the framework of a political community: first of all the author endeavors to clarify the goal to be pursued. In his view moral values are the same whether individuals or a political society are concerned.[56] In other words,

51. *Politica*, I, 2, 1253a2: In the doctrine of Aristotle it is important to emphasize that man is by *nature* (φύσει) a political animal; it is inherent in the very structure of a human being to be oriented to social life in a political community.

52. *Politica*, I, 2, 1253a9–29; G. Verbeke, *Les degrés d'humanité et le sens du progrès chez Aristote*, in: Ἀρετῆς μνήμη: *Mélanges en l'honneur de C. Vourveris*. Athens, 1983, p.121–141.

53. *Politica*, III, 11, 1282b1–3. Laws are general rules; they cannot deal with all possible particular cases; therefore, along with laws, practical wisdom of rules is necessary.

54. *Politica*, I, 2, 1253a1–9; III, 9, 1280b39–1281a4. In Aristotle's view man can only achieve the full development of his capacities in a political community; this society aims at the happiness and moral perfection of its members. It ought to be adapted to the nature of each population: each constitution should be chosen to promote the well-being of a particular population. (*Politica*, IV, 2, 1289a18–20).

55. W. Jaeger, *Aristotle: Fundamentals of the History of His Development*. Oxford, 1948, p.316–318.

56. *Politica*, VII, 13, 1333b37; 1334a11.

what is morally good for an individual will also be valuable for the state, which is created as an ordered community pursuing the most perfect development of all members. In Aristotle's view the state is not an entity that exists in itself and for itself; it is an organized society in view of the well-being of the individuals: if the members of a political community attain the most perfect way of life, then the republic itself will reach the highest goal it can achieve.[57] In this respect laws are a decisive factor: they are not the work of an individual only; they are shaped by the people as a whole. This is already a guarantee of their value. Many opinions put together are more valuable than the reflection of a single person: that is one of the reasons why Aristotle favors a limited democracy; opinions of the majority are to be taken into account.[58] The author also recognizes exceptional truth value to very ancient beliefs, which are generally accepted and persist throughout the course of time.[59] In a sense laws are not the work of one generation; they are transmitted from one generation to another and constantly corrected and improved[60]: what they aim at is not something distinct from the individuals who belong to the state; these are social beings and can only achieve their moral perfection in the framework of a political community. The most perfect republic is one in which all members are able to attain moral virtue and happiness. Of course, individual responsibility is not eliminated: laws should be compulsory, at least for young people, who do not yet possess the necessary experience and practice to make them fully understand the meaning of rules and consent to their regulations. More mature people, who already have experience of life and of moral conduct, will not need to be constrained; they will freely agree on the regulations settled by the community; they will understand that they have been established in view of their well-being.[61]

What then is this well-being in Aristotle's view? Let us state from the beginning that happiness is not a matter of good luck: it is not by chance that some people are happy, whereas others are not. There is no blind fate that decides arbitrarily on the course of human

---

57. *Politica*, VII, 13, 1332a31–38.
58. *Politica*, III, 11, 1282a14–23; 1281b34–38.
59. G. Verbeke, *Philosophie et conceptions préphilosophiques chez Aristote*, in: *Revue philosophique de Louvain*, 59 (1961), p.423; *Politica*, III, 6, 1281a42.
60. *Politica*, IV, 8, 1294a3–9.
61. *Politica*, III, 11, 1282b1–6; *Eth. Nic.*, X, 9, 1180a21–22.

life.[62] Such was a widespread prephilosophical belief particularly in connection with some tragic events: not being able to understand why some individuals were so severely afflicted and fell from one catastrophe into another, they attributed these misfortunes to blind fate. This power was believed to be blind, because it made no distinction between good and bad people: the blows of fate were apparently inflicted without taking into account the personal merits of each individual. Oedipus did whatever he could in order to avoid the tragic prediction of his future, and yet he was unable to escape from his destiny. The blindness of fate was a characteristic element in the Greek notion of "tragic": the destiny of Oedipus was tragic, because all his sufferings were not the result of some previous evil actions. This common belief in a blind fate was firmly dismissed by Aristotle: his interpretation of the world and of nature was decidedly teleological. Everything is oriented toward the good; all things tend toward what is perfect[63]: the First Act is loved by all beings; the movement of the universe is a constant aspiration toward the highest good.

Aristotle also rejects the opinion declaring that man's happiness depends upon the goodwill of some higher beings. In this sense again human destiny would not lie in the hands of each individual, but would be determined by divine powers that frequently interfere in human affairs.[64] According to mythological narratives such interventions occur in many circumstances: in the war of Troy, the gods are neither indifferent nor neutral; they side with one of the two conflicting armies. At the end of a Greek drama there may be a "deus ex machina," a divine intervention that puts an end to the evolution of the dramatic episodes. Such divine interferences are categorically rejected by the Stagirite: according to his metaphysical doctrine the First Act does not know the world or human beings; this perfect substance only knows its own thinking activity.[65] This

---

62. G. Verbeke, *Happiness and Chance in Aristotle*, in: *Aristotle on Nature and Living Things: Philosophical and Historical Studies Presented to David M. Balme on His Seventieth Birthday.* Ed. Allan Gotthelf, Pittsburgh, 1985, p.247–258.

63. *Eth. Nic.*, I, 1, 1094a1–3: Aristotelian teleology is certainly important with respect to the ethical teaching of the author. The universal tendency toward the good is also present in man: it is a permanent incentive to moral behavior.

64. The Greek term εὐδαιμονία is an expression of this ancient belief: it originally means that well-being is bestowed upon man by some divine beings (δαίμονες).

65. *Metaph.*, XII, 9, 1074b33–35.

viewpoint of Aristotle's is quite coherent, since he doesn't accept Pure Act as the creator of the universe: hence this Supreme Act cannot grasp the world without being passive and receptive toward it.

Aristotle is convinced that happiness, which coincides with moral perfection, is a matter that depends upon each individual subject, a matter of knowledge and choice. Man has to discover what is truly good, either in general as the final end of his life or in the variable circumstances of every day. Humans can be easily deceived and pursue things that are not really valuable. Aristotle dedicates a careful analysis to this question and comes to the conclusion that the highest happiness of man resides in the performance of his most noble activity, which is the activity of the mind.[66]

In an Aristotelian perspective, however, intellectual knowing cannot be separated from sensible experience; on the other hand, a life of contemplation is not possible without moral virtue, which ensures the rule of reason over irrational movements and emotions. The notion of potency plays an important part in Aristotle's ethics[67]: from the very beginning of his life man possesses the potency of becoming more and more perfect, but he has to actualize his possibilities and capacities constantly. He will attain his highest perfection and supreme happiness when he actualizes his most lofty capacity, the activity of thought, in an enduring and perfect way. When we apply all this to political communities, we may conclude that laws have to educate people to become able to attain this supreme degree of human happiness; the way to this goal is assiduous practice of moral virtue. In Aristotle's view education is the responsibility of political authority; it can never be a matter of private initiative.[68]

66. *Eth. Nic.*, I, 7, 1098a16–20. In discussing education Aristotle states that a well-educated person is able to formulate correct judgments of what is expounded by other people (*De partibus animalium*, I, 1, 639a4–8). Here again the activity of the mind is regarded as primordial.

67. G. Verbeke, *The Meaning of Potency in Aristotle*, in: *Graceful Reason: Essays in Ancient and Medieval Philosophy Presented to Joseph Owens, CSSR, on the Occasion of His Seventy-Fifth Birthday and the Fiftieth Anniversary of his Ordination*, ed. Lloyd P. Gerson, Toronto, 1983, p.55–73.

68. *Politica*, VIII, 1, 1337a21–27. Private education is repudiated by Aristotle, because it cannot ensure a common agreement on basic moral issues. Such agreement is indispensable to a coherent and stable society. Laws are considered to be the expression of these ethical values.

This theory is closely connected with the nature and role of a political community; this society is indispensable because individuals by themselves are unable to display their capacities adequately and to reach the perfection of their being. Everybody needs the assistance of others within the framework of an organized community; such a society can never be steadily grounded if its members do not agree on basic moral values.[69] So the state cannot be neutral or tolerant, because it belongs to the very nature of a political community that people agree with each other on fundamental values, such as the ideas of justice and mutual respect. According to Aristotle this agreement is neither arbitrary nor artificial: moral values are actually the same for all humans, since human nature is the same in all individuals. So the agreement of individual subjects on the idea of justice corresponds to the common nature that is present in all particular persons. The author does not accept moral relativism, stating that each individual has his own idea of moral life and cannot be blamed for acting accordingly. It is quite true that circumstances of life vary from one individual to another and from one period to another: hence it is not sufficient to know moral rules and values in general; everybody has to apply them to concrete situations in which he happens to be. Concrete moral judgments are quite delicate and require not only some general knowledge but also balanced wisdom based on practice and experience.[70]

This, however, does not suggest that moral values differ from one individual to another: Aristotle believes in political societies based on a common agreement regarding fundamental moral insights. In this view education is very important; it belongs to the essence of a political community and has to be ruled by the authority of the state: private initiatives cannot ensure the unity of views that is required in this respect. What is at stake is the subsistence of a political society. Aristotle is convinced that differences among

69. *Politica*, I, 2, 1253a14–18. Aristotle puts on the same level a political society and a family: in both communities an agreement on fundamental ethical insights is required.

70. *Eth. Nic.*, VII, 11, 1143b11–14. According to Aristotle people have to pay special attention to moral judgments formulated by aged and experienced persons or those who have acquired practical wisdom, even if they do not provide any demonstration of their viewpoint. Through their experience, such individuals have right intuitions (ὁρῶσιν ὀρθῶς) in the changing situations of life. These intuitions will be right because they are not obscured by irrational inclinations and they are grounded on previous experience of similar conditions.

members regarding basic moral values make common life and cooperation within the same political community impossible. The Stagirite was not against democracy, but even a democratic constitution
is to be ruled by laws that are the embodiment of a common view
of basic moral values. A democracy without laws is categorically
rejected by our author.[71] So it belongs to the responsibility of a
state to shape a coherent system of laws that ensures a common
moral sense of all citizens.

Education has to conform to the natural development of children
and youngsters: first comes the gradual growth of the body, then
the evolution of the irrational part of the soul, and finally the
progressive display of mental capacities.[72] In an early stage education
is mainly concerned with bodily growth: therefore, appropriate
nutrition is required.[73] Yet our author also mentions some other
aspects of this early education: until the age of seven, children
should have only few contacts with slaves, in order to avoid any kind
of indecent speech; such speech easily leads to indecent conduct.[74] A
similar rule is put forward with respect to paintings, representations,
and spectacles: any exhibition of what is morally evil is to be
avoided.[75] Within the framework of early education Aristotle is also
concerned with marriage and procreation of children: laws cannot
avoid dealing with sexual intercourse of married people. In Aristotle's view the age distance between parents and their children should
neither be too large nor too small; in view of this purpose law
should settle the appropriate age of marriage at eighteen for women
and at about thirty-seven (or a bit less) for men.[76] Procreation
should continue till about the age of fifty; after that age married
people may continue to have sexual intercourse for reasons of health
or some other reason but should not be permitted to procreate

71. *Politica*, IV, 4, 1292a4–37. A democracy without laws is strongly criticized and
rejected by Aristotle: it is comparable to a monarchy or a tyranny; in fact, it is ruled
by flatterers and demagogues who manipulate the people.

72. *Politica*, VII, 15, 1334b20–25. The author declares that the training of the body
is for the soul and the education of irrational impulses for the mind. (b 25–28).

73. *Politica*, VII, 17, 1336a3–8.

74. *Politica*, VII, 17, 1336a39–b12. There is a close link between manner of speaking
and way of behaving.

75. *Politica*, VII, 17, 1336b12–17.

76. *Politica*, VII, 16, 1334b38–1335a35. Cf. Plato, *Leges*, IV, 731 b–d: The age of
marriage is settled between thirty and thirty-five. Those who are not married at
thirty-five will have to pay a fine and will not be allowed public honors.

children.[77] No deformed child will be allowed to grow up; it ought to be eliminated. When population growth is too strong, abortion ought to be performed before the awakening of sensible life in the embryo.[78] From the age of seven the proper curriculum of education starts: in its first stage, until the age of puberty, it is oriented toward physical development, which is achieved by the practice of gymnastics. The exercises at this early age should not be too rigorous: Aristotle criticized the Spartan way of education, aimed primarily not at moral excellence, but at bodily strength.[79] In Aristotle's view reason and intellect are the final end of our nature; they are the highest power of a human being: education has to aim primarily at the development of the mind; even physical education should be directed toward the growth of the higher faculties.[80]

From the age of fourteen begins, for a period of three years, the study of some arts, those that are really useful or even indispensable. Young people should never learn arts that have a servile character, namely mechanical skills preparing for manual labor. In Aristotle's view manual work should be performed by slaves, not by free citizens. Under the influence of social circumstances in which he lived, his valuation of manual labor is indeed very low; it harms the body and is not worthy of a free citizen.[81] Even liberal arts are not unreservedly appreciated: they are approved insofar as they are really necessary in view of the education of character. In this context the author mentions grammar, music, and design; with respect to the last discipline, it is believed to be relevant because it draws the attention of young people to corporal beauty.[82] In his examination of liberal arts the author devotes an extensive exposition to the study and practice of music. The question whether music is intended mainly as relaxation or as part of the acquisition of moral virtue or

---

77. *Politica*, VII, 16, 1335b35–38; cf. Plato, *Respublica*, V, 459d–461d. In this context Aristotle unambiguously repudiates adultery, not only unconcealed adultery (cf. W. L. Newman, *The Politics of Aristotle*, Oxford, 1902, vol. III, p.477).

78. *Politica*, VII, 16, 1335b20–26.

79. *Politica*, VIII, 4, 1338b9–19; 1338b38–1339a4.

80. *Politica*, VII, 14, 1333b2–5.

81. *Politica*, VIII, 2, 1337b4–11; cf. *Eudemian Ethics*, I, 4, 1215a26–32. With respect to the real development of human existence, the performance of manual labor is not taken into account.

82. *Politica*, VIII, 2–3, 1337b22–27.

a life of leisure is raised. In Aristotle's view music is oriented toward this threefold goal[83]: what is most important is, of course, that music contribute to the shaping of character and moral attitude, since melodies are imitations and reflections of ethical behavior.[84] Music is able to exercise some influence on the moral character of the soul; hence it should play a part in the education of young people.[85] Aristotle recommends some practice of musical instruments: thanks to this performance people become more able and prepared to judge musical works correctly. This practice, however, should be limited and should not be oriented toward competitions: such activity is considered to be vulgar; it does not possess any worth in view of education.[86] With respect to instruments Aristotle repudiates the use of flutes and harps: they have no educative worth.[87] As to the modes, the author particularly recommends the Dorian, which is the expression of a balanced manly character, yet he takes into account the age of young people and the use in some circumstances of the Lydian mode.[88] As in the case of tragedy the author believes that music is able to purify the soul of excessive emotions and passions: therefore, one has to choose the modes that have the most explicit moral character.[89] After three years of liberal arts study more intense bodily exercises may be performed and a strict nutrition regime ought to be imposed.[90] Neither bodily exercises nor liberal arts are able to provide a complete education: they are only a kind of preliminary stage. True education is the work of philosophy; it is the privilege of philosophy only.

Aristotle is an eminent representative of Greek education. Belonging to the tradition of Socrates and Plato, he not only transmitted the doctrine of education he had inherited but perfected this theory in the light of his own philosophy. Refusing to accept the theory

83. *Politica*, VIII, 5, 1339b14–25.

84. *Politica*, VIII, 5, 1340a38.

85. *Politica*, VIII, 5, 1340b10–19. Aristotle draws the attention to the fact that there is a connection between harmony and moral life: many wise men, he says, declare that the soul is harmony or possesses harmony.

86. *Politica*, VIII, 6, 1340b20–39.

87. *Politica*, VIII, 6, 1341a17–28.

88. *Politica*, VIII, 7, 1342a2–30.

89. *Politica*, VIII, 7, 1342b27–33. With respect to education three criteria are put forward: whatever is used ought to be balanced, possible, and suitable.

90. VIII, 4, 1339a4–10.

of transcendent Forms and the doctrine of reminiscence, he stresses the importance of personal observation and experience as well as the necessity of exercise and training. The three factors of moral life, namely nature, knowledge, and training, are at the very heart of ethical progress and education.

[2]

IS LIFE WORTH LIVING?

THE question formulated in the title is closely connected with the subject of education: in Aristotle's view happiness is not the result of fortune, nor is it merely a gift of nature; it can be reached only by man's activity.[1] The appropriate way to attain the full development of human possibilities implies moral conduct. In this perspective life becomes valuable indeed; if human destiny were determined by some higher powers that rule over the world and fix the course of events, education would be meaningless and useless. If everything in the cosmos is settled by an inexorable fate, man has nothing to decide; no choice is to be made. On the contrary if a person is a responsible being, able to achieve perfection and happiness within the boundaries of a lifetime, existence becomes meaningful. Within this context education also has an important function to accomplish; it has to prepare people for a fruitful and happy life. But if life is considered to be worthless, or even evil, full of misfortunes and disasters inflicted on man without any apparent reason, education inevitably loses its meaning. The question concerning the worth of life was not ignored in Greek culture; it

---

1. *Eudemian Ethics* (*Eth. Eud.*), I, 3, 1215a12–19. In this context Aristotle formulates a very important statement: if happiness were the result of fortune or provided by nature, not many people could ever hope to obtain it, since they could not achieve it by means of their own efforts and activity. On the contrary, if people can reach it through their behavior and way of life, it will be more widely spread and more divine. By their efforts many people will try to participate in it; besides, this perfection will be more divine since it will be the outcome of man's endeavor and actions. In conformity with his teleological doctrine Aristotle believes that many people participate in moral conduct and happiness. At first glance it seems to be puzzling that not many people could hope to reach happiness if it were the work of nature. What Aristotle wants to say is that the work of nature does not depend on man's free choice and activity: if happiness were provided by nature, man would not be able to change a given situation.

was asked by ordinary people, by poets, and also by philosophers. Aristotle could not avoid facing it in his ethical inquiry.

At the end of his *Apology* Socrates treats a similar problem: to live or to die: which is preferable? According to the Greek philosopher a death sentence could not be regarded as a real punishment; if the judges wanted to punish him for what he did, his religious conduct, and his talks with young people, they had to invent some other penalty instead of condemning him to death. In Socrates' view death is either an endless sleep or a move to another place where those who have completed their life are gathered.[2]

A deep sleep without dreams is far from being a punishment: according to daily experience most people enjoy that kind of rest. Being totally unconscious, a man who sleeps has no feeling of pain or suffering. If this hypothesis is true, death means a final release from all troubles and hardships.[3] Quite obviously this hypothesis does not fully correspond to religious beliefs in the Greek world. It was usually accepted that people after death continue to exist in some way, although it be on a lower level of activity. The souls moving to Hades are not fully themselves: crossing the river Lethe they lose all memory of the past; in a sense they do not keep their personal identity and they pursue a kind of diminished existence. They are like shadows of what they have been during their lives. This weak existence, however, is not an endless sleep without consciousness and without dreams. If Socrates praises the sweetness of an unlimited sleep, he clearly endeavors to convince his audience without expressing his own view. The whole life of Socrates was devoted to the search for truth; how could he believe the end of this noble activity to be complete unconsciousness or a dreamless sleep? This consideration is not put forward as a personal teaching of Socrates.

2. *Apologia*, 40c. In Socrates' view what happened to him, his condemnation to death, could not be something evil: he did not receive any warning from what he calls the divine sign (τὸ τοῦ θεοῦ σημεῖον). People commonly imagine death to be the supreme evil. Socrates states that the sign would certainly have warned him if this opinion were true. According to him it must be erroneous.

3. *Apologia*, 40c–e. Socrates believes in divine providence: God is not indifferent to the course and context of human existence. Not receiving any warning from the divine sign, Socrates could not accept the common assessment of death; people must be wrong in adhering to such opinion. Looking for a more positive appreciation, he formulates his two hypotheses, that of an endless sleep and that of the soul's moving to another place. Both hypotheses should be understood in the light of the former statement: death could not be regarded as something evil.

As to the second hypothesis, it also does not correspond to popular belief. Socrates imagines that life after death may be a continuation of what he constantly did on earth: meeting people, talking with them, and asking penetrating questions. He would be pleased to encounter some outstanding persons and to start fruitful conversations with them. Several names are mentioned; not a single philosopher is among them.[4] Does Socrates deliberately avoid proposing names of previous or contemporary philosophers? Does he not appreciate their teaching? The reason for this attitude could be that Socrates' main philosophical interest and concern are different from the subjects treated by his predecessors. He is not dealing with questions of natural philosophy, such as the origin and structure of the cosmos; his inquiry is related to man, to moral behavior, man's destiny, the nature of truth, and the real good.

But who are the people Socrates wants to meet in Hades? There are, of course, the traditional judges, examples of rightness and justice, very different from those who claim to be judges without possessing the essential qualifications of their duty.[5] Socrates is speaking to his own judges. He is strongly persuaded to be innocent; he was a deeply religious person and was very concerned with the moral education of his fellow citizens, especially of young people. He will be condemned in Athens, but he is sure not to be found guilty by the true judges in Hades; his real religious and moral attitude will be finally acknowledged. Socrates does not expect any penalty; on the contrary, he will be allowed to continue his philosophical activity as he did on earth, without threats or danger.

Among the prominent persons Socrates wants to meet are four

4. *Apologia*, 40e. Socrates does not refer to previous philosophers, not even with respect to people he wants to meet in Hades. The trial of Socrates took place in Athens. Before the fifth century this city was not a center of philosophical activity. Until that time Greek philosophy developed in the Near East, the south of Italy, and Sicily. There is a dialogue of Plato in which Socrates discusses with Parmenides the most basic issues of Platonic thought, yet the name of Parmenides is not mentioned in the list of persons whom Socrates wishes to encounter in Hades.

5. *Apologia*, 40e–41a. Socrates mentions Minos, king of Crete; Rhadamanthus, brother of Minos; his brother, Aeacus; Triptolemos (subject of one of the plays of Sophocles); and some demigods who in their life gave an example of right behavior. Three of these names also occur in the myth at the end of Plato's *Gorgias*, viz. Minos, Rhadamanthus, and Aeacus (*Gorgias*, 524a).

ancient poets: Orpheus, Musaeus, Homer, and Hesiod.[6] They are eminent people indeed, since they have been for generations the educators of their countrymen; their works were read and studied by everybody, their ideal of life was communicated and assimilated on a large scale, they effectively contributed to the building of Greek culture. And yet after the oracle of Delphi, Socrates had already met with some poets in order to learn the meaning of what the Pythia had declared. The experience, however, had been negative: poets do not really know what they believe they know. Like political people and craftsmen they do not truly understand what they are doing: in fact, they are ignorant without being aware of their lack of knowledge. Plato's valuation of poetry is equally negative; how could it be otherwise? The author is in search of truth, not of mythological narratives; in his dialogues he uses myths, but in a rational way: he has recourse to mythical stories in order to illustrate or support his philosophical doctrines. In addition, his pattern of education is hardly comparable to the traditional one: strong emphasis is laid on mathematical training and dialectical contemplation. If Socrates wants to talk with these ancient poets, it is not to learn what they have to say, but to examine their understanding critically. Socrates also is in search of truth: he himself is conscious of his ignorance; he wants to learn whether these famous poets truly grasp what they expound in their writings.

Socrates also wishes to meet Palamedes and Ajax[7]: the first has been innocently sentenced to death, the latter was an outstanding warrior in the Trojan conflict; after the death of Achilles he wanted to inherit his arms equipment, but it was bestowed upon Odysseus. Ajax was so disappointed that he died as a result of this misfortune. Quite obviously Socrates wishes to talk with them because both have been victims of a lack of understanding and recognition. Socrates discovered in them the image of his own destiny; he probably

6. *Apologia*, 41a. Orpheus is mentioned in the first place: according to a legend he married Eurydice, and when she died, he was inconsolable. He went down to Hades to bring her back: Eurydice was allowed to return to the earth, but she had to walk behind Orpheus, who was not permitted to look back at her. This condition, however, was not observed and Eurydice was compelled to return to Hades. Musaeus was the son or pupil of Orpheus. Both were regarded as the authors of some religious poems used by the Orphic associations.

7. *Apologia*, 41b.

desired to learn their evaluation of the events in their life.[8] Finally Socrates mentions the leader of the Greek army in the Trojan war, Agamemnon. The whole conflict between Agamemnon and Achilles was a matter of serious reflection on human behavior. He further wants to have talks with Odysseus, who was famous for his cleverness and diplomatic abilities. He finally desires to speak with Sisyphus, who had been condemned in Hades to hard and meaningless labor: he had to push a heavy stone to the top of a hill; when he reached the top the stone immediately returned to the spot from which he started moving it.[9] Undoubtedly Socrates is eager to ask questions about the conduct of those people: what they did and why they acted in such and such a way.

The ultimate interest of Socrates is the meaning of life and human conduct.[10] He must have been deeply disappointed by his trial and condemnation. And yet he never states that life is worthless: the question is asked, but it receives a positive answer in his own conduct and his teaching. Despite all misfortunes he still believes in the worth of human existence, as he still believes in divine providence.

The question concerning the worth of life is present also in the works of Aristotle. It is explicitly formulated at the beginning of the *Eudemian Ethics*: within this context the author expounds a series of arguments that may support a negative assessment of life.[11] This passage is not a mere collection of popular opinions; it is rather an aporematic inquiry on the question of whether life is worth living. Aristotle realizes that this issue is of fundamental importance at the outset of an ethical treatise: if the answer is negative, it makes no sense to examine the nature of happiness and the way in which

8. In this context Socrates mentions all those who died as a result of an unjust trial (διὰ κρίσιν ἄδικον); he wants to compare his own sufferings with theirs. He hopes it will help him to understand his misfortunes better when he compares them with those of other persons.

9. *Apologia*, 41b–c.

10. *Apologia*, 41b: By asking questions Socrates endeavors to discover above all those who are really wise and those who are imagined to be wise without truly being it. Wisdom implies consciousness of one's ignorance; this awareness is a starting point in each search for truth.

11. *Eth. Eud.*, I, 5. According to Aristotle everybody believes that it is easy to make right judgments (τὸ κρῖναι καλῶς) about what is truly valuable in life and what will fully satisfy man's aspirations. The author thoroughly disagrees on this opinion: even the worth of life may be questioned.

it may be attained; moral education becomes meaningless. More-over, the answer to the formulated question is not evident; it is not immediately obvious that it is more valuable to live than not to be born. The arguments put forward in support of a negative valuation of life are taken from daily experience within the context of Greek culture and to some extent from basic insights of Aristotelian thought.

A first consideration refers to the fact that some people reject their life and commit suicide. Aristotle mentions three causes that are at the origin of these negative attitudes: disease, unbearable pain, and physical calamity.[12] Not only are the people directly involved concerned; so are many others who, taking into account that these misfortunes may occur in each human existence, believe that it is preferable not to be born. If people had the opportunity of deciding whether they agree to exist or not, they would prefer not to live for the reasons mentioned; everybody runs the risk of having to face illness and disastrous events.[13] This viewpoint may recall a Heideg-gerian argument concerning human existence: everybody exists without his previous agreement; people are thrown into existence (*Geworfenheit*) without having consented to live.[14] According to the Aristotelian argument they would rather refuse to exist, taking into account the enormous dangers threatening human life.

A second consideration is related to childhood. For human beings the period of childhood is rather long, particularly in a time when the average duration of life was much shorter than it is now.[15]

12. *Eth. Eud.*, I, 5, 1215b18–22. The question of suicide has been repeatedly discussed by Stoic philosophers. In one of his letters to Lucilius Seneca writes that people should not be excessively attached to their life or excessively hate it. Man ought to be cautious, as there is in him some spontaneous inclination toward suicide (libido moriendi, *Epistolae ad Lucilium*, 24, 25). In Seneca's view man is allowed to commit suicide only when he has reached the firm conviction that he is unable to achieve the moral goal of his life. A similar viewpoint is adopted by Marcus Aurelius (III, 1, 2; V, 29, 1; VIII, 47, 5). In the context of the *Eudemian Ethics* Aristotle points to the fact of suicides in his time without formulating a moral evaluation. On the other hand, he states that most people cling to life as there is some happiness and sweetness in it (*Politica*, III, 6, 1178b25–30).

13. Aristotle declares that a magnanimous person will not in all circumstances cling to his life (*Nicomachean Ethics* [*Eth. Nic.*], IV, 3, 1124b6–9).

14. M. Heidegger, *Sein und Zeit*, Halle an der Saale, 1935 (4th ed.), p.179. Heideg-ger, however, does not conclude that humans would refuse to exist if they had the opportunity of choosing (cf. A. De Waelhens, *La philosophie de Martin Heidegger*, Louvain, 1942, p.83–84).

15. *Eth. Eud.*, I, 5, 1215b22–24.

According to the Stoics the awakening of reason takes place at the age of fourteen; in Plato and Aristotle too the learning program does not start early.[16] The growth of a human being to full maturity takes a long time; it is well known that in Aristotle's view children are on a lower level of humanity. They are not fully human persons because their rational capacity is not sufficiently developed.[17] Therefore, Aristotle's valuation of childhood is undeniably negative: the author writes that no sensible person would ever endure going back to childhood, since it would mean a return to imperfection.

In a third argument Aristotle draws attention to the normal experiences of a human life. In his view some of them are thoroughly indifferent: they are neither pleasant nor unpleasant; they cannot be taken into account to support the worth of human existence. Other experiences provide pleasure, but not of a noble kind; in this context nonexistence seems to be better than existence. The sum of all those experiences cannot contribute to achieving true happiness.[18] Which are the experiences the author has in mind when he refers to ignoble pleasure? In another passage of the *Eudemian Ethics* he mentions some activities that cannot be taken into account in view of achieving the ideal of happiness; such are activities devoted to vulgar and mechanic arts and those concerned with business. In the author's view vulgar arts are pursued only to gain popularity and mechanical arts roughly correspond to manual labor: they are wage-earning and sedentary; as to business, the term refers to market purchase and retail selling. It is a kind of commerce, an activity that had already been censured by Plato.[19] Noble activities are those that contribute to the attainment of happiness; they are mainly political life and philosophical contemplation.[20]

The next argument deals with a basic aspect of human life. Looking at the activities performed by humans all over the world, the author reaches the conclusion that they are generally performed

16. *Scholia ad Platonis Alcibiadem*, I, p.121E (S V F I, 149); *Jamblichi de anima apud Stobaei Eclogas*, I, 48, 8, p.317, 21 W. (S V F I, 149).

17. G. Verbeke, *Les degrés d'humanité et le sens du progrès chez Aristote*, p.140.

18. *Eth. Eud.*, I, 5, 1215b24–26.

19. *Eth. Eud.*, I, 4, 1215a26–32. Cf. Plato, *Leges*, V, 741e; V, 743d: Plato believes that commerce readily leads to conflicts and disagreements. Aristotle does not disapprove of any kind of exchanges of wares; what he condemns is commerce whose object is mere profit (*Politica*, I, 9, 1257b5–10).

20. In Aristotle's time manual labor had to be performed by slaves; it could not lead to achieving man's perfection and happiness.

unwillingly; they are not intended for their own sake and are not the result of a free choice. Circumstances of life and all kinds of influences induce people to do what they are actually doing; in other words, they do not freely determine the content of their daily life. They are compelled to do what they are doing in order to survive; how can such activities be taken into account in view of happiness? In this respect they are totally worthless, because they are not the outcome of a free personal choice. If such activities are supposed to be performed during an infinite extent of time, they still remain worthless: to make them everlasting does not transform their real nature and value.[21]

What about food and sexual intercourse? The question is whether pleasure connected with meals and sexual relations is sufficient to justify a positive valuation of life.[22] Aristotle intends to appreciate these experiences without taking into account cognitive activities that are normally included in them. Assimilation of food and sexual intercourse are conscious experiences, which in the case of humans involve intellectual and sensitive knowledge. The author, however, considers them in an abstract way as being vital functions oriented toward the subsistence of individuals and the preservation of the species. According to Aristotle's argument all these pleasures can never justify a positive valuation of life, since they don't have a specifically human character. They belong not only to human beings but also to irrational animals. When Aristotle examines the nature of happiness, he immediately states that it must be linked to a specifically human activity. One may object that sexual relations and meals present a different dimension in a human context from what they are in the case of animals. The Stagirite would certainly agree with this argument, but he considers these experiences in terms of their physiological nature.[23]

Finally remains the pleasure of sleeping. In this context the same

21. *Eth. Eud.*, I, 5, 1215b26–30. In Aristotle's view a truly moral action has to be performed for its own sake, not for something else; in other words, a good action should be accomplished because it is good (*Eth. Eud.*, VI, 2, 1139b3).

22. There is no universal agreement about the highest good for human beings: some people maintain it is intellectual knowledge, others believe it is virtue, and still others declare it is pleasure; in addition some individuals state that happiness is a mixture of two or even of the three values mentioned (*Eth. Eud.*, I, 1, 1214a30–b5). In his study of happiness Aristotle does not disregard pleasure; it is taken into consideration as a possible component of human development.

23. *Eth. Eud.*, I, 5, 1215b30–1216a2.

question arises again: the author does not deny the pleasure of a quiet sleep, but he wonders whether that kind of satisfaction allows one to conclude that existence is more valuable than nonexistence. According to the argument no such conclusion may be drawn, because sleeping does not belong to the realm of specifically human experiences; it is rather comparable to the status of vegetables. So it has no relation to happiness or human perfection; a sensible man will never prefer to live in order to enjoy the pleasure of sleeping.[24]

All these arguments have been framed by Aristotle in order to introduce his own inquiry; the question is put sharply: many pleasures experienced in life are not specifically human, some of them are not noble; on the other hand, there are many misfortunes that threaten human existence and most of man's activities are not initiated by a personal and free choice. Aristotle is quite conscious of the fact that the worth of life had been questioned by other authors: it was a traditional topic. Plutarch in *A Letter to Apollonius* refers to a passage in the *Eudemus* of Aristotle, where the author mentions the proverb telling that life is a punishment: to be born is the greatest disaster. "And this is such an old and ancient belief with us that no one knows at all either the beginning of the time or the name of the person who first promulgated it, but it continues to be a fixed belief for all time."[25] Aristotle mentions this very ancient opinion in connection with the story of Silenus, who had been captured by Midas. The latter wanted to learn from his captive what is the most desirable thing for mankind. Silenus first refused to answer this question and remained silent: he thought it better for man not to be informed of his message.[26] Finally, however, he yielded to the repeated insistence of Midas and declared that the best thing for all men and women is not to be born; the next best thing is, after being born, to die as soon as possible.[27] *Eudemus* is an

24. *Eth. Eud.*, I, 5, 1216a2–10. Aristotle dedicated a small treatise to the topic of sleeping. During sleep all sensitive perceptions are suppressed, whereas vegetative activities continue. Hence the author concludes that sleep must be connected with the role and activity of the *sensus communis*, which is the principal sensitive faculty, the source of all perceptions, and which is located in the heart (*De somno et vigilia*, 2, 456a21–24; 3, 457a33–b2; 3, 458a25–28).

25. *Plutarch's Moralia*, with an English Translation by Frank Cole Babbitt, vol. II, Cambridge (Mass.), London, 1956, *A Letter to Apollonius*, 115c.

26. *A Letter to Apollonius*, 115d. In Greek mythology Silenus was believed to be the son of Hermes and a nymph.

27. *A Letter to Apollonius*, 115e. Cf. Sophocles, *Oedipus Coloneus*, v. 1225–1237.

early work of Aristotle, in which the author maintains an outspoken dualistic philosophy of man: soul is a substance, which represents the true self of man; life on earth is an exile and a punishment. Man has to free himself as soon as possible from the body in order to become what he truly is.[28]

A similar story is found in Herodotus: the mother of Kleobis and Biton wanted to take part in a ceremony organized at Argos to worship the goddess Hera. The two youngsters intended to take their mother to the celebration, but unfortunately the oxen from the field arrived late. Finally they decided to put on the yoke and to pull the cart themselves over a distance of forty-five stadia. The people of Argos admired the strength of the youngsters and praised their mother. The latter was full of pride and joy: standing in front of the divine statue she prayed that the goddess would bestow on her children the very best gift that a man could ever get. After this prayer the youngsters presented their offerings and went to sleep in the sanctuary; they never got up again. By this the goddess showed that it is better for humans to die than to live.[29]

Theognis, who lived in the sixth century B.C., expresses the same pessimistic view of life: the author categorically states that the best thing for humans is not to be born, never to contemplate the light of the sun. As to those who are born, it is desirable for them to go to Hades as soon as possible and to be buried under the earth.[30] This statement again expresses a negative view of human condition. Dating back to the sixth century B.C. the topic was still worthy of consideration in the fourth century by a philosopher such as Aris-

28. *Aristotelis Dialogorum Fragmenta*, ed. R. Walzer. Florence, 1934, fr. 8, p.20; Jamblichus, *Protrepticus* 8 (47, 21–48, 9 Pistelli); *Fragmenta selecta*, ed. Ross, fr. 10b. Human existence is characterized by the union of body and soul: this union is compared by Aristotle to the famous torture of war prisoners who were tied to a dead body. The background of this pessimistic view of life is the tremendous difference between the two components of man: the body is not worthy to be linked to the soul.

29. Herodotus, *Historiae*, I, 31. In this little story the two youngsters are praised for various reasons: their devotion to their mother, their religious attitude toward Hera, their strength and perseverance. Their reward is a precocious death: in this way they are saved from all misfortunes and calamities that may occur in human life.

30. Theognis, *Elegiae* I, 425–428, ed. D. Young (Leipzig: Teubner), p.28. According to the second part of this message it is preferable to stay in Hades instead of living on earth, yet according to popular belief souls in the underworld have only a diminished existence. In any case, according to Theognis life is not valuable or desirable.

totle. Apparently the matter is taken seriously by the Stagirite as it represents an ancient belief that is widespread. If it were true, it would make any moral reflection useless and meaningless. Dealing with ethical issues, Aristotle endeavors to attain a universal agreement among humans, if not fully, at least to some extent: he believes such a consensus is possible since everybody bears within himself an appropriate inclination toward truth.[31] Everybody is craving for truth, so it must be possible to reach an agreement on basic ethical issues. That means that humans ought to keep faith in the worth of life: the ancient negative valuations should be replaced by a more positive view.

In a little poem on the goddess, *Hope,* Theognis presents a picture of the deplorable situation of mankind: all gods have left the earth; one after the other they abandoned mankind and returned to Olympus. Among the divinities who left Theognis mentions Faith and Temperance; he also cites the Graces and states that oaths are not reliable anymore. Humans do not worship the immortal gods; they have lost any sense of piety and do not keep the laws of their political community. The only divinity still remaining on earth, in the world of humans, is Hope; if this deity also decided to leave, man would be completely abandoned to his own destiny. So humans should be very cautious: they have to worship Hope as faithfully and carefully as they can in order to prevent this divinity from leaving them.[32] The picture is dark; within this context how could human existence be desirable? When Pindarus characterizes human beings, he particularly emphasizes their weakness: life is very short and vulnerable; man is like the dream of a shadow.

According to Euripides the birth of a child should not be celebrated; it should not be an opportunity for rejoicing, but rather a reason for sorrow and sadness, since a new being has been thrown into so many troubles and hardships. When somebody dies, there

---

31. *Eth. Eud.,* I, 6, 1216b26–31. In ethical matters Aristotle endeavors to attain a universal agreement among all humans, and he believes it is possible as everybody bears within himself some kinship with truth (οἰκεῖόν τι πρὸς τὴν ἀλήθειαν). This consensus certainly is necessary with respect to political communities, which are grounded on a common moral sense of what is right and wrong.

32. Theognis, *Elegiae* 1, v. 1135–1150, ed. D. Young (Teubner), p.69. In Theognis' view the poor condition of mankind is a consequence of moral decline. The departure of the gods to Olympus results from the disappearance of basic moral values. This situation confirms the author's pessimistic and negative assessment of human life.

are many reasons for being pleased and joyful, because a man has been released from his sufferings.[33] The same consideration is expounded by Cicero,[34] whereas Seneca writes that souls would decidedly refuse to return to earth if they had not forgotten the misfortunes of former lives.[35]

It would be erroneous, however, when dealing with ancient thought, to mention only negative valuations of life: these are certainly present in Greek culture, but there are also very positive appreciations of human existence. One of the most famous and eloquent is a passage of Sophocles' *Antigone* in which man is depicted as the most wonderful being in the universe. And yet even in this picture there is a pessimistic accent: man is very ingenious and powerful, but he is unable to overcome the threat of death.[36] When Anaxagoras was asked why people might prefer to live rather than not to be born, his answer was quite characteristic. According to the Greek philosopher it is worthwhile to contemplate the heavenly bodies and the harmonious disposition of the universe.[37] In this opinion the worth of life is connected with the contemplation of the cosmos, which is regarded as a perfectly ordered arrangement: this cosmos is a model of what human life ought to be and actually will be if, like the universe, it is governed by the mind. Anaxagoras does not mention any possible improvement of human life and society; apparently this social perspective is not among his concerns. However, his valuation of life is positive. Yet it is undeniable that in Greek culture many statements about human existence are rather negative. What is the background of this pessimistic trend?

Let us look at some factors that may throw light on this attitude. One of the most important may be the widespread belief in fate. It is not easy to give an adequate definition of this notion; in any case, it means that human existence is inexorably dominated by some higher power, which is considered to be blind.[38] Fate does not

33. Euripides, *Cresphonte*, fr. 452 (Nauck).
34. Cicero, *Tusculanae Disputationes*, I, 48, 115.
35. Seneca, *Epistolae ad Lucilium*, IV, 36, 10: "veniet iterum, qui nos in lucem reponat dies, quem multi recusarent, nisi oblitos reduceret."
36. Sophocles, *Antigone*, v. 332–375; v. 361: Ἅιδα μόνον φεῦξιν οὐκ ἐπάξεται.
37. *Eth. Eud.*, I, 5, 1216a10–14.
38. D. Amand, *Fatalisme et liberté dans l'antiquité grecque*, Louvain, 1945. The author mainly studies the antifatalistic arguments developed by Carmeades and repeated again and again by later writers, non-Christians as well as Christians.

make any distinction between good and bad individuals, between innocent and guilty people: the blows of fate hit all kinds of persons, making no distinctions; they are unpredictable and unavoidable. It is hard to say why particular individuals are struck rather than others. Each individual feels threatened by this dark power.[39] Greek tragedy presents the lives of some famous characters who at some stage of their life were powerful and highly regarded and afterward became deplorable victims of fate. As a result man was not regarded as the author and autonomous principle of his own destiny: he always felt endangered by this higher power, whose impact and interference were unpredictable. In the light of such popular belief, it becomes quite understandable that human existence was not positively assessed. In view of escaping from the threatening of fate, it seemed better not to be born. This influence of fate was highly depressing; it jeopardized man's mastery over his own life and could push someone guiltless to a tragic end. If Oedipus, Antigone, Iphigenia, and many others had known beforehand the content of their life, they most probably would have chosen not to be born.

Another element of popular belief was related to the envy of the gods toward man. Greek religion was characterized by anthropomorphism: divine beings were not regarded as belonging to a transcendent level, very different from that of humans: on the contrary, they were rather conceived as immortal humans. The latter are mortal, whereas divine beings are immortal. Of course, this distinction is not unimportant; nevertheless, in many respects gods behave as human beings do: they have their personal character, their passions and emotions, their sympathies and antipathies. Even moral faults are not excluded from the realm of the gods: robberies, lies, deceits, unfaithfulness occur not only among humans but also among divine beings. In the temples the gods are represented as human beings: the Greeks entering to worship their gods did not feel estranged. In a sense they went to their own world and were confronted with a kind of more powerful humans. In this respect

39. Various Greek terms correspond to the notion of fate: τύχη, ἀνάγκη, μοῖρα, μοῖραι, εἱμαρμένη. Dealing with the question of how happiness can be achieved, Aristotle also mentions the hypothesis of a divine μοῖρα or τύχη (*Eth. Nic.*, I, 9, 1099b9–11): If there are other divine gifts, why cannot happiness also stem from God? In Aristotle's view this topic rather belongs to another inquiry (1099b13–14). As a matter of fact, the answer to this question depends on the nature of God and his relation with man. Such issues are treated in Aristotle's metaphysics.

ancient Greek religion was very different from the Jewish and later from the Islamic cult: both religions are monotheistic and repudiate any representation of the divine being. The Greek gods are not considered to be infinite, whereas lower beings are finite: before Plotinus the notion of infinite means something undetermined, not completed, not finished; later the term referred to the highest degree of perfection.[40] The Greek gods were immortal but finite; they were believed to be jealous of man's perfection. Man should never forget to be a mortal being; he should not be too wealthy or too powerful; he should keep measure in everything.[41] So human life is endangered again by some powerful and highly envious divine beings: instead of divine love and providence, there is constantly a threat of jealous divinities. Men should always be cautious and careful: they should avoid provoking the envy of the gods. This atmosphere is also depressing; it does not favor a joyful confidence in life. In Plato's opinion this belief has to be firmly rejected. In the transcendent world of Ideas the highest Form is that of the good: everything participates in this divine goodness; jealousy cannot be found in the realm of the divine beings.[42] According to the *Timaeus* the world has been made in conformity with immutable patterns.[43] In Aristotle's philosophy, too, there is no room for the jealousy of the gods, since the First Substance cannot possess a direct knowledge of the world.[44]

In popular belief life after death is not denied but is far from being attractive: man continues to exist as a shadow of what he has been. The proper characteristic of the gods is that they are immortal; man can never become immortal, for in that case he would be a divine being. Death is the end of a mortal individual; existence in Hades is weakened; all memories have been taken away from the

40. R. Mondolfo, *L'infinito nel pensiero dell' antichità classica*, Florence, 1956 (2d ed.), p.635.

41. "Nothing too much" (μηδὲν ἄγαν). This proverb is attributed to Solon (cf. C. J. de Vogel, *Greek Philosophy*, I, *Thales to Plato*, Leyden, 1950, p.3).

42. *Phaedrus*, 247a. This view of Plato's is quite coherent with his philosophy of the divine: if God coincides with the highest Idea, religious anthropomorphism ought to be radically repudiated.

43. *Timaeus*, 28a; 30c–d.

44. *Metaphysica* (*Metaph.*), XII, 9, 1074b33–35. Since God is not regarded as the creator of the world, he cannot directly know it without being passive in some way.

dead; they have lost their identity.[45] So the gods have no reason to be envious of the dead, and yet they continue to exist, whereas irrational animals do not. The Greeks always showed a high valuation of reason: man is able to think, to speak, and to create a world of culture. Thus man represents the highest level of perfection in the universe. It is understandable that in this context some existence after death is attributed to humans, but it could hardly enhance the value of life.[46]

Finally there is the prephilosophic notion of time: man is a temporal being; he is part of the universe, inserted in a ceaseless evolution, in which the present instant constantly passes away and is replaced by another moment. In ancient Greek culture time was considered to be cyclical: there is nothing new under the sun, what happens now is not new; it has happened before an indefinite number of times, and it will come back again. So the development of the universe is not the story of a constant progress: the evolution of the world is composed of a limited number of events, which are repeated indefinitely. The present cycle brings nothing new, it repeats what has happened many times before, and the future will bring a repetition of the present time. It is always the same drama that is repeated.[47] In this perspective life could not be highly valued: nothing is new, all beings already existed in the past, all events already occurred. Is it worth being born, if man has to repeat the same story indefinitely? If the successive cycles of time reproduce the same beings and the same events, one will seriously question the meaning of his life. Here again a rather negative valuation of human existence is quite understandable.

Is life worth living? What is the answer of Aristotle? It is quite

45. E. Rohde, *Psyché: Le culte de l'âme chez les grecs et leur croyance à l'immortalité,* Paris, 1952; especially chapter VII: "Comment on se représentait la vie dans l'au-delà." The situation of those who stayed in Hades was not the same: it did not depend upon former moral behavior, but mostly on whether or not they had been initiated into the mysteries of Eleusis.

46. According to Fustel de Coulanges the most primitive belief in the Greek world was that humans after death continue to exist in their graves; they did not give any account of their former life and did not receive any reward nor punishment. Relatives, however, were expected to bury their dead and to bring them some food and beverage. In this early stage dead people were highly respected and were regarded as a kind of divine beings (*La cité antique,* Paris, n.d., p.12–20). The work of Fustel de Coulanges is mainly based on funeral ceremonies.

47. The cyclical character of time has been most strongly emphasized by the Stoics.

clear that the Stagirite does not approve of the traditional belief in the negative worth of life; in his view life is worth living. The end of human existence is happiness, which is the outcome of steady moral behavior. The author acknowledges that moral behavior is difficult; it can only be pursued through constant effort and endeavor.[48] And yet happiness is not confined to a small number of humans: it belongs to many people; it is reached by all those who are not unable to practice virtue.[49] Of course, the level of happiness is not always the same: the highest degree, represented by constant philosophical contemplation, could hardly be attained by the majority of the people, but most of them are able to practice virtue and to attain a limited happiness within the boundaries of their existence on earth.

In Aristotle's view the worth of life is not connected with immortality of the soul and existence after death. As will be explained later on, the author does not accept the immortality of the human soul, since all human activities, even intellectual knowing, are linked to the bodily organism.[50]

In this respect the teaching of Aristotle is decidedly different from that of Plato: whereas the latter stresses the immaterial character of the soul, the former rather emphasizes the unity of man. Nor is the worth of life linked to religious belief in divine providence; from a philosophical viewpoint, Aristotle repudiates this prephilosophical opinion. It is incompatible with the notion of Pure Act: the first principle is totally immutable and impassible; its substance does not include any potential aspect.[51] On the other hand, it is not considered to be the efficient cause of the world, but only its final cause: within this framework the first substance could not grasp the world without being passive. Therefore, the author excludes any kind of providence.

Finally, a positive valuation of life cannot be based on Aristotle's

48. *Eth. Nic.*, II, 9, 1109a24: Virtue is a mean between two extremes. It is easy to yield to irrational impulses and tendencies, but it is difficult to adopt a balanced and reasonable attitude in all circumstances of life.

49. *Eth. Nic.*, I, 9, 1099b18. This doctrine corresponds to Aristotle's universal teleology.

50. G. Verbeke, *Comment Aristote conçoit-il l'immatériel?* in: *Revue philosophique de Louvain*, 44, 1946, p.205–236.

51. *Metaph.*, XII, 6, 1071b19–26. In Aristotle's view there must be an ontological priority of act toward potency: what is in potency can only be actualized by something that is already in act.

notion of time: in his view time never started and will never come to an end; it is linked to the ceaseless evolution of the universe.[52] In this sense time plays some part in the development of ethical conduct: virtues are abiding habits that are gradually acquired by repeating the same acts; they are like technical skills that are the result of repeated efforts in the course of time.[53] Nevertheless, the general valuation of time in Aristotle is rather negative: time is not primarily a source of progress and growth, but rather of decline and forgetfulness. It is not so much a principle of wisdom as a cause of oblivion and weakening.[54]

Despite all these considerations Aristotle maintains the worth of life: he must have some strong arguments to cling to his viewpoint. Apparently the most basic reason for this conviction is universal teleology: everything in the universe is oriented toward the good, the whole world strives toward this supreme value, nature permanently tends to what is good.[55]

In this respect Aristotle is a faithful disciple of Plato, although he rejects his theory of transcendent Ideas. Consequently man also is naturally oriented toward the good: how could human existence be evil if it is basically directed toward what is valuable? Could nature fail to attain the goal to which it strives? Next to nature Aristotle also accepts the impact of chance. But the orderly arrangement of the world cannot be due to fortune. All living beings, whether animals or plants, spring from a determinate seed: olives from the seed of olives and men from the sperma of men. This orderly disposition, which may be observed on earth, is much more manifest in the movements of the celestial bodies, in which nothing due to chance may be noticed.[56] In Aristotle's opinion chance is an accidental cause[57]: it implies some essential or principal cause, which is

52. *Physics*, VIII, 1, 251a10–28.

53. G. Verbeke, *Moral Behaviour and Time in Aristotle's Nicomachean Ethics*, in: *Kephalaion: Studies in Greek Philosophy and Its Continuation*, Assen, 1975, p.78–90.

54. *Physics*, IV, 13, 222b16–27. Any change is by nature ecstatic (ἐκστατικόν): it pushes things out of the condition in which they happen to be. Time is a constant manifestation of the instability of the world.

55. *Eth. Nic.*, I, 1, 1094a1–3. This teaching of Aristotle also corresponds to the doctrine of Plato: if the Idea of the good is the highest transcendent Form, everything is subordinated to this supreme value and oriented toward it.

56. *Physics*, II, 4, 196a28–b5.

57. *Physics*, II, 5, 197a5. In fact, Aristotle makes a distinction between chance (τύχη) and spontaneity (τὸ αὐτόματον): the first term refers to deliberate acts by which an unexpected result is reached. Spontaneity does not include reflection and choice.

prior to it, either nature or human choice.[58] With respect to the universe, the author strongly emphasizes that there must be something prior to chance, either nature or intellect or some factor of that kind.[59] Chance is an efficient cause, a principle of movement, but it is undetermined, inscrutable, and unsteady.[60] Hence it cannot be the principal cause of an orderly arranged universe.

What about happiness; can it be the result of chance? In Aristotle's view the highest moral perfection can never be the result of chance. A moral action, in order to be moral, ought to be consciously and deliberately intended; even more, a good act should be implemented because it is good.[61] Does the moral agent pursue anything beyond the ethical value of his act? Not according to Aristotle: the goodness of the act is the ultimate end that ought to be intended. What about a subject who by acting morally wants to obtain some reward or avoid some punishment in this life or after death? This perspective is hardly taken into consideration by Aristotle. A moral act can never be the accidental and exceptional result of an activity performed to reach something else. In his *Eudemian Ethics* Aristotle states that if moral life depended upon fortune or nature, it would be beyond the hopes of many people, but if it depends on man himself and his conduct it will be more common and more divine.[62] That is indeed the conviction of the Greek Master: man is the author of his own destiny; he is by nature a moral being and so happiness is widely diffused. Most people participate in moral life leading to the full perfection of human existence.[63]

However, Aristotle recognizes that some auxiliary or secondary elements of happiness may be referred to chance: in order to implement the full development of his life, man needs not only personal moral behavior, but some other factors that rather belong to the sphere of fortune. In this respect the author points to the possession

58. *Physics*, II, 6, 198a9–13.
59. *Physics*, II, 4, 196a28–31.
60. *Physics*, II, 5, 197a9; 197a30; 198a2–5.
61. *Eth. Nic.*, VI, 2, 1139b3; VI, 5, 1140b7. Moral action does not coincide with making or producing something: these latter terms refer to acts that are oriented to something distinct from the activity itself. A moral act does not intend anything beyond the action itself.
62. *Eth. Eud.*, I, 3, 1215a13. In Aristotle's view ethical behavior is not merely a natural phenomenon, although man is by nature a moral animal.
63. *Eth. Nic.*, I, 9, 1099b18.

of some material goods, some economic wealth[64]; external goods are desirable in order to make the practice of some moral virtues, such as liberality and magnanimousness, possible.[65] In this context the author also mentions the practice of friendship: it is desirable in all ages of life; it is the source of coherence in all communities from the family to political society.[66] Yet Aristotle does not consider the relation to friends to be an essential constituent of happiness.[67] The same viewpoint is adopted with regard to political power: those who are invested with political responsibility have the onerous duty but also the opportunity of constantly practicing the virtue of justice in the exercise of their functions.[68] The author also mentions good birth and satisfactory children[69]: good birth contributes to the development of moral life. As to the rearing of children Aristotle teaches that the family is the basic human community out of which the self-sufficient society of the city-state grows: it is the first cell in which moral life awakens and develops.[70]

Life is worth living: it generally leads to some degree of moral life and happiness within the limits of human existence on earth. So it is preferable to be born than not to be born; life is the greatest gift one ever may receive; being the principle of their existence, a father is more than anybody else a benefactor of his children.[71] Man is by nature a moral animal, he is the author of his own destiny, of his ethical perfection and happiness. The goal of life does not depend upon fate or chance: it is achieved by each individual, whatever the circumstances of life may be. What is essential is moral conduct.

64. *Eth. Nic.*, I, 8, 1099a31–33. The Aristotelian notion of happiness essentially means the full development of human capacities: such development could hardly be achieved without some material wealth.

65. *Eth. Nic.*, IV, 1–2; particularly IV, 2, 1120a23–27; 1120b4–9.

66. *Eth. Nic.*, VIII, 1, 1155a5–31.

67. *Eth. Nic.*, IX, 9, 1169b3ff.

68. *Eth. Nic.*, I, 8, 1099b1; 13, 1102a7–10.

69. *Eth. Nic.*, I, 8, 1099b2–3.

70. *Politica*, I, 1, 1252a24–b15.

71. *Eth. Nic.*, VIII, 11, 1161a15–17; VIII, 12, 1162a4–7; *Politica*, I, 12, 1259b10–17.

[3]

A MORAL ANIMAL

ACCORDING to Friedrich Nietzsche man is a diseased animal. In his work *Zur Genealogie der Moral* the author criticizes the overturn of values that occurred in Western thought, mainly under the influence of Christian religion.[1] Values have been overthrown and falsified; in the author's view the origin of this radical transformation is a kind of resentment, which is an imaginative revenge of defeated individuals.[2] When weak subjects feel overcome, all kinds of negative reactions and judgments regarding strength, vitality, and whatever they are unable to get arise in them. In the mind of people without force, such resentment gives rise to the construction of a moral system, which repudiates whatever is strong and noble; in this way resentment as suppressed relief tries to find a justification of its own weakness. Consequently a metaphysical and anthropological doctrine is invented, maintaining that man does not coincide with his actions: in this opinion man is regarded as a substantial and free being. According to Nietzsche this theory is totally false: each individual coincides with his actions and ought to be reduced to the activities that he performs; hence actions can never be attributed to a human subject as if it could act differently from the way it actually does.[3] Moral doctrines are considered to

---

1. According to Nietzsche, in moral life there has been a rebellion of slaves: it started with the Jews and it has been fully successful (cf. *Zur Genealogie der Moral*, Leipzig, n.d. p.260: "dass nämlich mit den Juden der Sklavenaufstand in der Moral beginnt"; p.262: "Gewiss ist wenigstens, dass sub hoc signo Israel mit seiner Rache und Umwertung aller Werte, bisher über alle anderen Ideale, über alle vornehmeren Ideale immer wieder triumphiert hat").

2. *Zur Genealogie der Moral*, p.263.

3. S. Vanni Rovighi, *Uomo e natura. Appunti per una antropologia filosofica.* Milan, 1980, p.43; *Zur Genealogie der Moral*, p.272: "Aber es gibt kein solches Substrat; es gibt kein 'Sein' hinter dem Tun, Wirken, Werden; der 'Täter' ist zum Tun bloss hinzugedichtet—das Tun ist alles".

be a construction of weak individuals who attempt to justify their weakness.

Moreover, resentment also raises in man a feeling of culpability and bad conscience. Remorse is considered to be an illness that arises when man happens to be in a peaceful condition: in this situation feelings unable to be discharged outwardly turn into the self and produce an internal dissatisfaction and suffering.[4] The author firmly opposes ascetic ideals that involve renunciation and praises the will to power and the supremacy of vital values. In Nietzsche's view religious asceticism is merely negative, whereas the one promoted by philosophers such as Plato, Descartes, Spinoza, Leibniz, and Kant is not authentic: their ideal is that of a divinized and winged animal, which hovers beyond real life.[5]

Aristotle was not a Christian, and yet in his view a moral man is not a weak individual who endeavors to justify his weakness. On the contrary he is a strong personality, who because of adequate ethical knowledge and constant training gradually effects the full perfection of his being, which coincides with happiness.[6] The fundamental moral virtues, such as wisdom, courage, temperance, and justice, far from being consequences of weakness in character, are the result of a perseverant effort toward the implementation of the highest human possibilities. These virtues correspond to the deepest nature of man, and yet they are not present from the beginning of life. Moral behavior is not a mere gift, something that belongs to man's natural equipment; it is the result of both fundamental natural propensity and potency and personal effort and assiduous practice.[7]

According to Aristotle man is by nature a moral animal: he is not only a political being but also a moral person. The two aspects are closely linked to each other; they belong to the very nature of each

4. In Nietzsche's view feeling of remorse and culpability originates from some primitive and basic relations among humans, particularly those between sellers and buyers (*Zur Genealogie der Moral*, p.300–301; concerning the origin of bad conscience, p.318–319).

5. Vanni Rovighi, *Uomo e natura*, p.47–48.

6. In Aristotle's view the term happiness, or εὐδαιμονία, primarily has an objective meaning: it does not refer in the first place to an internal feeling of pleasure, but to a state of perfection, in which the highest capacities of a human being have been actualized (*Nicomachean Ethics* [*Eth. Nic.*], I, 7, 1097b22: τὸ ἄριστον).

7. *Eth. Nic.*, II, 1, 1103a31–1103b2: Moral virtues are acquired through practice and assiduous exercise; in this respect, virtues are comparable to technical skills.

human individual.[8] These features are not accidental qualities, nor even permanent properties that always proceed from the essential structure. In Aristotle's view the concept of nature plays an important part: the universe is not a chaotic whole of individual things existing on their own, but a well-ordered cosmos in which everything has its place and its function. Not only do the four elements have their natural location, to which they always tend when they are at some distance from it, but all beings have their specific nature and their appropriate position in the totality. Sensible beings are compounded of undetermined matter and form; the latter is the source and principle of determination and perfection. This substantial form is also dynamic: it is the origin of the specific activity that is proper to each being. So everything in our sensible universe is a compound of potency and act: in the structure of a being potency is always present; matter does not disappear when it is joined to form, it remains present in sensible things as a permanent source of potentiality. Form, on the contrary, is the dynamic cause of a specific development. Humans also are a compound of matter and form: at every moment of their existence they bear within themselves a principle of indetermination and potentiality; is it because of this material component that man is a moral being? Not exactly, although in the case of human beings and their moral behavior the material principle is to be taken into account.[9] Man is not only some finite act; he is constantly in potency toward new achievements and new perfections. If man is by nature a moral animal, that means that moral behavior, moral development, corresponds to his twofold structure, to the potentiality of the material component and to the rational perfection of the formal constituent.

8. *Politica*, I, 2, 1253a1–4: Aristotle is very formal in his statement. Man is by nature a political animal; it is part of the essential structure of humans to be incorporated in a political community. If somebody by nature were unfit to live in a political society, he would be below or beyond human condition; such animal would rather belong to the category of irrational beings or would transcend the level of human perfection.

9. The notion of potency plays an important part in moral life: ethical perfection is the outcome of a gradual development by means of repeatedly accomplished virtuous actions. In Aristotle's view there are various degrees of moral behavior; some individuals achieve progress more and faster than others. This doctrine of gradual moral development was not accepted by the ancient representatives of the Stoic School: to be a wise man one has to possess all virtues; as long as he lacks one of them, he must be counted among the majority of the unwise (cf. G. Verbeke, *Les Stoïciens et le progrès de l'histoire*, in: *Revue philosophique de Louvain*, 62, 1964, p.5–38.).

As a result, the ideal of moral life is not the privilege of a small group of selected individuals, but a way of life and conduct to which all humans are oriented and spontaneously inclined.[10] Humans are able to attain moral virtue, to establish the ruling of reason over passions and emotions, and to reach in this way balanced behavior, avoiding the excesses of irrational movements. It is true that not everybody behaves in conformity with reason; many people deviate from the right way by all kinds of impulses and do not follow the instructions of their rational faculty; even moral judgment may be disturbed by irrational tendencies.[11] Yet everybody is called to the perfection of ethical life, since moral conduct corresponds to the essential structure of a person. According to the Stoics, the number of wise individuals is very limited; only very few reach the highest level of moral perfection. The great majority of the people belong to the group of those who are called insane or foolish, since their life is not directed by reason.[12] When somebody asked Seneca whether he believed himself to be wise, the answer was negative; in his view only exceptional individuals are really wise, perhaps only one in five centuries.[13] Nevertheless, according to the Stoics also, man is by nature a moral being: the soul of every individual is a particle of divine Reason, which permeates the whole universe. Each human individual bears within himself the seeds of moral conduct: ethical life is the development of what is initially present as a germ, which has to grow and to increase according to its

10. *Politica*, VIII, 5, 1339b27–31. According to Aristotle it rarely happens that men achieve their final perfection: the level of permanent intellectual contemplation is not attained by the mass, yet the author maintains that it is the real end of human life and that everybody is naturally oriented to this goal.

11. In Aristotle's view, as more generally in the Greek tradition, there is a close connection between reason (λόγος) and order or harmony: reason is considered to be a principle of harmonious arrangements and dispositions in the universe as well as in human conduct. In this respect the viewpoint of D. Hume is quite contrary to that of Aristotle; he writes, "Reason is and ought only to be the slave of the passions and can never pretend to any other office than to serve and obey them" (*Human Nature*, III, 1, 1). Regarding the valuation of passions, Aristotle continues the tradition of Plato; as to the position of the Stoics, it was much more negative.

12. Plutarchus, *De Stoicorum repugnantiis*, cp.31, p.1048e (SVF III, 662). Some of Aristotle's considerations about moral conduct as it is actually practiced are also rather pessimistic: the author believes that most people are governed by their feelings, particularly by pleasure and pain (*Eth. Nic.*, X, 9, 1179b10–16; *Politica*, VI, 4, 1319b32–33).

13. Seneca, *Epistulae ad Lucilium* (*Epist.*), 42, 1: "nam ille alter fortasse tamquam phoenix semel anno quingentesimo nascitur."

hidden possibilities. Every individual knows and loves himself; man spontaneously endeavors to protect, to preserve, and to develop his own substance. From this initial and spontaneous tendency derives the inclination toward moral behavior.[14] Although the highest perfection of ethical life is exceptional, the natural orientation toward moral conduct is present in everybody. Both the Stoics and Aristotle agree that moral life is not something foreign to human individuals, that it is not imposed from without as a compulsion, but corresponds to the deepest aspiration of a person.

According to the Stoic view all humans are equal; they all participate in the light of divine Reason, even slaves and barbarians. Nobody is a slave by nature; if some people are in this social condition, it must be as a result of some contingent events.[15] Seneca stated that nobody could ever be a slave as far as his soul is concerned. As to the barbarians, the Stoics wanted them to be incorporated into one and the same universal republic,[16] ruled by the same laws; they also recommended an all-embracing philanthropy, since all humans are children of the same family, all born from the same father.[17] In this respect Aristotle is more critical, presumably under the influence of the society of his time. Slavery was generally tolerated and had become a kind of normal social institution. Yet as a true philosopher he put it into question: he wanted to know whether it was really justified and tried to ascertain whether slaves were actually deprived from the use of reason. He reached the conclusion that at least some slaves do not deserve to be in that condition; prisoners of war do not necessarily have a lower degree of rationality; even Plato had been a slave.[18] According to our author some individuals are slaves by nature because of their low degree of

14. Diogenes Laertius, VII, 85–87.

15. Seneca, *Epist.* 44, 2: "Nom omnes curia admittit . . . , non reicit quemquam philosophia nec eligit: omnibus lucet"; *De Beneficiis* III, 18: "Nulli praeclusa virtus est, omnibus patet, omnes admittit, omnes invitat, ingenuos, libertinos, servos, reges et exsules; nudo homine contenta est."

16. Seneca, *De Beneficiis* III, 20: "Errat, si quis existimat servitutem in totum hominem descendere: pars melior eius excepta est. . . . Corpus itaque est, quod domino fortuna tradidit. Hoc emit, hoc vendit: interior ea pars mancipio dari non potest."

17. Cicero, *De Officiis* I, 43, 153: "Illa autem sapientia, quam principem dixi, rerum est divinarum et humanarum scientia, in qua continetur deorum et hominum communitas et societas inter ipsos."

18. *Politica*, I, 6, 1255a21–32. Aristotle points to the fact that the origin of a war may be unjust: in such a case a prisoner does not deserve to be a slave.

rational capacity: they are not able to assume the full responsibility of their conduct and are to be directed by other people. They are only capable of understanding instructions given by somebody else and of implementing them.[19] This doctrine is far from being a mere justification of the existing institution of slavery: it makes an essential distinction among individuals happening to be in that situation. Hence slaves are not excluded from moral life: they participate in the rationality of their masters and of the laws. As to barbarians, they also are moral beings by nature, although they are on a lower level of cultural evolution: they are not devoid of moral sense, but they do not reach the degree of rational activity that exists in the area of Greek civilization.[20] In this area rationality developed gradually: in the first stage people were only concerned with daily needs of food and clothing. Then followed the discovery of technical skills and abilities. In a third period political societies were grounded, in order to promote the well-being of all members by means of the rule of law. Then came the study of sensible nature, followed in the last period by the investigation of suprasensible reality.[21] In Aristotle's opinion Greek civilization is the kingdom of reason: barbarians, particularly those from Asia, did not attain the same degree of evolution. With respect to women, Aristotle is convinced that their rational capacity is lower than that of men; generally speaking they are weaker than men, since their degree of natural warmth is lower.[22] So their life is more strongly influenced by emotions and passions: this, however, is not an obstacle preventing them from practicing moral behavior. They participate in the rational life of their family as well as that of the political community to which they belong.[23] Children are in a provisional prerational

19. *Politica*, I, 5, 1254b20–24. Aristotle has in view a very low degree of rationality: the difference among humans is compared to that between body and soul or between men and animals. If some individuals happen to be on such a low level of rational knowing, it is better for them to be slaves, so that they may be guided by the insights of other persons.

20. *Politica*, III, 14, 1285a19–22. With respect to their way of behaving barbarians are closer to slavery than Greeks: their conduct is less ruled by reason.

21. Philoponus, *In Nicomachi Isogogen*, I, 1 (*Aristotelis Fragmenta selecta*, ed. W. D. Ross, Oxford, 1955, fr. 8).

22. *De generatione animalium*, IV, 6, 775a5–7; 14–16. According to Aristotle male embryos are more active and restless than female, as their natural warmth is higher; hence there are more deficiencies among male children than among females.

23. *Politica*, I, 13, 1260a10–14. All parts of the soul are present in every human being, but in a different way (διαφερόντως). Slaves are deprived of the deliberative faculty, whereas women do not lack it, but it is not powerful in them.

stage[24]: the study of liberal arts starts at the age of puber
as they are in an early stage, they can only participate in t
life of the communities in which they are incorporated,
are called to moral life and happiness.[25] Consequently,
many differences among humans with regard to rational capacity,
every individual is by nature a moral animal.

In Aristotle's view all humans are oriented by nature toward
ethical life and happiness, yet ethical behavior is far from being a
natural gift; it is the result of much effort and training. Man is not
naturally equipped with the virtues of wisdom, courage, temperance, and justice: some natural capacity and disposition are at the
outset of ethical development, but this capacity is only a potency.
It is not, as it is in Stoic philosophy, a seminal presence from the
very beginning of life. In this latter view all elements of moral
behavior are present in each individual from childhood: the development of moral life is comparable to the growth of a germ; the
seed of a tree or an animal already contains all factors of the later
evolution; nothing really new can ever arise.[26] In the case of man,
each individual ought to become what he truly is from the very
beginning of his life: it is the duty of everybody to favor and
promote the growth of what he bears within himself. In Aristotle's
view moral capacity is a potency, not a germ: according to the
author's general doctrine a potency can never come to act without
being actualized from without. A thing that is movable can only
pass to actual movement when it is moved by something else; the
same rule obtains with regard to ethical potency: it cannot be
actualized without some impact from outside. In Aristotle's opinion
moral education is indispensable: all humans are potentially ethical
agents, but the potency of becoming moral beings must be actualized, and that is the proper duty of an appropriate *paideia*.[27] In some

24. *Politica*, I, 13, 1260a13–14.
25. *Politica*, VII, 17, 1336a39–1336b1; *Eth. Nic.*, III, 12, 1119b5–7. Until the age of
seven, children ought to be educated at home: contacts with slaves should be avoided
as much as possible.
26. G. Verbeke, *Les Stoïciens et le progrès de l'histoire*, p.7ff., with respect to the
doctrine of moral progress, p.31–37. This issue is connected with an important topic,
which is called οἰκείωσις (cf. G. Verbeke, *L'humanisme stoïcien*, in: Festschrift in
honour of Prof. E. Moutsopoulos, in press).
27. *Politica*, VIII, 1, 1337a18–27. With regard to the process of moral education
Aristotle refers to the influence of shame or self-respect: he states that people praise
youths who are gifted with this spontaneous sense that withdraws them from wrongdoing. (*Eth. Nic.*, IV, 9, 1128b18–26).

passages of his ethical works the author presents a rather dark picture of average people: what moves them in their behavior is not shame but fear; if they refrain from wrongdoing it is not because such conduct is blamable, but because they want to avoid punishment. In their activity they are driven by passion, they pursue pleasure and try to escape from pain, they have no sense of what is really good and truly delightful, as they have never tasted it.[28] Ordinary people lead a kind of servile existence, rather similar to the life of cattle.[29] This negative description is not in disagreement with Aristotle's teaching on the moral nature of man: however, it manifestly shows the necessity of a strong ethical *paideia*. In a first stage this education will lead to premoral practice: people will perform acts that correspond to ethical rules without having the intention of accomplishing what is good for the sake of the good. In this respect there is a clear difference between technical training and moral *paideia*. In the first case, the internal disposition of the agent does not play an essential part, whereas in the latter it is of decisive importance.[30] Aristotle believes that the transition from a premoral to a moral stage will be achieved through personal experience of ethical conduct. Possessing a natural sense of right and wrong, the agent will discover gradually in his own activity the concrete meaning of moral values. Moreover, as he is spontaneously oriented toward the good, he will pursue these values in his behavior. Finally, his knowledge of the truly good will constantly grow, insofar as his irrational propensities have already been guided and directed by his conduct. In this way moral virtue is acquired by performing acts that conform to it: these acts, which at the outset are premoral, will become more and more truly ethical.[31] The most decisive influence with regard to moral education is the rule of law in a political community; without these regulations ethical behavior is considered to be impossible.[32] As has already been mentioned, there are three factors that contribute to the development of moral

28. *Eth. Nic.*, X, 10, 1179b11–16.

29. *Eth. Nic.*, I, 3, 1095b19–20.

30. *Eth. Nic.*, II, 1, 1103a31–b2.

31. D. J. Allan, *The Philosophy of Aristotle*. London, New York, Toronto, 1952, p.170–171.

32. *Politica*, IV, 4, 1292a4–37; IV, 8, 1294a3–9. In Aristotle's view a democracy without laws inevitably leads to tyranny: when the people is invested with all power, it will be dominated by the harmful influence of demagogues.

life: nature, knowledge, and training. What Aristotle means by knowledge is practical wisdom, the ability to make right ethical judgments in the variable circumstances of life. This ability ought to be acquired through moral experience and practice: it is not a matter of merely theoretical insight, it largely depends upon ethical conduct and experience.[33] The last factor is exercise or training: if somebody wants to become a craftsman, a carpenter, or a sarton, he has to learn the skill by frequently repeating the same acts under the direction of a master. So he will gradually acquire a habit allowing him to perform the work in an appropriate way and without much effort. The same can be applied to virtue: a moral habit is the outcome of many previous actions, which have imprinted their traces in the character of an individual. One swallow does not make the spring: only when similar actions have been frequently repeated will they be performed in an adequate way.[34]

Moral virtue is a personal conquest, and yet Aristotle states that humans are ethical animals by nature: in what sense should we understand this view? In each individual there is some spontaneous intuition of right and wrong: some actions are believed to be good, whereas others are repudiated and considered to be evil. This distinction between right and wrong acts may differ from one country to another, from one period to another, or from one person to another, but the distinction is present always and everywhere. The distinction itself is not questioned; what is sometimes controversial is whether particular ways of behaving belong to the one or to the other category.

The question, however, as to the origin of this universally accepted distinction between right and wrong arises: is it an inborn knowledge that belongs to the original structure of human mind? Not really, since Aristotle always stresses the necessity of experience

33. *Eth. Nic.*, VI, 12, 1144a34–b1; III, 5, 1114a31–b5. Aristotle is persuaded that immoral conduct influences ethical judgments: irrational factors disturb the functioning of reason.

34. *Eth. Nic.*, II, 2, 1104a33–b13. In this context Aristotle deals with what he calls "right education" (ὀρθὴ παιδεία). It ought to start early (ἐκ νέων) and is mostly concerned with pleasure and pain, for people commit wrong actions to obtain pleasure as they neglect to do what is good because they try to avoid pain. The outcome of an adequate education ought to be that people take pleasure in doing good and suffer pain when they do wrong.

and practice.[35] No human knowledge is merely innate: inborn knowledge would require the preexistence of the soul, a doctrine firmly repudiated by our author. Intellectual knowledge always derives from sensible experience, and that is true also of ethical intuitions. This viewpoint, however, does not mean that understanding is nothing more than sensible perception: the data of sensible knowledge are a necessary starting point, on which intellectual insight is based. On the other hand, there is in each individual a natural tendency toward the good, a kind of universal love animating all beings and driving them toward Pure Act.[36] Man knows himself, and so he is conscious of this internal tendency pushing him toward the highest good. If man is aware of this aspiration, he must also grasp, at least vaguely, the object to which it is oriented. Starting from this internal and natural craving that belongs to the structure of a human being, man realizes more and more the true meaning of these fundamental notions, right and wrong. Hence the understanding of good and evil is not really inborn; nor is it merely derived from sensible experience. It is true that even self-knowledge requires some sensible experience: in his contact with the world man discovers his own being and becomes aware at once of the world and of himself; so he discovers in his own nature the permanent inclination toward the good and understands better and better the goal of his internal longing. At the beginning, however, this understanding remains vague and uncertain: it gradually becomes more explicit in the course of time both through philosophical reflection and through the experience of ethical behavior in the world. It is not an easy task to disclose what is truly good, what is

35. *Eth. Nic.*, I, 3, 1095a2–11. According to Aristotle young people are not an appropriate audience for ethical lectures: the main reason is their lack of experience in the field of human actions. The author adds that in moral teaching arguments deal with human conduct and proceed from it: arguing is not theoretical and abstract; it is mainly based on the experience of life. The notion of experience is clearly described in *Analytica Posteriora* II, 19, 100a4: "So from perception there comes memory, as we call it, and from memory (when it occurs often in connection with the same thing) experience; for memories that are many in number form a single experience" (*Aristotle's Posterior Analytics*, translated with Notes by J. Barnes, Oxford, 1975).

36. *Eth. Nic.*, I, 1, 1094a1–3. Apparently Aristotle's teleological interpretation of the universe is the result of a global intuition, based on innumerous observations in the field of biology and astronomy. The universe is a cosmos (κόσμος), in which all things are orderly put together as to constitute a harmonious whole. The internal principle of this harmony is the substantial form of each being.

really beneficial, in view of a harmonious development of human existence.[37]

In moral knowledge a capital distinction ought to be introduced: there is first a general intuition of the ethical ideal to which all humans are called and that coincides with the full development of man's capacities and with happiness. Which are the characteristic features of human perfection, and how can it be achieved? This question is a general one, which does not deal with a concrete act in its particular context; what is at issue is the worth of human conduct in view of attaining the ethical ideal. In Aristotle's perspective the end of life is to reach what he calls *eudaimonia*, which means both the highest perfection and the true happiness of a person.[38] The end of life is not sensible pleasure; nor does it coincide with honors and political power: it decidedly consists in moral virtue and intellectual contemplation, which represent the highest performance of which an individual is capable.[39] In this way the end of life is a reflection of divine perfection, which resides in permanent self-contemplation.

Next to the general knowledge of right and wrong are the concrete ethical judgments concerning a particular act in the variable and complex circumstances of life. It is not always easy to make an adequate choice about what to do in situations that are never the same. What particularly jeopardizes one's appreciations in these concrete cases is the disturbing influence of passions and desires;

37. The main reason why it is difficult to grasp what is truly good, particularly in the changing circumstances of life, is twofold: each human action is unique; it occurs in a situation that never took place in the past and will never be reiterated in the future. In addition, man is not merely mind: in each individual there are irrational impulses that may strongly influence and distort moral judgments (*Eth. Nic.*, II, 1, 1104a3–11).

38. The subject is formally treated in *Eth. Nic.*, I, 6. In order to discover man's highest perfection and happiness, the author starts from what is considered to be the proper activity of humans. Act is superior to potency; moreover, intellectual knowing is superior to any other human activity. In this context Aristotle is not directly concerned with other aspects of an individual, such as emotions, passions, social relations, manual labor, wealth, or poverty. These other factors, however, will be treated in the further development of the ethical discourse.

39. *Eth. Nic.*, X, 7, 1177a12–18. In Aristotle's view happiness must be connected with the activity of the highest power that is present in human beings; it is a faculty that is able to grasp what is good and divine; it is invested with a leading function in human life. Is it the mind? The author is very cautious: it is the most divine power present in man, whether it be the mind or something else. In Aristotle's view it must be the mind: he never mentions a human faculty superior to the intellect.

these emotions obscure the mind and prevent agents from having a clear view of what is to be done. In Aristotle's opinion only a virtuous individual is able to discover what is truly valuable in the unstable circumstances of life.[40] This doctrine seemingly involves a vicious circle; as a matter of fact, in order to grasp what is truly good one has to behave morally and in order to behave morally one has to seize what is really good in the various situations of life. This problem, however, is solved by Aristotle in the framework of political society: in the early period of life youths should be constrained to behave morally in conformity with the regulations of laws, and when they have acquired the necessary experience and practice of ethical conduct, they will be able to make personal choices regarding their behavior.[41] This viewpoint is extremely important for moral education; it will be treated more adequately in a later inquiry.

Summarizing our previous considerations, we may conclude that man is by nature a moral animal, since he bears within himself a natural sense of right and wrong. Moreover, man is an animal that deliberates: before acting, he ponders over what to do; he considers various possibilities; he may even spend a long time before taking a decision and afterward reflect on what he did and assess his behavior. In this respect human conduct clearly differs from that of irrational animals[42]: it is by no means an automatic reaction produced by an external stimulus; there is some distance between external influences exerted on an individual and his own reaction. This response is not merely caused by external forces; it is mainly the outcome of a personal reflection in which the subject tries to uncover and to evaluate the various aspects of an envisaged action.[43]

40. *Eth. Nic.*, VI, 12, 1144a34–b1; III, 4, 1113a29–33. A virtuous man is able to formulate correct moral judgments in all situations: everybody assesses what is good and pleasant according to his habits. An individual with moral habits will valuate rightly what is good: he is like a rule and a criterion in these matters.

41. *Eth. Nic.*, X, 9, 1179b31–1180a5. Aristotle's view on the compulsive character of laws is quite categorical: many people obey in response to constraint and punishment rather than to reason and moral beauty. This judgment is related not only to children but to individuals of all ages.

42. *Eth. Nic.*, III, 1, 1111a25; b8–10. Aristotle makes a distinction between voluntary actions and choices: in his view children and irrational animals are able to perform voluntary actions but not choices: these latter, however, are also voluntary.

43. *Eth. Nic.*, III, 2, 1111b29–30. Aristotle carefully distinguishes between willing (βούλησις) and choice (προαίρεσις): willing concerns the end, whereas choice

As a matter of fact, deliberation does not deal with the past, with acts already performed, but with the future, with what remains to be done. In fact, man is also able to draw his attention to some acts he has already performed and ask himself whether his conduct was right or wrong. This consideration, however, is not properly a deliberation; it is not concerned with a project or an initiative. It actually refers to the area of moral judgments following the implementation of an act. Of course, the past cannot come back again—it is irreversible—and yet it remains present in the mind: many facts fall into oblivion and disappear from our memory, but important actions and decisions do not easily fade away. Each individual bears within himself, in his mind, not only present events and actions but some past decisions and choices: everybody feels responsible not only for his present conduct, for what he chooses and implements in the present situation, but also for his former behavior and his future projects.[44] In this way every person is responsible for his past and prepares his future; everybody has his own past, and in a sense he already possesses his future, although this future is contingent. Man lives in the present; he constantly has to face situations and events he did not expect; he is involved in all kinds of new situations in which he has to find his way. But he also lives in the past and the future. In a sense each individual experiences in each moment the totality of his existence as a unity: the present blends with past and future.[45] Stoic philosophers insisted on this aspect of man's consciousness of time: whereas irrational animals live only in the present and are unable to go beyond the successive instants of time, man is capable of transcending these limits and of collecting into one whole past, present, and future.[46] The meaning

deals with the means used to reach the end. Everybody wishes to be healthy and chooses the means to attain this goal; similarly everyone wants to be happy, yet it is not accurate to declare that everybody chooses to be happy (1111b26–29).

44. *Eth. Nic.*, III, 5, 1113b6–17. Everybody is responsible for his moral character, whether good or bad: to state that nobody is voluntarily evil is false, but to declare that nobody is involuntarily happy is true. Happiness corresponds to a basic tendency in all humans, whereas moral deviations are the responsibility of each individual. Man naturally strives toward happiness and is able to attain this goal by means of virtuous conduct.

45. G. Verbeke, *La perception du temps chez Aristote*, in: *Aristotelica: Mélanges offerts à Marcel De Corte*, Brussels-Liège, 1985, p. 376–377.

46. Cicero, *De officiis*, I, 4, 11 (*Panaetii Rhodii fragmenta*, ed. M. Van Straaten, Leyden, 1952, fr. 80): "homo autem . . . facile totius vitae cursum videt ad eamque degendam praeparat res necessarias."

of deliberation, which plays a central part in Aristotle's ethics, ought to be understood in this context. Encompassing the totality of his life and not living only in the present moment, an individual is able to judge the true worth of an act in the perspective of his existence as a whole.

Differing from all other beings in nature, man is conscious of his spontaneous inclination toward the good: the whole universe is animated by the same tendency. In this respect man is not an exception, and yet he is a privileged being since he is aware of this fundamental longing. He looks at all other things in the world and may discover in them the same aspiration he finds within himself, and yet other beings never become conscious of what they are and what they want. Man represents the awareness of the universe: the Divine Substance knows his own perfection and intellectual activity, not the material universe.[47] Man introduces consciousness into the cosmos: here again there is a noticeable difference between Aristotle and Stoic philosophy. According to the Stoics God is the consciousness of the universe: Divine Reason is present everywhere; each human soul is a particle of the Divine Logos, which is present also in other beings; all things in the world are shaped, permeated, and animated by Divine Reason.[48] In Aristotle's view divine consciousness is confined to the highest perfection. Being the consciousness of the universe and being able to embrace the whole course of his existence, man is able to judge the true worth of his conduct. With regard to the past he is able to valuate his actions and is also able to judge his personal responsibility, taking into account the various factors of his behaving.[49] The matter becomes more difficult when the future is concerned: in order to deliberate adequately, man has to foresee the future, which always remains uncertain, unpredictable; yet man has to make a choice, to take a decision. Finally he will always do this in a climate of uncertainty: even when a deliberation is carefully achieved and extends over a long time, it will only emerge

47. *Metaph.*, XII, 9, 1074b33–35.
48. M. Pohlenz, *Die Stoa: Geschichte einer geistigen Bewegung.* Göttingen, 1948, p.95–96. In Aristotle's doctrine God is Pure Act: he could not know the world without being passive in some sense: hence his knowledge is confined to self-consciousness. In Stoic philosophy the Divine Logos penetrates everywhere and produces the variety of cosmic beings.
49. *Eth. Nic.*, III, 5, 1113b6–14. Man may be responsible even for his ignorance (*Eth. Nic.*, III, 5, 1113b30–1114a3).

into a reasonable and justified option; it will not be carried out with a clear view of the future. Man has to make decisions in uncertainty, and yet he is truly responsible of his conduct: his deliberation will be morally correct when he avoids in his judgment the influence of irrational movements, passions, and emotions.

Besides, man is able to learn and to acquire abiding habits and abilities; in Aristotle's view moral education is essentially the acquisition of enduring dispositions that are called *virtues*. Man is a potential being and human existence is a constant passage from potency to act. Is it a mere movement? Not exactly: when something potential is actualized, the movement is completed. In the case of human evolution there is something more: frequent performance of similar acts produces an enduring ability, on the level of knowing as well as on the level of acting.[50] According to Aristotle the knowledge of an individual may really grow and some new information may be acquired. Learning is not merely the recollection of an already present knowledge: it is the introduction into the mind and the assimilation of some new objects as a result of sensible experience. So there may be a progress of moral knowledge as well as of grammatical or mathematical learning. The question whether virtue may be learned has repeatedly been asked; the meaning of the question is whether moral behavior is a mere matter of knowledge. The answer of Aristotle is shaded: he acknowledges that knowledge is a very important factor in our moral behavior, but it is not the only one. Man's conduct does not derive automatically from his understanding; many other factors, both internal and external, interfere in it.[51]

Aristotle frequently compares the acquisition of virtues to the learning of practical skills. Technical abilities are not inborn; they are the outcome of previous acts, which will gradually be performed

---

50. *Eth. Nic.*, II, 4, 1105b9–12; II, 1, 1103a31–b2. Moral behavior is not the outcome of some theoretical speculation but of repeatedly accomplished ethical actions. Many people erroneously believe that they will become virtuous by philosophical reflection: they are comparable to sick individuals who listen carefully to physicians but do not do anything they prescribe.

51. *Eth. Nic.*, VI, 13, 1144b28–32. Aristotle does not agree with Socrates, who states that all virtues are a kind of science: moral habits are reduced to rational insights (λόγους). Aristotle agrees that it is impossible to be fully virtuous without moral wisdom or to possess moral wisdom without ethical virtue. In the area of moral behavior, knowledge and conduct are mutually linked. Cf. J. D. Monan, *Moral Knowledge and Its Methodology in Aristotle*, Oxford, 1968, p.79.

in an increasingly capable manner. Moral conduct develops in the same way: nobody is by birth wise, brave, temperate, and just; each virtue is the result of previous actions. By behaving courageously man becomes brave: he may only be called brave if he possesses courage as an abiding habit.[52] Yet it remains true that man is by nature a moral animal; what happens in human life could never occur to irrational animals. They could be trained and acquire some habits, but these are not virtues, because they are not ruled by ethical insight and personal choice.

Moreover, human actions, when they have been implemented and completed, do not totally disappear without leaving some trace of their performance; on the contrary they survive in the agent; an individual is at each moment the result of what he has done. Man not only remembers what he has achieved but is the outcome of his previous actions: being the result of deliberation and choice, these actions are not anonymous; they bear the stamp of the acting person. An individual always bears within himself the traces of his previous behavior.[53] According to J. P. Sartre, man invents man: in his view an individual not only is at the origin of his acts but also freely creates his moral values.[54] Aristotle would only partly agree with this viewpoint: moral values are discovered by man on the basis of experience, ethical practice, and awareness of the fundamental orientation of everybody toward the good. The author would, however, accept that man is at the origin of his moral character, since he is the principle of his ethical habits, which cannot easily be changed when they have been acquired. Aristotle would certainly not agree with the Stoics when they maintain the passage from immoral life to virtuous conduct to be instantaneous.[55] According to the Stoics humans are to be divided into two groups: few of

52. *Eth. Nic.*, VI, 2, 1139a33–34. A moral choice cannot be achieved without insight and reflection, but it also requires ethical habits: both factors are necessary. A moral man accomplishes what is good because it is good: hence he must know it. Moreover, he must decidedly will it: this implies that he has acquired firm and abiding virtuous habits.

53. G. Verbeke, *Moral Behaviour and Time in Aristotle's Nicomachean Ethics*, in: *Kephalaion: Studies in Greek Philosophy and its Continuation*, Assen, 1975, p.84.

54. *L'existentialisme est un humanisme*, Paris, 1946. According to Sartre, there is no human nature that can guide man in his moral choices (p.53). As a result man has to create his values: "Mais si j'ai supprimé Dieu le père, il faut bien quelqu'un pour inventer les valeurs" (p.89).

55. Plutarchus, *De communibus notitiis*, c.10, p.1063a (SVF, III, 539).

them are wise; all the others are insane. A passage from the second
group to the first is possible, but exceptional and very hard: an
individual can only be considered to be wise if he possesses all virtues
without a single exception. This theory stems from a monolithic
conception of the unity of moral behavior: according to this view
a man cannot be wise if one virtue is lacking; the absence of one
virtue not only is a gap in moral life but has an immediate impact on
other virtues.[56] Later Stoics, however, have mitigated this teaching:
between wise men and foolish individuals they accepted an intermediary category, those who are in progress; the latter do not possess
all virtues, but they are gradually approaching the ideal of wisdom
by extending more and more the power of reason over the emotions.[57]

Aristotle decidedly maintains the progressive character of moral
conduct: a habit is not acquired suddenly, but gradually. In our
author's view everybody is in progress: through perseverant ethical
behavior one reaches abiding habits that become more and more
stable. And when an act proceeds from a steady disposition, its
ethical worth will be higher and purer: an enduring disposition
implies that the agent is totally dedicated to the act he implements.[58]
A variable and unsteady attitude cannot guarantee such total devotion, even when the action itself entirely conforms to the require-
ments of moral virtue.[59] Like the Stoics, Aristotle also maintains a
connection among moral habits, particularly between wisdom and
the other virtues: in his view it is impossible to have right moral
intuitions without possessing the other virtues (courage, temperance, and justice). The reason is that under the influence of emotional movements moral judgment will be disturbed. An ethical
insight could never be right if it was attained under the impact of
irrational impulses. When moral wisdom increases, the other virtues
also develop, and when ethical dispositions achieve some progress,

56. Stobaeus, *Eclogae* (*Ecl.*), II, 7, 11g, p.99, 3 W (SVF, I, 216); cf. O. Luschnat,
Das Problem des ethischen Fortschritts in der alten Stoa. Philologus, 102 (1958), p.178–
214; G. Verbeke, *Les Stoïciens et le progrès de l'histoire*, p.27ff.

57. G. Verbeke, *Les Stoïciens et le progrès de l'histoire*, p.31–37.

58. *Rhetorica* (*Rhet.*), I, 11, 1370a6–9. In Aristotle's opinion habits are pleasant:
acts that proceed from a habitual disposition are virtually natural.

59. G. Verbeke, *Moral Behaviour and Time*, p.84: "In his (Aristotle) view, a real
assent to the good for its own sake is only possible if it originates from a permanent
disposition or a habit."

wisdom also will follow. Ethical knowledge is not merely theoretical; it is essentially practical: it is not only concerned with human behavior but is constantly dependent on the conduct of an individual. Ethical insight is in fact a personal conquest: in the field of moral action conduct and insight cannot be separated.[60] Moral behavior may be compared to the work of a craftsman: this man also is able to judge rightly in the area of his skill, not on the ground of theoretical speculations but on the basis of practice and experience. An experienced individual not only works better but also correctly judges things to be done. Ethical insight cannot be right if the mind is obscured by passions.

Being able to acquire abiding ethical habits and to develop them by his own activity, man must be by nature a moral animal. In addition, each individual bears within himself a sense of friendship: man is not locked within his own being and isolated from other subjects; he is spontaneously inclined to meet them and communicate with them. This is clearly shown in the various types of society, from family to political community. Man constantly transcends the borders of his own being in order to meet other people: this openness toward others is a characteristic feature of human consciousness.[61] In his *Nicomachean Ethics*, a work that comprises ten books, Aristotle devotes two of them, a fifth of the whole treatise, to the topic of friendship[62]: this relationship with others both reveals the deeper structure of human individuals and plays an important part in their striving toward happiness.

60. *Eth Nic.*, VI, 12, 1144a34; J. R. Moncho, *La unidad de la vida moral según Aristoteles*, Valencia, 1972, cap. IV: La connexion general de las virtudes y su fundamento, p.150–187; J. D. Monan, *Moral Knowledge and Its Methodology in Aristotle*, p.152–153.

61. Some irrational animals also live together and form a kind of community; instead of living isolated, they display some common activities. In this context Aristotle mentions, besides humans, bees, wasps, ants, and cranes. Only humans, however, are capable of true friendship (*Historia Animalium*, I, 1, 487b33–488a10).

62. *Eth. Nic.*, VIII–IX. In his ethical inquiry Aristotle pays much attention to friendship. The reason is obvious. Friendship is a virtue, or at least it cannot be achieved without virtue: friendship contributes to human happiness and perfection. Man is by nature a social being: he can only attain the full development of his being within a political community, which is an extension of family life. To love the true self of other people in a permanent way is a virtue or implies virtue: it really promotes the development of each individual toward happiness, as it is the basis and ground of each community. In this sense Aristotle can state that friendship is indispensable for human life (*Eth. Nic.*, VIII, 1, 1155a3–5).

In a philosophical inquiry about this issue the main question is related to the object of this relationship: man is a compounded and complex being; hence the question as to what exactly is loved in the other person. In the *First Alcibiades* the same topic is treated in a dialogue between Socrates and Alcibiades. When the latter was young, he had many lovers, when he advanced in age he gradually lost all these friends. And yet Alcibiades was still the same person; his identity had not changed; why did he lose all those friends? Trying to solve this problem, Socrates reaches the conclusion that all those lovers were not properly friends of Alcibiades, but of the body of Alcibiades.[63] Hence the further question whether Alcibiades coincides with his body. Is a lover of the body of Alcibiades truly a friend of this young man? To this question the answer of Socrates is negative: the body is not the center of a human person; it is only a tool used by the soul in order to implement its functions, just as a craftsman needs various instruments in order to perform the works he intends to effect. The true center of a person is the soul and in the first place its highest principle, the mind. Hence to be a friend of someone means to be a lover of this noble and worthy component of human soul.[64] True friendship is not an easy relationship, as is clearly shown in the case of Alcibiades. In fact this gifted young man never had many friends; he only had some lovers of his bodily beauty. His only true friend was Socrates, who remained faithful in the course of time. What he loved in Alcibiades was his true personality, the very core of his identity. The background of this teaching is clearly a dualistic theory of man. What has been called "Platonic love" is based on an interpretation of man according to which body and soul are linked together without representing a real unity. In Aristotle's view the unity of undetermined matter and substantial form is much deeper: soul is considered to be the first act of a body that possesses life in potency; in this view even the organic structure of the body is derived from the soul.[65]

63. *Alcibiades,* 131c–e. Socrates is the only true friend of Alcibiades, since his love is oriented toward the true self of the young man, not toward some secondary constituent of his being.

64. *Alcibiades,* 133b–c.

65. *De anima,* II, 1, 412a27. It is important to notice that human soul is the *first* entelechy of an organic body: consequently even the organic structure derives from the soul. If the body already possessed an organic arrangement by itself, the soul could not be the first entelechy: the constituent that corresponds to the first entelechy must be undetermined matter.

In Aristotle's opinion the activity of an individual does not belong only to one of the two components, body or soul: even the highest activity of man, namely thinking, is not confined to the mind or to the soul. The body also is involved, since intellectual knowledge always requires sensible experience. Aristotle is compelled to repudiate the immortality of human soul: there is in man not a single activity in which the body is not involved. If the body is decomposed, the activity of the soul must be blocked: if the soul is unable to perform any activity without the collaboration of the bodily organism, it can no longer subsist when the body perishes.[66]

Yet with respect to the very center of a person, the teaching in Aristotle is not so different from the one of Plato: the author states, with some hesitation, that the core of an individual is the mind. This doctrine is expounded within the context of an inquiry on friendship, which is related to the highest component of a human being, the mind.[67] This viewpoint is confirmed by Aristotle's concept of happiness: the highest level of human perfection is contemplation of the most intelligible object. These statements, however, should not be interpreted in the light of Platonic spiritualism: they have a coherent meaning also within the framework of Aristotle's psychological doctrine: the main difference between the two philosophers is the valuation of the body and of sensible knowledge. In Aristotle's view friendship is a virtue, or at least it cannot be practiced without virtue[68]: everybody needs friends in order to achieve his true and proper perfection. A friend is called an other self: there is always a resemblance among friends; when two individuals are very different, friendship is difficult or even impossible.[69]

In all circumstances friendship already has a moral meaning, because it is a steady and benevolent relationship between the true

66. *De anima*, I, 1, 403a7. In Aristotle's view even intellectual knowing is always linked to some sensitive activity, with respect to not only the origin of our intelligible objects but also to each mental operation (*De anima*, III, 7, 431a14–17; 8, 432a3–9). Cf. G. Verbeke, *Comment Aristote conçoit-il l'immatériel?*, in: *Rev. philos. de Louvain*, 44(1946), p.205–236.

67. *Eth. Nic.*, IX, 4, 1166a31: ἔστι γὰρ ὁ φίλος ἄλλος αὐτός; IX, 9, 1169b6; 9, 1170b6; VIII, 12, 1161b28. The true self of man seemingly coincides with the rational principle (*Eth. Nic.*, IX, 4, 1166a17).

68. *Eth. Nic.*, VIII, 1, 1155a3–4. Virtue is a habit, an abiding disposition, which is the result of former actions. In this perspective friendship is a permanent love of the true self of another person.

69. *Eth. Nic.*, VIII, 1, 1155a32–35; 3, 1156b20; 8, 1159b2–4.

self of one individual and that of another. A superficial relationship mainly based on external factors may be easy, but it is not a guarantee of a stable connection between the true self of one person and that of another.[70] This attitude implies that one is conscious of his own true self, as he is aware of the real self of other individuals. In fact, the teaching of Aristotle is a purification and transposition of the love of boys as it was practiced in Greek society. A friend will be concerned with the real good of his fellow. Such help is needed by each individual who endeavors to reach the ideal of human perfection; an isolated individual is unable to achieve ethical conduct in a steady manner: he is comparable to an isolated piece in a game of dice.[71] True friendship is impossible among immoral individuals because their behavior does not correspond to the true self: it develops on a lower level. True friendship is a privilege of virtuous people. The highest level of friendship will be attained when virtuous people wish for the sake of their friends and for themselves whatever is good: in this case the relationship is not based on some accidental feature, but on what they are in themselves, their moral goodness.[72] When these conditions are fulfilled, the relationship will also be enduring and stable: virtue is not something transitory and precarious; being the result of many previous acts, it is an abiding disposition. A moral individual not only performs good acts but implements them for their own sake, because they are valuable. True friendship also is devoid of any kind of egoism: a friend endeavors to achieve the good of his friend for the sake of this latter. What he loves in his friend is the true self, or more specifically the highest perfection of this real self: he does not want any advantage or material benefit for himself. Whatever he undertakes is in view of his friend, for the sake of his friend. Needless to say, in this perspective friendship has a basic moral dimension.

In Aristotle's teaching friendship is a communion; it is actually

70. *Eth. Nic.*, VIII, 3, 1156b25; 3, 1156b31. Friendship requires some time: it cannot be suddenly achieved: friends ought to know of each other that they are worthy of love and reliable.

71. *Politica*, I, 2, 1253a6–7. Aristotle speaks of humans who by nature or accident are without a city: if they are so by nature, they must be defective; something must be lacking in their natural structure. If not, they must be superior to ordinary human beings as they must be able to attain the full development of their being without being incorporated in a political society.

72. *Eth. Nic.*, VIII, 4, 1158b9–12.

achieved when friends live together and communicate with each other: in this sense friendship is important for all kinds of societies, particularly for political communities. It brings people together and keeps them united in a steady way. An individual is related to his friend in the same manner as he is related to himself: as he enjoys his own existence, he will also enjoy the existence and presence of his friend. He will perform various kinds of activities together with his friend: one of them may be a common dedication to the study of philosophy and quite obviously a reciprocal support in moral conduct.[73] According to Aristotle life is worth living: this worth is considerably enhanced when it is spent in an enduring communion with true friends, a communion that will be steadily actualized in common activities.

In his *Eudemian Ethics* Aristotle wonders whether real friendship is possible between God and man, that is, between a human self and Divine Substance. A first difficulty is quite obvious: Divine Substance is Pure Act, whereas man is always both act and potency; of course, man is by nature oriented toward the good, toward the highest perfection, and he wants to contemplate the fullness of goodness. Nevertheless, there is a great distance between a human being and the Divine Act. Moreover, God does not create the world to which human beings belong: God exists from eternity and the world also is without beginning, but individuals come to be and pass away. Can this gulf ever be bridged? Finally the Aristotelian notion of God excludes providence: divine knowledge is confined to the most perfect object, which is divine understanding itself. A personal relationship such as friendship can only be based on reciprocal knowledge: the two friends must know each other. And yet Aristotle accepts that some kind of friendship is possible between God and man: it will be a friendship of unequal levels, in which one of the two friends notably transcends the other.[74] In his opinion a man who attains the highest level of perfection through contemplation is particularly loved by God.[75] These considerations are rather amazing: they are seemingly a yielding to popular beliefs, which in

73. *Eth. Nic.*, IX, 12, 1171b32–1172a8.
74. *Eth. Eud.*, VII, 3, 1238b27–28; 4, 1239a17–21.
75. *Eth. Nic.*, X, 8, 1179a22–24; a29–30. Love of man for God does not entail special difficulties: friendship, however, implies more, since it is a mutual relationship. In this respect various questions arise, not only because the level of perfection is very different but because divine knowledge is confined to self-consciousness. Yielding

our author's view may contain some elements of truth, when they belong to an ancient tradition and are universally accepted.

All these reflections show that man is by nature a moral animal: man possesses a spontaneous sense of right and wrong, he is able to deliberate before proceeding to an action, he is able to learn and to acquire abiding ethical habits, and finally he is oriented toward friendship, toward benevolent and stable relationships with the true self of other individuals. For all humans moral behavior is the way leading to perfection and happiness.

---

to popular belief, Aristotle seemingly does not totally exclude some divine awareness of the world, insofar as God is conscious of being an object of universal love and aspiration (*Metaph.*, XII, 7, 1072b3: κινεῖ δὲ ὡς ἐρώμενον).

[4]

MAN AND SOCIETY

IN THE middle of the eighteenth century J. J. Rousseau published a discourse on the origin and foundation of inequalities among men; some ideas expounded in this work had already been treated by him in a former essay on sciences and arts.[1] What is at issue is mainly the impact of society on human condition. According to the French author man should go back to his original status, to the very beginning of his history. At that early period inequalities among men were very small: primitive humans lived in a simple and natural way; their body was stronger than it was in later generations, when it had been weakened by various kinds of illnesses. When humans came together and founded societies, they were gradually reduced into slavery, subdued to some of their fellow-countrymen who had become wealthy and powerful: thus people became weak and devoid of courage. Life in society was the origin of a progressive degeneration.[2] Moreover, scientific and technical discoveries were also a source of many evils; they actually contributed to removing men from their original innocence and equality. In the beginning humans were guided in their conduct by natural instincts, which were less harmful than laws in political communities.[3] Under the influence of society people became avaricious, ambitious, and evil; the history of civil society is an accumulation of robberies, deceits, and tyrannies. Having become degenerate through society man

1. *Discours sur l'origine et les fondements de l'inégalité parmi les hommes* (1755); *Discours sur les sciences et les arts* (1750): In this latter work the author maintains that sciences actually originate from human vices: astronomy springs from superstition; eloquence stems from ambition, hatred, flattery, and deceit; geometry derives from avarice, physics from vain curiosity. All sciences, even moral doctrine, proceed from human pride (*Oeuvres complètes*, ed. B. Gagnebin et M. Raymond, Paris, 1959–69, III, p.17).
2. Rousseau, *Oeuvres complètes*, III, p.139.
3. Rousseau, *Oeuvres complètes*, III, p.152.

ought to return to his original condition: his natural propensity to love and sympathy mitigates egoism and contributes to saving the species.[4] Despite the profound decline of mankind Rousseau believes a collective restoration still possible: it must be achieved by means of a social agreement, since no individual by nature possesses any authority over his equals. When society is grounded on a social contract, freedom and equality of all members will be respected; all humans will be equal by contract as they are by nature.[5] A similar theory had already been proposed by T. Hobbes concerning the origin of political society: people come together in order to protect themselves against egoism and destruction; entering into a freely accepted contract they entrust a sovereign with absolute power. In order to survive they renounce their spontaneous striving for power and wealth.[6] According to Rousseau the kind of government is secondary: what matters above all is individual freedom and equality of all men; in this respect he clearly differs from Hobbes, who advocates absolute power of the sovereign, even in religious matters. With regard to education Rousseau maintains the same principles: natural freedom of children and youths ought to be secured; each form of constraint or punishment should be avoided.

According to Rousseau life in society is the origin and cause of human degeneration. This view is radically opposed to the one expounded in Aristotle's writings: let us look more closely at his doctrine. In the history of Greek thought Socrates is known as a symbol of philosophy, the embodiment of ancient wisdom: his whole life was dedicated to philosophy, and even his death was a philosophical act, a detachment from sensible reality and a return to the true self.[7] His trial and death deeply impressed and hurt the

4. Rousseau, *Oeuvres complètes*, III, p.156. Cf. *Émile:* at the beginning of this work the author writes, "Tout est bien sortant des mains de l'Auteur des choses, tout dégénère entre les mains des hommes."

5. Rousseau, *Du contrat social*, I, 4. Every citizen remains free since he freely gave up his freedom: "Chacun de nous met en commun sa personne et toute sa puissance sous la suprême direction de la volonté générale."

6. *Leviathan*, I, 17. According to Hobbes man is not by nature a social being. Cf. K. Schuhmann, *The Interwovenness of the Natural History of Reason and the State in Hobbes*, in: *Tijdschrift voor Filosofie*, 49(1987), p.438: "It is therefore not difficult to predict that men will be prone to live together in groups large enough to provide for the defense of their havings."

7. In his *Apology* (30a–b) Socrates declares that he will never give up his divine vocation, even if he is sentenced to death; he will never cease exhorting people to be more concerned with the well-being of their soul than with their body and property. In Socrates' view to die is not a punishment: it is rather a benefit (40c).

young Plato, whose philosophical dialogues are an uninterrupted conversation with his Master. Death in prison was not the end of Socrates' life; philosophy could not be jailed or killed. Socrates was still alive: philosophical discussions went on and the great Master was at their center. Plato always wondered how it had been possible for a man like Socrates to be sentenced to death: in this exceptional trial a noble and wise man was repudiated by a corrupt society, a deeply religious person was killed by superstitious and superficial people. In short, reason was slaughtered by mythology. The death of Socrates was not an accidental or contingent event: it was the expression of an essential conflict, an unavoidable opposition, a tension and constant battle between rational philosophical reflection and mythological tradition. Both were present in Greek culture and the struggle was inevitable.

As a result of Socrates' condemnation Plato dedicated an important part of his philosophical inquiry to political matters, above all to the role and structure of an ideal republic. In his dialogue *Protagoras* the author presents a mythical narrative dealing with the origin of political society. In ancient times humans lived spread all over the country: there were no villages or towns. This situation, however, was full of danger: people were repeatedly threatened, attacked, and killed by wild beasts. Becoming more and more aware of this peril humans finally decided to come together in order to protect themselves against the attacks. So they founded towns, where they were able to defend their lives adequately. Unfortunately this life in common quickly proved to be impossible because of ceaseless conflicts, oppositions, and tensions: people never stopped struggling against each other. Finally towns were dissolved and people again started living separately: the same dangers and attacks occurred as in the past and many were killed. After those hardships people again wanted to gather and to establish political communities, but the outcome was the same.[8] At this stage Zeus became concerned with this really tragic situation: he wondered what humans were lacking, preventing them from living together and estab-

---

8. *Protagoras*, 322b. According to the myth man has been created by Epimetheus, who already had distributed all his gifts to other animals and was unable to endow man in an adequate manner. Fortunately Prometheus came to inspect the work and provided man with practical skills and the use of fire. In this way man was able to survive, but there was still something lacking in him: political wisdom.

lishing enduring political societies. Then he realized that men were actually in need of two qualities or gifts: sense of justice and respect for the self and the others.[9] The original terms used ($\delta i\kappa\eta$ and $\alpha i\delta\tilde{\omega}\varsigma$) offer a rich variety of meanings, especially the second, which translated literally means sense of shame. But in the context of the myth, dealing with the possibility of living together, the term refers to respect for other humans and one self. Fearing that the human species would disappear, Zeus sent Hermes to earth: he was entrusted with the distribution of the two gifts to all human beings. When Hermes asked whether he could possibly confine himself to bring these gifts to some individuals, as happens in the case of technical skills (not all men are bakers or shoemakers), the answer was categorical: everybody ought to possess the sense of justice and respect for oneself and the others.[10]

The meaning of this myth is not questionable: political society is grounded on justice and respect for human dignity. Plato wants to establish a new kind of republic, one in which it will be impossible to condemn a man like Socrates, in which the ideas of justice and respect regarding the dignity of man are fully incorporated.[11] In this new republic philosophy will neither be persecuted nor oppressed; on the contrary it will be invested with the highest authority. The rule of the state should be committed to philosophers; only philosophers have a direct and immediate intuition of the transcendent forms.[12] The ruler should contemplate perfect justice or the Idea of justice so that he is able to apply it in the fulfillment of his office; the same obtains with regard to the other ethical values. Contemplating the Idea of justice a philosopher will be able to organize the republic in such a way as to come as near as possible to the ideal society. The reforms proposed by Plato are radical, since they stem from the intuition of a perfect pattern. In order to realize fully the

9. *Protagoras*, 322e. In Plato's ethical doctrine justice plays an important part: as a virtue it does not belong to a particular part of the soul, unlike wisdom, courage, and temperance; rather it ensures the harmony of the three parts with each other. Everybody has to fulfil his own work or function (*Politeia*, IV, 433a).

10. *Protagoras*, 322c–d.

11. *Protagoras*, 322d. The last recommendation of Zeus is characteristic: if an individual is unable to participate in the sense of justice and in the respect of the self and the others, he ought to be eliminated. Socrates, who possessed these two qualities in the highest degree, had been sentenced to death by Athenian society: this event was in radical contrast to Plato's teaching on political philosophy.

12. *Respublica* (*Respubl.*), VI, 484c–485a.

Idea of justice, Plato envisages not only suppression of private property but even family life in a part of the community.[13] Communism of wives and children is an expression of this philosophical radicalism: Plato does not start from concrete experience but from a theoretical ideal. Aristotle repudiates this theory because it does not correspond to the reality of human existence. Plato never was able to put his ideal into practice: it remained a philosophical dream, a splendid utopia.

In Aristotle's view political society gradually developed from a primitive cell, which is the family: from this germ city-states progressively came to be.[14] Of course, the notion family corresponds to the Greek *oikia,* which includes not only parents and children but also the next generation as well as servants and slaves.[15] A Greek family is a small community that enjoys to some extent economic self-sufficiency (*autarkeia*). In this sense a city-state is considered to be an extension of this primitive community, which is a family, where the first moral education is provided.[16] In Aristotle's opinion families and political societies are based on a common consciousness of moral values: there ought to be a universally shared understanding of right and wrong, of just and unjust and other moral values; otherwise families will be disrupted, unable to endure as a coherent unity.[17] Of course, there is a natural friendship between men and women: by nature they are inclined to each other and want to live

13. *Respubl.,* V, 457c–d. In Plato's view common possession of wives and children is intended to ensure unity, agreement, and harmony in political society: such coherence implies a community of pleasure and pain among all citizens.

14.*Politica,* I, 1, 1252b12–15. Family is a community of husband and wife for the purpose of procreation: Aristotle stresses the natural character of this primitive community. It is not a matter of choice, since nature has determined the way of procreation: man and woman need each other in order to give birth to children. Cf. C. Despotopoulos, *Aristote sur la famille et la justice,* Brussels, 1983, p.11ff.

15. *Politica,* I, 3, 1253b4. Dealing with family structure, Aristotle strongly emphasizes the importance of an authority: the head of a family must be somebody who, through his intellectual capacity, is able to foresee the future. Those who are dedicated to manual labor are in a subordinate position. In this context Aristotle mentions that in barbarian civilizations women and slaves are put on the same level, since they are not able to command on the basis of their rational capacities (*Politica,* I, 2, 1252a26–b15).

16. *Eudemian Ethics* (*Eth. Eud.*), VII, 10, 1242a40–b2.

17. *Politica,* I, 2, 1253a18. In Aristotle's opinion the unity of a family is stronger than that of a political society. Plato's theory on political communism is wrong: the author does not sufficiently realize the difference between families and political societies (*Politica,* II, 2, 1261a16–22; II, 5, 1263b34–35).

together, not only in view of the procreation of children but also for the development of their own life.[18] In a sense families are more fundamental and prior to political societies, but on the other hand political communities are regarded as naturally preceding families and individuals.[19] In the gradual development of human society families are obviously prior, but an adequate evolution of individuals and families depends on their incorporation in a political community. When an organic whole is destroyed, the parts lose their function and meaning; a hand or a foot is no longer what it was when integrated into the organic whole of a living body. Families are the most elementary communities from which political societies developed. There is, however, an intermediate stage, that of villages: a village already represents a first extension of family life, since it groups some neighboring families together. The basis of this small community is vicinity or location within the boundaries of the same territory.[20] From villages a larger community comes to be: a polis that fully enjoys self-sufficiency. According to Aristotle such political society is required in view of a harmonious development of human life, not only for satisfying material needs but above all in view of moral education. Man is considered to be by nature a political being; this viewpoint is strongly emphasized at the beginning of Aristotle's political treatise.[21]

Man is naturally gifted with a sense of what is just and unjust: as has been already explained in connection with our knowledge of right and wrong, this intuition is not really inborn; it is largely based on experience and practice.[22] True, everybody bears within

18. *Eth. Nic.*, VIII, 12, 1162a16–22. Correct behavior of a husband toward his wife is regarded as a kind of justice: it is comparable to the relationship between friends (1162a29–31).

19. *Eth. Nic.*, VIII, 12, 1162a18: man is by nature a political being, but his inclination to marriage and procreation of children is more fundamental; *Politica*, I, 2, 1253a18–22.

20. *Politica*, I, 2, 1252b15–27.

21. *Politica*, I, 2, 1252b27–34. *Eth. Nic.*, I, 5, 1097b8–11; IX, 9, 1169b18–19. Political communities exist by nature: they are not the result of a contingent choice or a common agreement. They correspond to a fundamental human need and inclination. E. Berti draws the attention to the fact that the Aristotelian polis does not coincide with the notion of state as it developed in modern time: the polis of Aristotle represents the full dimension of political society (*La notion de société politique chez Aristote*, in: *Antike Rechts- und Sozialphilosophie*, herausg. O. Gigon and M. W. Fischer, Frankfurt a.M., Bern, New York, Paris, 1988, p.80–96).

22. *Politica*, I, 2, 1253a15–18. Sense (αἴσθησις) of right and wrong is a proper characteristic of human beings.

himself a spontaneous inclination toward justice: being conscious of this striving, man will become more and more aware of the precise meaning of its object. But this progress in understanding cannot be effected without experience of social life: one has to learn from experience how to achieve an ideal of justice in the concrete structure of a political society. Starting from a general notion it is impossible to deduce from it how this moral value should be embodied in human relations within a particular society.[23] Practice also is required, because without exercise an abiding disposition cannot be acquired. Each political society ought to be a concrete embodiment of the idea of justice: humans need each other in order to reach the full development of their potencies, but they cannot live together in a stable manner without behaving in conformity with justice and mutual friendship.[24]

In a political community there ought to be an agreement on some basic moral values: if there is no consensus regarding fundamental ethical issues, people cannot live together in a steady way; such society must inevitably collapse.[25] In Aristotle's view there is only one notion of justice: ethical relativism, as it had been professed by the Sophists, is categorically repudiated by Plato as well as by Aristotle.[26] There is only one supreme perfection, and the whole universe is animated by the same tendency toward the good. Of course, circumstances will be different from one country to another, from one period to another: therefore, a legislator needs practical wisdom, as each individual needs it for his own conduct. But this does not mean that there are many notions of justice and that

23. *Eth. Nic.*, II, 2, 1103b34–1104a10. According to Aristotle the degree of *acribeia* in moral judgments concerning particular situations is rather low. The reason is obvious: concrete circumstances constantly change. Scientific knowledge properly deals with what is most intelligible, namely what is universal, necessary, and uncompounded. The object of metaphysical inquiry represents this highest level of intelligibility. Cf. S. Mansion, *Le jugement d'existence chez Aristote*, Louvain-Paris, 1946, p.91.

24. *Eth. Nic.*, VIII, 1, 1155a22–28. In a political community friendship is even more necessary than justice. The question of individual human rights did not play any part in the evolution of Greek society; it became important in the absolutist states of modern Western history (W. Kullmann, *Die politische Philosophie des Aristoteles*, in: *Antike Rechts- und Sozialphilosophie*, p.77).

25. *Politica*, I, 2, 1253a18.

26. *Eth. Nic.*, V, 7, 1134b27–30; *Rhetorica* (*Rhet.*), I, 13, 1373b6. What is just by nature is not necessarily invariable: Aristotle also accepts some variability in the field of natural justice, as he accepts it in the area of legal justice. Even nature allows some flexibility.

everybody may choose the one he prefers. There is only one justice, although there may be several interpretations of it according to the situations of life; members of the same community may discuss and perhaps disagree on some concrete applications, but they should agree on the basic concept of justice, as the foundation of every republic.[27]

In view of reaching this consensus on moral issues language plays an essential part. Man is gifted with the capacity of speaking: he is a speaking animal, able to communicate with other individuals by means of language. A dialogue includes at once acts of speaking and of listening. In Aristotle's perspective dialogue is necessary, since a political society is not possible without a consensus of the members upon basic principles of moral conduct: these principles or rules ought to be expressed and formulated in laws. Citizens are called to reach an agreement on the content of legal rules: such laws are the armature of the state.[28] As a matter of fact the republic envisaged by Aristotle is not neutral; it is grounded on a definite ethical pattern, which embodies traditional values of ancient Greece. The author does not ignore that these values are to be interpreted, explained, and concretized; therefore, articulated language is an appropriate means: it allows one to analyze some vague notions derived from popular beliefs and to invest them with an accurate and definite meaning.[29] In this process of clarification there is an enormous difference between humans and irrational animals: the latter also produce some sounds and are able to indicate an object to other animals; according to the sounds they perceive animals have their attention drawn to a particular thing. But in the case of

27. *Eth. Nic.*, V, 5, 1133b32–1134a6. As has been already explained, Aristotle draws a distinction between natural justice and legal justice: the latter depends on what has been settled by law (*Eth. Nic.*, V, 7, 1134b18–24). With respect to natural justice, the author declares that it has the same authority everywhere: in other words, its authority does not depend upon the fact that it has been decided by the people.

28. *Eth. Nic.*, X, 10, 1180a21–22: laws are considered to be the fruit of reason and wisdom.

29. *Politica*, I, 2, 1253a14–15. In this context Aristotle uses two significative terms: irrational animals are able to show (σημαίνειν) to other animals that some objects cause pleasure or pain; they inform other animals of their sensations of pleasure and pain. As to humans, they are able to clarify (δηλοῦν) what is useful and harmful, what is just and unjust. Two important differences may be noticed: there is quite a difference between a simple indication and a clarification. Moreover, what is at issue in the case of animals is a pleasant or unpleasant impression, whereas humans are concerned with the disclosure of basic ethical notions.

irrational animals the sounds produced are not articulated speech; they are merely a sign or token that points to an external object.[30] On the contrary, human language, being articulated, is able to explain what is referred to: by means of words and sentences man can elucidate the intelligible content of what he wants to disclose.

In his logical works Aristotle is very much concerned with the question of clarification: terms are clarified by definitions. Man always endeavors to explain the terms used in ordinary language and therefore elaborates definitions, which normally include a generic and a specific element. This method shows that the author first attempts to put an object within the boundaries of a general class and then to uncover its characteristic features. The outcome of a definition is the disclosure of the specific nature of an object.[31] Both generic and specific features together form the essential structure of a being: thus man is defined as a rational animal; the general category to which man belongs is that of animals, whereas the specific feature of humans is rationality. The author also stresses the importance of some proper characteristics, which do not belong to the essential nature, but necessarily spring from it: in this way such features contribute to the clarification of the essence by showing some properties that proceed from it. On the other hand, by knowing the essential nature, it is also possible to have a better insight into the properties that are linked to it: there is a constant interaction between our knowledge of the essence and that of the properties.[32] The Aristotelian definition is not a static formulation: when man is called a rational animal, the elucidation is not finished; it goes on mainly by disclosing the proper characteristics that are necessarily linked to the essence. Thus in the case of man the capacities of speaking and of laughing are not considered to be essential features, but properties proceeding directly from the essence. Finally, even

30. *Politica*, I, 2, 1253a9–14.

31. G. Verbeke, *La notion de propriété dans les Topiques*, in: *Aristotle on Dialectic, the Topics*, ed. G. E. L. Owen, Oxford, 1968, p.260–261, p.264.

32. G. Verbeke, *La notion de propriété dans les Topiques*, p.270–275: "Qu'on parte de l'essence pour découvrir les propriétés, ou qu'on s'appuie sur les attributs propres pour arriver à la compréhension de l'essence, le savoir scientifique est toujours, aux yeux d'Aristote, une connaissance nécessairement corrélative de l'essence et de la propriété. Plus particulièrement la 'science à faire' par opposition à la 'science faite' est une sorte de mouvement oscillatoire, allant de l'essence à la propriété et de la propriété à l'essence, et ce mouvement sera sans doute aussi illimité que celui du monde" (p.275–276).

accidental and contingent factors contribute to some extent to uncover the essence, since there is at least a possible connection between them

In his logical inquiry Aristotle went even further and tried to
justify or to demonstrate definitions, but in this attempt he did not
entirely succeed: a definition is never the conclusion of a syllogism.
In this context the author proposes a syllogism of the essence; this
arguing, however, is not a proper syllogism. It is nothing more than
the justification of a vague and imprecise description by means of a
more accurate indication.[33] The Aristotelian definition could not be
proved, at least not according to the author's rules of scientific
theory. A definition is the starting point of an argument; it is not
attained at the end of a reasoning process. Man always tries to
elucidate the notions he uses: this clarification is possible because
of language, which allows him to analyze the hidden constituents
of an idea and to express them in a coherent formulation.

In contemporary thought many questions about the Aristotelian
method of definition have been raised. When man is called a rational
animal, the question arises whether man is an animal in the same
sense as irrational animals. In Aristotle's perspective the answer is
decidedly negative, since man is characterized as a unitary being; he
is not a juxtaposition of two or three joined substances, but one
single compounded substance.[34] In the case of humans the animal
character is penetrated by reason: the rational faculty is not merely
joined to an already constituted animal; rationality and animality
belong to the same substance.[35] Moreover, one may wonder
whether rationality truly characterizes all humans: if indeed rational-

---

33. S. Mansion, *Le jugement d'existence chez Aristote*, p.186–192.

34. *De anima*, III, 7, 431b2; 8, 432a7–9. The unity of man is clearly expressed in
the fact that human understanding is always linked to sensible knowledge: not only
is the origin of our concepts connected with perception but at any time the activity
of the mind is dependent upon sensible objects. T. Tracy writes: "Aristotle holds
that the intelligible forms or unchanging essences exist only in particular, concrete
sensible things. Hence they are always presented to the intellect under a particular
sensible form. For though the act of sense-perception is of the particular, its content
is universal—is man for example, not the man Callias" (*Post. Anal.*, 100a17–b1)
(*Physiological Theory and the Doctrine of the Mean*, p.262).

35. *Eth. Nic.*, I, 13, 1102b13–28. In humans the irrational part of the soul is not
merely irrational: it is able to conform to reason and to follow the injunctions of this
higher power. On the other hand, the activity of the rational part may be hampered by
emotions and passions. In man reason permeates sensible knowledge and emotional
inclinations.

ity is present in all human individuals, its levels are obviously very different. Some individuals are in their way of behaving, in their understanding and knowledge, much more rational than others. A general statement declaring that all humans are rational may easily be questioned: human conduct does not always manifest an undeniable rational inspiration; Aristotle frequently points to the obscuring influence of passions.[36] As a result we may conclude that by means of articulated language man is able to elucidate fundamental moral notions, to communicate with other individuals, and to reach a common understanding of these values.

In Aristotle's view man is by nature a political being: he needs an organized society with laws in view of his moral education.[37] Young people are not able to attend lectures on moral philosophy in a fruitful way; they do not have special difficulties when they study mathematics: this discipline is based on abstract reasoning and does not require experience and practice, whereas in the area of ethics knowledge is intimately linked to conduct, at least when the intuition of what is good in the variable situations of life is at stake.[38] Two arguments support this viewpoint: first, it is not possible to deduce from universal axioms what is to be done in particular circumstances; a general rule cannot foresee all concrete cases in which an agent happens to be. In some situations it is not even desirable to apply the law literally. If the legislator were confronted with some exceptional cases, he certainly would not want strict obedience to the law. Therefore, a ruler needs the virtue of equity (*epieikeia*) so as to be able to judge particular cases correctly.[39] A

36. *Eth. Nic.*, VI, 12, 1144a34–b1. In Aristotle's view the rational character of various individuals is not the same: it depends upon their moral conduct. If somebody constantly lives and behaves in conformity with reason, he will be more rational than another individual who usually yields to emotional impulses. Ethical conduct makes humans more rational: in this sense everybody is responsible for his level of rationality.

37. O. Gigon rightly declares about Aristotle's political theory: "Da wird also der Staat ein Erziehungsstaat, der sowohl weiss, was dieses Ziel des vollkommenen Lebens beinhaltet, wie auch bereit ist, alle seine Anordnungen diesem Ziele dienstbar zu machen" (*Die Staatsverdrossenheit in der Antike*, in: *Antike Rechts- und Sozialphilosophie*, p.211; cf. p.212.)

38. *Eth. Nic.*, VI, 8, 1142a11–19. Practical wisdom is largely based on experience, which can only be acquired after a considerable period of time ($\pi\lambda\tilde{\eta}\theta\sigma\varsigma\ \gamma\dot{\alpha}\rho\ \chi\rho\acute{o}\nu\sigma\upsilon$): young people, because they are young, cannot possess this required experience of human behavior. At their age they cannot have practical wisdom.

39. *Eth. Nic.*, V, 14, 1137b5–16.

man who knows all moral rules sufficiently well will not always be capable of formulating adequate judgments on ethical matters in special situations, which are constantly changing and may be very complicated. In addition, when an agent ponders a particular moral judgment he is always threatened by irrational movements that obscure the mind. Only a virtuous man is able to judge correctly what is to be done in the changing circumstances of life; an individual dominated by violent passions or emotions will not succeed in disclosing what is truly valuable: he will judge in conformity with his irrational inclinations.[40]

Aristotle has to face a complex problem, and he cannot avoid proposing a solution: moral action depends upon knowledge, namely upon our intuition of what is good in particular situations. But on the other hand the same ethical insight depends on our moral conduct: one has to behave morally in order to be able to grasp what is truly good.[41] The solution suggested by Aristotle refers to political society. According to our author the rules of moral conduct are embodied in the laws of the state: a republic without laws is not a true political society. Laws express the wisdom of the people: they proceed from a consensus and may be reformed and improved in the course of time. Lacking experience and practice young people cannot yet understand why such rules of conduct are imposed. In a first stage they have to accept the laws without understanding them and to behave in conformity with them: at this early stage of their life they should act under compulsion of the laws and so they will gradually understand that the rules are justified and truly moral.[42] Intuition of ethical values with regard to concrete situations is not a matter of merely theoretical understanding.

Consequently Aristotle does not side with those who maintain that all human inclinations and tendencies are good and that no restriction whatsoever ought to be imposed upon individual freedom. He disagrees with authors like Rousseau who declare that moral degeneration does not proceed from natural propensities but

40. Being the author of his moral character, man is responsible for what appears to him as good or evil; in this sense everybody is to some extent responsible for his ethical judgments and valuations. It is true that everyone evaluates concrete situations according to his character, but it is also true that man is at the origin of this character inasmuch as he is the principle of his habits (*Eth. Nic.*, III, 5, 1114a31–b5).

41. *Eth. Nic.*, VI, 12, 1144a36.

42. *Eth. Nic.*, X, 9, 1180a1–5.

from life in society. According to Plato and Aristotle each individual bears within himself a permanent conflict between reason and passions: in the *Phaedrus* passions are compared to a restless and unruly horse, which the driver has to break in so that he may come to the contemplation of the ideal Forms.[43] To master the unruly horse means to subdue passions and emotions to the rule of reason. Plato and Aristotle do not suggest extirpating all irrational movements; this view was later adopted by the Stoics, who proclaimed that man ought to become what he is by nature, namely reason, a particle of the Divine Substance. In their opinion passions cannot be tolerated, since by their very nature they oppose reason.[44] The valuation of passions is certainly more positive in Plato's and Aristotle's thought, and yet both believe that some compulsion is required in moral education in order to subordinate passions to reason.

The question whether the compelling authority of laws refers only to young people, or also to other members of society may arise. Aristotle believes that as individuals become more mature and have some experience of life and moral conduct, they will gradually come to grasp the meaning of laws and be ready to accept these regulations without constraint.[45] This viewpoint is mainly based on his teleological conception of the universe and of man. A natural tendency toward the good is present in each individual: thus everybody is inclined to implement what is good when he grasps it and is not prevented from achieving it by unexpected obstacles. A political society has to secure the knowledge of what is truly good; young people are not able to discover it independently; they should be guided by laws that ought to be imposed with a compulsory authority.[46] Later on, when they have acquired more experience and more

43. *Phaedrus*, 246b; 247b; 248a–c: it is quite difficult for human souls to reach the plane of truth (τὸ ἀληθείας πεδίον). Authentic reality belongs to a transcendent level: what is offered in sensible things is only an imitation of the immutable Forms. In a sense sensible perception may contribute to grasping the Ideas, but at the same time man has to go beyond these imperfect beings if he wants to seize what is truly real.

44. Diogenes Laertius, VII, 110.

45. *Eth. Nic.*, VI, 12, 1143b21–28: in Aristotle's view moral education mainly aims at acquiring practical wisdom (φρόνησις), which is able to guide man in the variable situations of life. This intellectual virtue however is linked to courage, justice and temperance.

46. *Eth. Nic.*, X, 9, 1180a21. Aristotle declares that law has a compulsory force (ἀναγκαστικὴν ἔχει δύναμιν): it is a rational rule that proceeds from practical

practice of moral behavior, they will become able to take ethical decisions in all circumstances of life. So they will implement what is good not as a result of compulsion but of their own personal insight.

In Aristotle's view a political society plays an important part in moral education,[47] particularly with respect to young people. In this context it is necessary to look more closely at the specific nature of a political community: like Plato, Aristotle endeavors to disclose the proper characteristics of an ideal republic, in which all members will be able to realize their highest degree of perfection and true happiness. According to the Greek Master the end of the state coincides with the end of an individual. In other words, a republic does not possess an end in itself, distinct from that of its individual members: it is established for the benefit of its members; individuals do not exist as a means for the development of the state. Aristotle is strongly convinced of the capital importance of political communities, but this importance is entirely related to the development of individual members: there is no worship of the state as a subsistent entity. The state is important because the full development of individuals depends upon it. Hence the question which kind of constitution is the best one: in Plato's view an ideal republic ought to be ruled by a king-philosopher. Only philosophers are able to contemplate the transcendent Forms, which in the field of moral conduct represent the highest values: perfect justice, the basis of a political society, is grasped only by philosophers.[48] All other members of a

wisdom and intellectual insight. Laws are largely responsible for the moral education of a community: they ought to be settled by reason (λόγος), and since they deal with human behavior in all kinds of situations, they should proceed from practical wisdom (ἀπὸ φρονήσεως). In this context Aristotle also mentions intellect (νοῦς) since this power is concerned with basic principles (*Eth. Nic.*, VI, 6, 1141a5–8): the ultimate ground of legal regulations must be found in the fundamental principles of moral life. Only those who are supremely virtuous should not be submitted to legal rules (*Politica*, III, 13, 1284a13–14).

47. Political society is in a sense a result of moral education and a source of it. According to Aristotle, ethical education secures the necessary coherence and unity of all members of a political community (*Politica*, II, 5, 1263b36–37). This community is not a neutral body, in which many ideologies and different conceptions of life are represented by the members: according to our author there ought to be an agreement on basic moral values.

48. *Respubl.*, V, 475b: in Plato's view a distinctive feature of a philosopher is that he loves the whole of truth. A philosopher will certainly direct his attention to the Idea of the Good, which is the highest Form: all other Ideas are linked to it and

republic will participate in the transcendent values through the mediation of philosopher-rulers: since other people do not have direct and personal access to the transcendent values, they need the help of those privileged individuals gifted with wisdom. These are able to build a society that corresponds to the ideal patterns: their fellow-citizens will benefit from their ruling, as they will be incorporated in the same community. So according to Plato the best constitution is a philosophical aristocracy. This viewpoint, however, does not mean that knowledge of truth is confined to a small number of individuals: everybody bears within himself a hidden treasure of knowledge; each human soul had immediate intuition of the Ideas before it was joined to the body. Apparently Plato believes that most of the people are prevented from discovering this hidden truth as a result of their concern with sensible things; they seemingly ignore that these things are only an imitation of true reality. They are like the famous prisoners in the cave, looking at shadows and believing that they are dealing with real beings.[49] When a philosopher is king, everybody partakes of his wisdom.

Aristotle dedicated his whole life to the study of philosophy. He certainly shows a very high regard for this kind of intellectual activity. When he describes the supreme level of human perfection, he points to philosophical contemplation performed in an assiduous and capable way. And yet he does not entrust philosophers with the highest political authority.[50] Wanting to discover the best constitution, the author understandably starts from the study of existing political systems: this method conforms to the author's theory of

---

subordinated to it. In the transcendent world Forms do not exist separately from each other: they are mutually connected and constitute in this way the ground of judgments and arguments in human thought. So a philosopher is concerned with the whole of authentic reality, up to the highest principle.

49. *Respubl.*, VII, 514a; 515c. The tragedy of the prisoners was that they so firmly believed they were dealing with real things that they killed the man who endeavored to show them their true situation. Did the prisoners really want to be deceived? In Plato's view they did not: they were victims of their condition, but they had the capacity of discovering that true reality could not coincide with the shadows they were watching. All prisoners bear within themselves a treasure of true knowledge that they are able to discover.

50. The question whether philosophers should engage into political affairs has been answered in different ways: according to Epicurus a wise man should withdraw from politics, except when special circumstances compel him to be involved; as to the Stoics, they teach that a wise individual will be concerned with political matters, except when special circumstances prevent him from doing it (Seneca, *De otio, 3, 2*).

knowledge. Intellectual understanding stems from sensible experience, although it transcends perception. Studying various constitutions, comparing them with each other, knowing also how they work and to which results they lead, the author tries to find the best form of government. Within the area of Greek culture he noticed three main kinds of constitution: monarchy, aristocracy, and democracy. He does not deal with the evolution and possible decline of these various systems; according to Polybius there is a constant degeneration of each of these constitutions. Monarchy evolves to tyranny; such a system cannot last; it is overthrown and replaced by aristocracy. But aristocracy also degenerates to oligarchy; this government also is opposed and eliminated; it is replaced by democracy, which in its turn develops to ochlocracy, or arbitrary domination of the mass. Again this government is eliminated and replaced by monarchy; in this way the cycle of successive constitutions starts again.[51] Aristotle is quite conscious of possible deviations of political systems and wants to avoid them; therefore, he endeavors to discover a pattern of government able to be lasting and promoting the well-being of all members of the community. From a rather theoretical viewpoint the Stagirite believes that the best constitutions are kingship and aristocracy: they are grounded on the moral and intellectual excellence of either one or a small number of eminent persons. When such outstanding individuals are available, they should assume the responsibility of ruling the polis. As a matter of fact, it is impossible to determine which constitution is the best without taking into account the kind of population that is concerned.[52] At the time of Aristotle most city-states were oligarchies or democracies, so they were governed either by the great majority of the poor or by a small group of wealthy individuals.[53] Obviously

51. Polybius, *Historiae*, VI, 1–10. Living in the second century B.C. Polybius must have been familiar with some Stoic ideas. In his view history is a kind of philosophy: it does not teach, however, by arguing and reasoning but by expounding some concrete examples of the past. The author was not interested in sectional investigation of various peoples and countries: in his view all parts of the world are related to each other and constitute an organic whole. As to the theory of gradual decline of each given society and of cyclical evolution of history, it is certainly present in Stoic thought.

52. *Politica*, III, 18, 1288a32–b2; IV, 2, 1289b18–20.

53. *Politica*, IV, 11, 1296a22–23. The main reason for this situation is that the middle class is generally small. In the conflict between the property owners and the mass, one of the two groups prevails and adopts a political system that conforms to its own interest.

these constitutions are regarded as deviations; they ought to be corrected. In conformity with his moral teaching on the mean as an intermediary between two extremes, he proposes a constitution located between oligarchy and democracy, which might be called "a limited democracy" or *politeia*. This kind of government is not merely democratic, nor is it purely oligarchic: it is a mixture of the two, and the combination will be perfect when it may be called a democracy as well as an oligarchy. The constitution of Sparta is considered to be a good illustration of such a combination.[54]

A political system in which power is committed to a single person is generally to be repudiated.[55] People have to be involved in the ruling of a state. A strong reason in favor of this viewpoint is that in this way conflicts, tensions, and all kinds of opposition will be prevented: if people are excluded from participation in ruling, they will be inclined to revolt against the authority.[56] But there is in the mind of Aristotle a more profound argument that supports some kind of democracy, namely his valuation of common opinions. In his view everybody may contribute to the discovery of truth; each human individual has his own mind and his own experience; what people think, what they believe to be true, should not be dismissed. The views of many people are more worth than the opinion of a single individual.[57] Aristotle takes popular beliefs, even mythological narratives, very seriously when they are ancient and have been universally accepted up to the present day. This teaching corresponds to Aristotle's teleological doctrine: if common opinions that are universally accepted are false, the whole of mankind lives in a condition of permanent error, which is incompatible with universal teleology. If everything strives toward the good, human mind too tends to its perfection, namely to the knowledge of truth; in this perspective it is quite impossible that all humans persist in error.

54. *Politica*, IV, 9, 1294b13–40. Regarding the democratic character of the Spartan constitution Aristotle especially points to the system of education, which is the same for all children; the common meals, and the way in which all citizens are dressed.

55. *Politica*, III, 16, 1287a30. Aristotle firmly opposes the idea of entrusting one individual with all political power: in his view this coincides with giving all authority to a wild beast. Yet the author declares that a person who by far exceeds all other citizens could not be considered as an ordinary member of a political community (*Politica*, III, 13, 1284a3–8; III, 17, 1288a15–19).

56. *Politica*, V, 1, 1302a8–15.

57. *Politica*, III, 10, 1281b4–10; b34–38. This viewpoint fully corresponds to Aristotle's teaching on the worth of popular beliefs and prephilosophical opinions.

Therefore, people should not be excluded from participation in ruling power. On the other hand, it is also desirable that a society be ruled by the best of its members: not everybody has the same intellectual capacities or attains the same level of moral conduct. The aim of society is to promote the full development of its members: how can this ideal be attained if the ruling persons are on a low level of rational insight and moral behavior? For these reasons Aristotle wants a mixture of oligarchy and democracy, or a limited democracy.

Dealing with the proper nature of a democracy, the author mentions three main characteristics. The first is liberty of the citizens; each lives as he wants to live without any constraint from the political power.[58] This feature, however, does not imply that liberty is unlimited. In a democracy there are also laws that prescribe a way of conduct, but they are settled by the whole community, not only by a single ruler or by a small number of them.[59] In this context laws are like a self-imposed and freely accepted norm of behaving. Moreover, in a democracy all citizens are equal. When an individual is invested with ruling authority, it is only for a limited period of time: there is an alternation of responsibilities and nobody is privileged. Equality in a democracy is numerical: it does not depend upon birth, wealth, or property[60]; each individual is equal to the other members of the community, although some categories of people are excluded from government: slaves, foreigners, women, and children. Finally, a democracy is characterized by a specific concept of what is lawful: what the majority of the citizens decides is lawful. Decisions taken by the majority are considered to be right.[61]

In the framework of Aristotle's philosophy these characteristics of democracy cannot be unreservedly approved and accepted. Aristotle

58. *Politica*, VI, 2, 1317a40–b13: τὸ ζῆν ὡς βούλεταί τις. Democratic liberty is opposed to slavery: slaves have no possibility of living as they want to live. Still this characteristic of democracy should not be misunderstood: even a democratic society has to be ruled by laws invested with compulsory power. Within this framework, however, everybody chooses his own way of life.

59. *Politica*, IV, 4, 1292a7–11. A democracy that is not ruled by decent laws will inevitably fall under the influence of demagogues: on the contrary, when it is governed by laws, the best citizens will be entrusted with authority.

60. *Politica*, VI, 2, 1317b2–4; b7.

61. *Politica*, VI, 2, 1317b5–7. In a democracy the majority of citizens decides what is just and unjust. In Aristotle's view this decision is not arbitrary: the majority of the people will probably decide correctly on what is right and wrong.

never maintained the universal equality of all humans: in his view the most typical feature of a human being is rational activity. Other animals are not endowed with reason: thinking is a privilege of humans, who in this respect outdo all other sensible beings. Yet among humans the degree of rational activity is far from equal. Some humans are on a low level in this regard: we have already mentioned Aristotle's opinion of slaves, barbarians, women, and children; their rational capacities are not strongly developed.[62] Consequently they are excluded from ruling society: the ideal republic of our author ought to be ruled by Greeks who are free citizens, not slaves, and who are adult men, not women. Regarding rational activity Aristotle further distinguishes lower and higher levels, which, however, are not taken into account in view of political responsibility. On this point the author differs from Plato, who commits the full political responsibility to some outstanding scholars who have attained the highest degree of intellectual knowledge. This view is not adopted by the Stagirite: he believes that political leaders need above all practical wisdom ($\phi\rho\delta\nu\eta\sigma\iota\varsigma$): they need it for formulating good laws, which promote the moral education of the people, as well as for applying laws to particular situations, which are always unique since they constantly vary. As a moral man needs practical wisdom for his own life, so political rulers need the same virtue for their ruling responsibility. Regarding intellectual knowledge, Aristotle mainly distinguishes three levels: the lowest is confined to the knowledge of facts; particular events occurring in nature are observed and collected. A second level is the knowledge of causes: man tries to disclose why things happen as they do; the knowledge of causes represents a higher degree of understanding; it explains and elucidates what occurs.[63] The highest level of understanding is realized when the ultimate causes are grasped: a further clarification of reality is not possible. Everybody is oriented toward knowledge and truth: that means that each individual consciously or unconsciously strives toward the highest level

62. G. Verbeke, *Les degrés d'humanité et le sens du progrès chez Aristote*, in: Ἀρετῆς μνήμη (Festschrift C. J. Vourveris), Athens, 1983, p.123.

63. *Metaphysica* (*Metaph.*), I, 1, 981a24–30. It has already been explained that experience results from frequently repeated memories of the same thing (*Analytica Posteriora*[*Anal. Post.*], II, 19, 100a4–6). Scientific knowledge transcends the mere gathering of facts.

of understanding.[64] Aristotle does not wonder whether some free citizens are on too low a level of rational activity to be able to participate in ruling responsibility: are there not some citizens who belong to the category of slaves by nature? In Aristotle's perspective this question is not important, because the majority has to take decisions and the views of this majority are reliable.

The author, however, realizes that not all political communities are compounded in the same way: he favors a society in which there are neither too many wealthy nor too many poor people. In his view the best society is one in which there is a strong middle class: such people more readily behave in conformity with the prescriptions of reason. Wealthy people are hardly able to obey, and poor people living in miserable conditions are inclined to become envious and jealous.[65]

As to liberty in a democracy, it ought to be limited by legal rules, which should be approved by the majority of the people. All citizens take part in the deliberation of the assembly and in the assessment of the accounts of officials.[66] According to our author no technical ability is required for such political responsibility.[67]

A democracy without laws is firmly repudiated by the Greek Master: the highest authority should be held by laws, not by rulers.[68] Of course, laws are only general norms of conduct; they cannot take into account all particular and concrete cases. The interpretation of laws is committed to magistrates. Their duty is to apply those general rules to the changing situations of life. Such interpretation requires much practical wisdom and truly ethical conduct: when these conditions are not fulfilled, the interpretation may easily be mistaken and falsified.[69]

64. *Metaph.*, I, 2, 982b7–10. The highest level of scientific knowledge is concerned with the first causes: among them the author mentions the final cause and the good. Pure Act is indeed the final cause of the universe.

65. *Politica*, IV, 11, 1295b3–25. This viewpoint of Aristotle's is based on his more general ethical teaching on the mean as a norm of ethical behavior: extremes should always be avoided, including with respect to wealth and poverty. As to the question of external wealth and properties, according to the Stagirite they only depend on chance and fortune (*Politica*, III, 1, 1323b27–28).

66. *Politica*, III, 11, 1281b28–34.

67. *Politica*, III, 12, 1282a14–23. An architect is not always the best qualified judge of a newly built house: people who live in it are often in a better position to make an assessment.

68. *Politica*, IV, 4, 1292a4–37.

69. *Politica*, III, 11, 1282b1–6; 15, 1286a9–12; II, 8, 1269a9–12; IV, 4, 1292a32–37.

So we may conclude that in Aristotle's view political society plays a major part in the moral education of its members, particularly of young people; this education ought to be achieved by means of compulsory laws in a limited democracy, in which the middle class should be sufficiently strong.

ETHICAL INTELLECTUALISM

I S MORAL education only a matter of knowledge and learning, or is it something more? If somebody wants to become an expert in arithmetic, geometry, or astronomy, he has to learn these disciplines: he may need the help of a teacher, but his preparation will be merely intellectual.[1] In Plato's view, as we know from the *Meno,* the learning process is not an assimilation of new knowledge, of something that was previously ignored. It is considered to be a growing awareness of what was already present in the mind but must be awakened in order to become a conscious understanding. In the dialogue Socrates does not transfer his own knowledge to the slave; he only asks questions. As to the slave, he is not always able to formulate an answer immediately; he hesitates and also makes mistakes. But the solution of the problem is not easily given to him by an expert in the matter: it is really discovered by him with the help of Socrates. Thus the latter does not communicate a solution to somebody who is only receptive.[2]

In Aristotle's philosophy the theory of recollection is firmly repudiated: all knowledge is linked to sensible experience; progress in

---

1. This question is formally treated in Plato's *Protagoras:* at the end of his discourse on education, Protagoras comes to the conclusion that virtue may be taught (ὡς διδακτὸν ἀρετή); he further adds that the Athenians agreed on this viewpoint. As to the question why virtuous parents do not always have virtuous children, he replies that the reason may be found in the natural disposition of the children. In any case, in Protagoras' view this fact does not prove that virtue is not a matter of teaching (*Protagoras,* 328c). The same question has been treated by two disciples of Socrates, Crito and Simon: the first wrote a work entitled: Ὅτι οὐκ ἐκ τοῦ μαθεῖν οἱ ἀγαθοί (*That Men are not made Good by Instruction*); the latter composed the writing Περὶ ἀρετῆς ὅτι οὐ διδακτόν (*That Virtue cannot be Taught*) (Diogenes Laertius, II, 121–122). Nothing is known about the content of these works: the titles rather suggest that, according to the authors, virtuous conduct is not merely the result of learning.

2. *Meno,* 82a–85b.

knowing is not merely awareness of some hidden treasure of ideas that man bears within his mind. It really is the discovery and assimilation of something formerly unknown. In this perspective education and learning acquire a much more positive meaning than they have in Plato. An individual constantly increases his knowledge, since he meets new objects and assimilates them.[3] This development is regarded by Aristotle as a biological process: new elements of knowledge are not juxtaposed to the previous ones; they are acquired and integrated into the already existing patrimony, to form an organic unity with them. Elements that are not integrated into the formerly acquired information are not really part of our knowledge. In this sense learning is always a gradual increase and assimilation: the content of the mind becomes larger, although the unity is not broken: objects of knowledge are related to each other and form together the organic coherence of an individual's understanding.

What about moral education in this perspective? In Plato's view progress in moral knowledge is regarded as a growing awareness of ethical insights existing in the mind, whereas in Aristotle's thought it is a progressive acquisition of virtue and practical wisdom. Moral knowledge may really increase and be improved: through teaching and experience our understanding of ethical values develops. In this regard there is a parallelism between learning geometry and learning moral philosophy: in both cases a real growth of knowledge and understanding is possible. Yet there is also an important difference between the two disciplines: the study of geometry is merely theoretical, whereas moral knowledge is practical; it refers to practice and it also depends upon practice.[4] Hence the question whether

3. In Plato's opinion sensitive activity does not provide man with new knowledge and does not supply new information; its function is to stimulate consciousness, to evoke some knowable content that is already present in the mind. In this respect the role of sensible perception is very different in Aristotle: it supplies new information to be assimilated by the mind. In Plato's view intellectual insights do not proceed from sensible experience, whereas according to Aristotle universal notions stem from sensible data that have been made intelligible by the active intellect. According to *Anal. Post.* (II, 19, 100a17–b1) what one perceives is a particular, but perception is of the universal, for example, of man but not of Callias the man. According to J. Barnes "man" must be an incidental object of perception (*Post. Anal.,* Notes 100a); but Aristotle does not explain how such concept derives from sense data. In any case, Aristotle is convinced the substantial forms are present in sensible beings.

4. *Nicomachean Ethics* (*Eth. Nic.*), VI, 8, 1142a18–19. Practical wisdom is not a science, since it is concerned with individual acts (a23–25): as a matter of fact, human conduct is a series of particular actions, which occur in a variety of concrete situations. Practical wisdom is more like a special ability of formulating correct moral judgments

this question is positive, moral education is reduced to learning. Children have to be taught what is right and wrong: if they understand and assimilate this teaching, they will act rightly. In this perspective the cause and origin of moral faults is ignorance or error. Nobody can ever pursue what he believes to be wrong: consequently what is essentially needed is that people be informed of what is right and wrong, that they be acquainted with true moral values. Man will always pursue what he believes to be good: how could he ever strive for what he knows to be evil? This possibility is decidedly excluded as it is contrary to Aristotle's teleological view of man and the universe.

Such a doctrine, however, has to face serious difficulties, first of all that of man's responsibility: if human behavior is merely a matter of knowledge or ignorance and error, how can an individual be responsible for what he is doing, whether it is right or wrong? Some people have a better understanding than others; they may be also better instructed than others. Is an individual responsible for what he knows and what he ignores? Human knowledge mostly depends on the natural capacity of each person, and this capacity is far from being the same in all. Moreover, there is much wrongdoing among men: all kinds of immoral acts are constantly committed, some rather light, but also some that are grave, such as murders or acts of injustice in important matters. It is hard to believe that all those people are ignorant of what they are doing or happen to be mistaken about the ethical value of their conduct. If moral behavior depends upon our information on ethical matters, people very learned in this field must have the most perfect behavior; one would also expect in this case that progress of learning and education would always be beneficial for ethical conduct. Finally one could not deny that there is in human life a permanent conflict between reason and passion, between intellectual insights and irrational impulses. It is commonly accepted that individuals are driven to immoral actions under the influence of emotional drives, although they know their behavior to be wrong. In his *Metamorphoses*[5] Ovid writes, "Video meliora

---

Practical wisdom is more like a special ability of formulating correct moral judgments in the various circumstances of life: what are needed are above all some experience of human behavior and a clear intuition that is not obscured by emotional factors.

5. *Metamorphoses*, 7, 20. Cf. S. Paul, *Epistola ad Romanos* (*Rom.*), 7, 21. In a sense it is true that nobody does what he believes to be wrong: like all other beings, man always strives toward the good. In dealing with this question, Aristotle distinguishes

proboque, deteriora sequor" (I know what is good and approve of it, and yet I do what is wrong).

In Plato's *Protagoras* Socrates deals with the same question: people commonly believe that individuals who commit wrong actions actually know that what they are doing is evil, but that their knowledge is overcome by their inclination to pleasure; in fact, they perform what they know to be wrong, because their moral intuition is superseded by passion. Socrates does not agree with this interpretation: in his view nothing is stronger or more powerful than true knowledge[6]; such insight can never be overcome or suppressed by an irrational impulse. Moral faults must be explained in a different way: they are not the result of a conflict between ethical insight and passion, a struggle in which passion supersedes knowledge. Moral faults are the consequences of a deficiency or a lack in moral knowledge. This knowledge is mainly concerned with the valuation of pleasure and pain with respect to a future action; if this appreciation is right, man will act accordingly and his conduct will be right; if the valuation is erroneous, he will again behave in conformity with it and his behavior will be wrong. According to this viewpoint man's conduct always corresponds to his moral judgment; he behaves in agreement with his ethical intuition.[7] This interpretation of moral faults is a typical expression of Socrates' intellectualism. Let us look more closely at the background of this philosophical attitude.

The vocation and philosophical activity of Socrates are closely linked to a statement of the oracle of Delphi: Chaerephon wanted to know whether anybody was wiser than Socrates. At that time Greek philosophy had already some tradition: from the seventh

---

various kinds of knowledge: in his opinion it is possible to perform a wrong action, knowing that it is evil, provided this knowledge is only universal or habitual (*Eth. Nic*, VII, 3, 1146b31–1147a18).

6. *Protagoras*, 357c–d.

7. *Eudemian Ethics (Eth. Eud.)*, I, 5, 1216b2–10. In his account of Socrates' teaching Aristotle stresses the fact that moral behavior is regarded as a necessary consequence of knowledge: if someone truly knows what is courage and justice, he will automatically behave accordingly. The main problem, however, is which kind of understanding is intended by Socrates. According to Aristotle's interpretation what is at issue is to grasp the true nature of a virtue. The author categorically opposes this doctrine: it is much more important to know how to achieve virtuous conduct. The goal that is pursued is not mere knowledge but behavior: if one knows what is courage, without being courageous, this knowledge will be useless. A comparison is made with health: what matters is not to know what is health but to be healthy (*Eth. Eud.*, I, 5, 1216b10–25).

century onward philosophical questions had been repeatedly studied and investigated. In the fifth century Athens had become the center of philosophical inquiry and Socrates was not the only one dealing with such questions. Instead of examining the outside world, its origin, and its structure, philosophers at that time were concerned with the study of man and human problems. They concentrated their attention on epistemological and moral issues; above all they wanted to disclose the notion of truth. Is truth relative to each individual or is it universal and valid for every mind? If there is universal truth, can it ever be attained by human individuals who live at a particular time and place? Should we accept that individuals are the measure of everything?[8] Similar questions were asked about basic moral issues, the distinction between right and wrong, the origin of moral obligation, the nature of ethical conduct. Here again questioning was mostly related to the objective nature of moral values: are these values the same for all humans, or do they vary from one country to another, from one period to another, and from one individual to another? Are moral values merely conventional? Are they simply formulated and imposed by individuals who are in power?[9] The range of questions was very wide, but they were mainly concentrated on man and society. Socrates was one of many philosophers; his friend probably wanted to know whether he could trust him and rely on him, or whether he should rather turn to other representatives of Greek wisdom. The answer was negative: nobody was wiser than Socrates; within the group of philosophers at that time he represented the highest level of wisdom. Chaerephon must have been pleased; instead of moving to other masters, he could stay with Socrates.[10]

8. *Theatetus*, 152a: knowledge is reduced to sensible perception, which is considered to be infallible (cf.*Cratylus* [*Crat.*], 385e); 168d; 183b: Plato strongly opposed epistemological relativism: his basic argument was the existence of transcendent Forms that are immutable. These Forms represent true reality: they are participated in and imitated by sensible things, which are part of a ceaseless change. Human understanding intends to grasp these immutable Ideas.

9. *Theaetetus*, 152c ff., especially 157a–b: in Plato's view moral values are immutable: they exist on a transcendent level and are present in an imperfect way in human life and society. These values cannot be created by human initiative; they can only be accepted. Moral conduct is a constant attempt to take part more perfectly in the eternal patterns of ethical virtue.

10. *Apologia*, 20e–21a. Neither Chaerephon nor Socrates questions the authority of the Delphic oracle. Socrates himself did not consult the oracle; it is hardly

Yet Socrates himself was rather puzzled by the Delphic statement; he could have drawn the conclusion that his philosophy, which opposed the epistemological and moral relativism of the Sophists, had been confirmed by the Pythia of Apollo. His thought would have received divine approval and consecration.[11] But he did not go to other masters in philosophy to inform them of the oracle and to question them about its meaning. As a true philosopher he wanted to disclose the hidden significance of this concise statement: why was he proclaimed the wisest man of his time? Quite understandably he did not wish to consult other philosophers in Athens about the oracle, as he profoundly disagreed with them on basic issues. According to the *Parmenides* of Plato, when he was young, Socrates had a talk with his great predecessor: in this conversation the oracle of Delphi is not mentioned[12]; the main topic of the discussion is the theory of Ideas, subsisting in a transcendent world as perfect and immutable forms. Parmenides formulates a series of criticisms and objections; most of these objections remain unresolved; apparently the questions of Parmenides do not receive a satisfactory answer.[13] Nevertheless Plato did not abandon his theory. Socrates does not speak with Parmenides on the oracle of Delphi, nor does he consult representatives of Greek science on the same topic. He did not question astronomers, geometers, mathematicians, or physicists. In fact, he consulted nobody: what he did was not a consultation, but a questioning of some groups of people in order to ascertain whether they really knew what they claimed to know.[14] So he

believable that he could have done it. The report of Chaerephon should be interpreted within the context of the *Apology*. One of the charges against Socrates was that of impiety; the consultation of the oracle fits very well into the framework of a speech aiming at defending Socrates' religious attitude. Socrates did not disapprove of his friend, nor did he repudiate the Delphic statement.

11. *Apologia*, 21b: The first reaction of Socrates was a profound astonishment; in his own view he was not a wise man. In Aristotle's view amazement is a starting point of philosophical inquiry: being astonished at the statement of the oracle, Socrates endeavored to disclose its meaning.

12. *Parmenides*, 127c.

13. *Parmenides*, 132c–133a. In this famous encounter Parmenides formulates a series of criticisms of Plato's theory of Ideas: one of the best known is related to the paradigmatic character of the Forms. Resemblances among sensible things are explained by their common participation in the same Idea, but there is also a resemblance between the Ideas and sensible reality; here again a transcendent principle will be required, and so indefinitely. Hence the theory of Ideas necessarily involves a *regressus in infinitum*.

14. *Apologia*, 20c–22c.

met politicians, poets, and craftsmen, but he did not mention the oracle; he questioned them about their own activity. The conversation dealt with political matters, poetry, and technical skills. Socrates reached the conclusion that all these people did not possess a true understanding of what they were supposed to know: there was an undeniable lack of insight and reflection.[15]

At this stage Socrates believed he had reached the understanding he was looking for: he actually was proclaimed wiser than his countrymen because he was aware of the limits of his knowledge, conscious of his ignorance. He did not know more than the people he had questioned; he was also unable to give satisfactory answers to all the questions he had asked. But he differed from them because he knew the frontiers of his understanding. Other people were unaware of their ignorance.[16] This conclusion is rather pessimistic: people live in darkness and do not realize it; even Athens is full of darkness, and people live as if they were acquainted with many disciplines. They are like the prisoners in the cave: they look at shadows and are persuaded that they are dealing with real things. And when somebody gets out of prison and has the privilege of looking at real objects, he wants to go back to his fellow prisoners to inform them of their mistake: the end is tragic, since he is killed by the fellows he wants to save.[17] And yet that is the vocation of Socrates, corresponding to the message of the oracle. He has to meet his fellow-citizens and to uncover the limits of their knowledge; he should show them that they believe they know what they do not really understand. Is Socrates entrusted with the mission of humiliating his countrymen? Not really; the true goal of his vocation is to bring people, particularly young people, to deeper reflection and

---

15. *Apologia:* With respect to poets Socrates declares that they say a lot of beautiful things but without understanding what they are talking about (22c); the same obtains in the case of politicians and craftsmen.

16. *Apologia,* 23b. The awareness of one's ignorance has been called *docta ignorantia* which implies an adequate assessment of the limits of one's knowledge, and in this sense it is a stimulus for further inquiry. The aporematic method, frequently used by Aristotle in his philosophical treatises, is closely related to this attitude; to undertake effective research implies that one be aware of the deficiencies in his knowledge.

17. *Respublica (Respubl.),* VII, 517a. In the allegory of Plato a philosopher is a privileged person: he gets outside the cave and contemplates true reality. However, he is unable to persuade his fellows, as they only deal with shadows, yet it is not impossible to disclose the nature of these shadows and to go beyond them, even for people remaining in the cave.

understanding, especially in moral matters. Socrates is convinced that human conduct corresponds to understanding of ethical values: nothing is more powerful than true knowledge. Virtues are sciences[18]: they are the result of a deep and true understanding of moral values. Man is inclined to all kinds of pleasure, but such propensities can never supersede true knowledge. And thus to bring people to reflection, understanding, and truth is to bring them to moral behavior. Moral depravity is the result of ignorance and error. The vocation of Socrates is to make people conscious of their lack of understanding: in this way he will convince them of the need of true insight, particularly with respect to moral issues.

Nevertheless there is a difficulty: if we look at the *Meno*, should we not accept that everybody bears within himself a treasure of true knowledge? How can man be called ignorant if he possesses this hidden science within his soul?[19] Socrates could face this objection easily: it shows, in fact, that his mission is possible and may be carried out with success. The knowledge that everybody bears within his soul is not active: it is not an actual understanding until it has been stimulated and awakened. Thus a man may be both ignorant and omniscient: he is ignorant as long as hidden knowledge remains inactive; he is omniscient because he is not a passive recipient of knowledge that is communicated from without. Moral education is carried out by activating the knowledge everyone bears within his soul; when in this way man reaches true insight, moral behavior will necessarily follow.

Aristotle repudiates the theory of reminiscence; he also opposes moral intellectualism as it was maintained by Socrates. At the beginning of the *Eudemian Ethics* the author wonders how moral education is achieved: in which way should one proceed in view of attaining eudemony, or happiness? Five possible answers are proposed and successively examined. Moral perfection may be regarded as a gift of nature: some individuals are tall, whereas others are small; some people are white, whereas others are black, and these

18. *Eth. Nic.*, VI, 13, 1144b17–21, 28–30. Aristotle opposes the Socratic teaching: virtues are not reduced to knowledge; they imply rational insight (μετὰ λόγου).

19. The initial question of the *Meno* is whether virtue is an object of teaching. At the end of the dialogue Socrates comes to the conclusion that virtue cannot be taught, since there are no teachers in this matter (96c); with respect to human behavior, true opinion may be as powerful as scientific knowledge (97b–c). Yet scientific understanding, being based on causality arguing, is more stable than true opinion (98a).

differences depend upon the natural endowment of each person.[20] In the same way one may suppose that some individuals are virtuous by nature, whereas others are not; in this view the absence of virtue would be comparable to a physical defect, whereas virtue would be considered as a privilege of nature. According to Aristotle humans are by nature moral animals[21]: hence the question whether ethical life and behavior are not merely the result of a natural endowment. In this case personal responsibility would be suppressed: nobody could be responsible for his acts if each way of life is the consequence of a natural disposition. This hypothesis is not merely discarded by Aristotle: the author makes a distinction between natural virtue and ethical virtue in the proper sense of the term. Natural dispositions are not acquired; they belong to the inborn structure of living beings, not only of humans but also of animals. They are not the result of free choice and personal effort. According to the Stagirite such natural dispositions may even be harmful when they are not directed by understanding and insight[22]: bodily strength without sight is a rather dangerous quality. The same obtains with regard to natural virtues: as long as they are not guided by the mind, they are not beneficial and cannot promote the true development of human life. These dispositions only become true virtues when they are directed and permeated by reason and moral wisdom.[23] In the light of this teaching moral education intends to achieve the transition from natural virtue to truly moral virtue.

According to the second hypothesis moral conduct may be learned by means of teaching and instruction in the same way as people learn grammar and arithmetics.[24] What Aristotle has in mind is not simply recollection but a real process by which new knowledge is assimilated. In this view people have to be informed of what they should do in order to reach happiness.[25] Young people particularly

20. *Eth. Eud.*, I, 1, 1214a14–18. This hypothesis should be understood in the light of Aristotle's universal teleology.

21. Among all animals only man has a sense ($\alpha\ddot{\iota}\sigma\theta\eta\sigma\iota\varsigma$) of right and wrong; other animals are aware of what is pleasant and painful, but they have no notion of what is good or evil (*Politica*, I, 2, 1253a12–18).

22. *Eth. Nic.*, VI, 13, 1144b1–9.

23. *Eth. Nic.*, VI, 13, 1144b12–17.

24. *Eth. Eud.*, I, 1, 1214a18–19.

25. Aristotle uses the expression $\delta\iota\grave{\alpha}\ \mu\alpha\theta\acute{\eta}\sigma\epsilon\omega\varsigma$ (1214a18); the author specifies that according to this hypothesis there would be a science of happiness (1214a18–19). Science is more than a mere observation of facts; it is also an inquiry and disclosure of the causes of what is observed.

should acquire this knowledge, in the same way as they have to learn grammar in order to write and speak correctly. There are teachers of grammar; likewise there should be teachers of moral conduct and happiness: the first will teach how to write without mistakes, the latter how to behave in order to attain happiness. In this perspective rules of grammar and rules of behavior are on the same level: they may be learned in the same manner. It is further supposed that human behavior proceeds directly from ethical insight: if somebody knows what is good, he will do it, or at least he will not perform what he knows to be evil.[26]

According to the third supposition ethical conduct and moral perfection would be the outcome of practical training and exercises.[27] Moral education would be similar to gymnastic training or to apprenticeship of technical skills: a craftsman is educated gradually by implementing some works under the direction of a master: nobody becomes a carpenter or a tailor by mere theoretical instruction. In this opinion emphasis is put on practical training; the result of such exercises is twofold: the act that is carried out becomes more and more skilled. In the case of gymnastics, a performance becomes more competent, and with respect to technical skills the process of production as well as the product will be gradually improved.[28] Another consequence will be that by performing similar acts repeatedly, an individual acquires an enduring ability or habit. In this supposition no attention is paid to the internal disposition of the agent, to his deliberation and intention: what is stressed is practical training, instead of merely theoretical instruction.[29]

In a fourth hypothesis Aristotle wonders whether happiness is a gift that springs from some higher power, a kind of divine inspiration or enthusiasm.[30] In the *Meno* also the question whether virtue

---

26. If moral conduct is merely a question of learning, it will be sufficient to inform people: their behavior will always be in conformity with their knowledge.

27. *Eth. Eud.*, I, 1, 1214a19–21.

28. *Eth. Nic.*, II, 1, 1103a32–34. In the field of technical skill people learn by doing. At the beginning performances will inevitably be imperfect and deficient; they will gradually become more adequate through training and experience.

29. *Eth. Nic.*, II, 1, 1103b6–22: ἐκ τῶν ὁμοίων ἐνεργειῶν αἱ ἕξεις γίνονται. Reiterating the same acts does not always effect improvement or progress: if acts are badly accomplished, the result will be a habit, an abiding disposition of performing acts in an inadequate way. In this respect the direction of a master is important.

30. *Eth. Eud.*, I, 1, 1214a22–24. Popular opinions and religious belief are not simply repudiated in Aristotle's philosophical reflection: they are regarded as being worth critical consideration.

is a divine gift is asked.[31] Such a viewpoint can hardly fit into Aristotle's philosophical system; it rather derives from popular opinions and religious belief. According to Greek mythology the gods are not indifferent toward humans: some people are believed to be favored through all kinds of privileges and special protection. Within this context it may be supposed that virtue is a kind of privilege, bestowed on some persons as a special favor from a divine being. In this case personal responsibility disappears: moral conduct is regarded as a divine benefit.

Finally the author wonders whether virtue is merely the result of good fortune or chance: those who happen to be virtuous should not be praised, and those who are not should not be blamed. The first are lucky, whereas the latter are not. Opinions about good luck and chance were widely spread in ancient Greece: in his *Physics* Aristotle dedicates a careful inquiry to these notions and asks whether the cosmos may be caused by chance, as some philosophers maintain. The author does not totally exclude the impact of chance, but in his opinion it is only a secondary cause: the main forces that govern the universe in its arrangement and evolution are nature and intellect. Moreover he introduces a distinction between chance and fortune: chance belongs to the physical world, whereas fortune is related to human activity when it results in something that was not intended.[32]

Aristotle decidedly rejects the two last hypotheses: ethical perfection cannot depend upon chance; it is not some unexpected accidental event that was not intended by human activity. Man is by nature a moral being: he naturally strives toward the good and has to bring about his full development through virtuous conduct. If man attains happiness, it will be as a result of constant efforts in the various situations of life.[33] Nor is happiness a privilege that proceeds from

31. *Meno,* 99e–100a.

33. G. Verbeke, *Happiness and Chance in Aristotle,* in: *Aristotle on Nature and Living Things* (Festschrift D. M. Balme), Pittsburgh-Bristol, 1985, p.247–258. In the context of the *Eudemian Ethics* the author uses the term τύχη. In the *Physics* two terms are put forward: τύχη and ταὐτόματον. The latter refers to accidental events in the physical world.

33. In Aristotle's view moral education ought to start early in life (εὐθὺς ἐκ νέων, *Eth. Nic.,* II, 3, 1104b11–13). Young people ought to be educated in such a way that their behavior corresponds to moral norms and standards, even if they do not understand why they should act in such a way. Through practice and experience they will gradually disclose the true meaning of ethical values. Moral practice is necessary in order to reach ethical understanding.

a higher power: each individual is considered to be the author of his own destiny, which does not depend upon fate, nor on a divine being. Everybody has to achieve his destiny by means of his personal behavior. In order to reach the end of his life, one needs some knowledge as well as some practice or training: both are the development of a natural disposition.[34] Consequently our author accepts and brings together the three first hypotheses, introducing, however, some specifications. In acquiring virtue and promoting moral conduct theoretical knowledge does not play an important part; the author even states that such knowledge contributes nothing or little to the progress of moral life.[35] When somebody knows the definition of courage or temperance, he does not yet possess the corresponding habits. There is an important difference between learning a theoretical science and acquiring moral education. To become a geometer, one needs to study geometry; to become an architect, one ought to learn architecture. These disciplines are theoretical: if somebody assimilates the necessary theoretical knowledge, he will acquire the habit of the art and become an expert in that matter.[36] When productive sciences are concerned, the situation is different: in this case the goal of learning is not mere knowledge; what is intended is to effect something, such as health or good government. Hence medical or political art is not reduced to a merely theoretical knowing: a physician ought to find out what to do in order to restore or promote the health of a patient.[37] Such knowing is practical and must be learned by experience and exercise. The same obtains with regard to the political art: it also endeavors to establish a good and appropriate government; the end is practical and requires some experience of political life and some active preparation. The condition of moral philosophy is comparable to that of technical skills: with respect to ethical virtue what matters is not knowledge or understanding but human behavior. By means of actions steady

34. In Aristotle's view nobody will ever perform an act if he actually believes it evil (*Eth. Nic.*, V, 9, 1136b7): such behavior would be contrary to the basic tendency of human nature.

35. *Eth. Nic.*, II, 4, 1105b2. The term used by Aristotle in this context is τὸ εἰδέναι: it refers to theoretical knowledge, such as knowing the definition of justice or of another virtue.

36. *Eth. Eud.*, I, 5, 1216b8–16. Dealing with theoretical disciplines Aristotle declares that they may accidentally be quite useful in terms of many necessities of life.

37. *Eth. Eud.*, I, 5, 1216b16–25.

habits are brought about: they are the principles of a more and more truly ethical conduct.[38]

Moral intellectualism is categorically dismissed: the main argument developed by Aristotle refers to the nature of ethical knowledge, which is not merely theoretical but practical. The goal pursued is virtuous conduct: it is not sufficient to know the definition of a virtue in order to be able to practice it. Virtues are the outcome of an assiduous moral training, which, of course, involves ethical insight or practical wisdom (φρόνησις). The proper features of this wisdom are studied in the *Nicomachean Ethics* (book VI). In this context the author wonders whether it is really able to promote ethical conduct.[39] The first opinion taken into consideration provides a negative answer: moral wisdom attempts to disclose what is just, right, and beautiful. But a moral agent spontaneously pursues these ethical values; he does not need prudence or moral wisdom.[40] As to individuals who are not virtuous, they have to conform to the views formulated by those who possess that wisdom. If somebody is ill, he will not study medicine in order to be able to cure himself: he will appeal to the help of a physician who will treat him and endeavor to deliver him from his illness. According to this opinion people who are not virtuous should not act according to their own judgment but according to the intuition of others[41]; this opinion implicitly supposes that society will always include a number of individuals who are not virtuous and who have to be guided by the insights of others.

Besides, Aristotle knows that Socrates reduces moral behavior to

38. *Eth. Nic.*, II, 4, 1105b9–10. To become just or temperate is a matter of practice: by performing just or temperate acts, one becomes just or temperate. Although man is by nature a moral animal, education remains indispensable: he will never become just or temperate without accomplishing actions that correspond to these virtues.

39. *Eth. Nic.*, VI, 12, 1143b18–21. According to P. Aubenque, "La prudence ne sera jamais pour Aristote qu'un pis aller, le *substitut* imparfait d'une sagesse plus qu'humaine" (*La prudence chez Aristote*, Paris, 1963, p.19). I could hardly agree with this interpretation: Aristotle's teaching on moral wisdom is one of the most remarkable elements of his ethics; it is really at the center of his ethical treatise. It allows him to elaborate a coherent moral system after rejecting Plato's Idealism and Socrates' intellectualism. Aristotle is rightly persuaded that different kinds of reality require appropriate methods of knowledge.

40. *Eth. Nic.*, VI, 12, 1143b21–29.

41. *Eth. Nic.*, VI, 12, 1143b30–35. According to this extreme position moral wisdom is totally useless: it is useless for those who already are virtuous as well as for those who are not; the latter may be compared to people who are ill and who need the help of a physician. If they are not virtuous, their own moral judgment cannot be reliable.

a kind of knowledge: virtues are forms of prudence, or, as he states in another passage, they are reasons or logoi.[42] The basic idea of this doctrine is obvious: a man who knows what action is good will certainly perform it, since everybody by nature strives to the good. If somebody performs wrong actions, he must do so because he does not grasp what is truly valuable: this man is mistaken; he has fallen into error. He could not do what is wrong if he did not believe it was good.

The two opinions are radically opposed to each other. Aristotle rejects both, the first because it only deals with theoretical knowledge: to grasp the definition of a virtue is a theoretical insight; it is not concerned with a particular action in the concrete and complex circumstances of life. Aside from this kind of knowing, there are judgments concerned with the moral value of a particular act. Whereas theoretical insight has little or no impact on ethical conduct, practical and concrete valuation of a particular way of behaving is a determining factor.[43] As to the second opinion, which coincides with Socratic intellectualism, it is also repudiated insofar as it declares human conduct to be regulated by universal and theoretical knowledge of moral values.

The solution of this problem, as it has been elaborated by Aristotle, mainly relies on the unity of moral conduct or the mutual connexion of virtues: one aspect of moral life and action is not independent from the others; it is not a separate entity that can exist in itself without any relation to the other ethical attitudes.[44] As a matter of fact, this doctrine would be contrary to Aristotle's teaching

42. Eth. Nic., VI, 13, 1144b19–20; 1144b28–30. In dealing with the doctrine of Socrates, Aristotle does not always use the same terminology: virtues are considered to be moral intuitions (φρονήσεις), or rational insights (λόγους), or scientific knowledge (ἐπιστήμας). In any case, understanding is regarded as the determining factor in moral behavior.

43. Eth. Nic., VI, 5, 1140b12–19; VII, 2, 1145b26–27. In a sense nobody can ever perform an act, knowing actually that it is wrong. There cannot be a chasm between man's behavior and his actual insight in the ethical value of a particular act. The teaching of Socrates is more radical: true human knowledge can never be superseded by something else; passions and emotions are unable to overcome intellectual intuitions.

44. Eth. Nic., VI, 13, 1145a1–2. Aristotle, however, agrees that natural virtues may be separated from each other (VI, 13, 1144b35–36). There may be in the same individual a natural disposition to one virtue and not to another: even children and brute beasts may possess this disposition (1144b8–9). But when properly moral virtues are concerned, such separation is impossible: ethical wisdom implies the presence of all other virtues and each moral virtue includes ethical knowledge.

about the unity of each human individual. The Stagirite emphasizes this unity much more than his master Plato: Aristotle's theory of the relationship between body and soul is an attempt to discard any kind of psychological dualism. Body and soul are not two substances joined together: they constitute one single substance, since the corporeal character of the body and its organic structure spring from the psychic principle. Man is a unitary being, and so also is his moral behavior. And yet this unity is less radical than it is in Stoic philosophy: according to the Stoics there is only one virtue, which manifests itself in various ways according to the different kinds of ethical activity. People usually distinguish several virtues, but these ethical habits could not exist without each other: it is impossible, for example, to be courageous without being prudent, temperate, and just. A moral man is one who possesses all virtues in an indissoluble unity.[45] Could a wise man ever become unwise? This possibility is totally excluded because there is no weakness in his moral equipment, as he possesses all virtues.[46] Could an unwise man ever become wise? That is possible, provided his ethical structure is complete: as long as one virtue is lacking he cannot be truly moral.[47] In the Stoic vocabulary a man is wise when he has suppressed all passions: only under this condition does he become what he really is, namely reason.

The teaching of Aristotle is more flexible: he declares that it is impossible to have prudence or moral wisdom without possessing the other virtues.[48] In his view prudence is concerned with particular moral actions and elaborates judgments about their ethical value. Such valuations cannot be deduced from some general axioms or rules; they are not a conclusion of a syllogism; they are rather right intuitions of a person who can rely on experience and moral conduct.[49] A virtuous man fulfills all necessary conditions to formulate a

45. Cicero, *Academica Posteriora (Acad. Post.)*, I, 38 (SVF I, 199); Diogenes Laertius (Diog. Laert.), VII, 161 (SVF I, 200). Stoic thought is basically biological: in the universe everything is linked to all other things, since the whole cosmos developed out of one germ. Similarly in human life there is a firm coherence among the various aspects of man's behavior.

46. Diog. Laert., VII, 128 (SVF I, 569).

47. Diog. Laert., VII, 125 (SVF III, 295); Hieronymus, *Epistolae (Epist.)*, 66, 3 (SVF III, 300). If one virtue is lacking, not only is one area of human conduct jeopardized: all aspects of ethical behavior are endangered.

48. *Eth. Nic.*, VI, 12, 1144a36.

49. *Eth. Nic.*, II, 2, 1104a3–5; II, 9, 1109b22–23. Aristotle is quite aware of the considerable differences existing in the various situations in which man has to decide and to act.

correct assessment: his mind is not obscured by passions, as his reason governs and dominates irrational movements.[50] Moreover, a virtuous individual will also possess experience of moral conduct: he is in the same condition as a physician or a craftsman; both can rely on their experience in exercising their art. A physician who can refer to extensive experience is more able to treat illnesses than a colleague with little or no experience. The same obtains in moral behavior: here also experience is important in order to disentangle complex situations and to reach right valuations.[51] Finally a virtuous man is trained in the practice of virtue: this practice not only leads to the acquisition of ethical habits but makes the performance of virtuous acts more easy and efficient.[52] For all these reasons a man cannot have the virtue of prudence without possessing the other virtues.

On the other hand, prudence is required in view of exercising moral virtues. In order to clarify this issue the author examines the relationship between prudence and ability: this relation is similar to the one that exists between natural virtue and ethical virtue.[53] Natural virtue only resembles ethical virtue, and yet it may become a properly moral habit, if reason is joined to it.[54] The definition of virtue specifies that the action conforms to right reason.[55] This characteristic is essential: moral conduct cannot be reduced to the material fulfillment of right actions; one ought to do what is good because it is good.[56] In Aristotle's view there is no motive more basic than this one; it is a feature of any truly moral attitude. An

50. *Eth. Nic.*, VI, 12, 1144a34.

51. *Eth. Nic.*, II, 2, 1104a5–10. Situations in the course of time are never the same: relying on the experience of acting in similar situations and knowing the results of his former way of behaving, an agent is better prepared to take the right decisions.

52. *Eth. Nic.*, II, 4, 1105a32–33; 1105b9–10.

53. *Eth. Nic.*, VI, 13, 1144b1–4. Natural virtue is a spontaneous inclination to perform right actions: such actions are not the outcome of a rational deliberation and decision. Cf. P. Aubenque, *La prudence chez Aristote*, p.62: "la prudence est médiatrice entre la vertu naturelle et la vertu morale, mais la vertu morale est médiatrice entre l'habileté et la prudence."

54. *Eth. Nic.*, VI, 13, 1144b12–17. True virtue is animated by moral wisdom: a particular way of conduct is always chosen because it is good.

55. *Eth. Nic.*, VI, 13, 1144b21–24. According to Aristotle moral wisdom is not merely cognitive: it is also imperative (*Eth. Nic.*, VI, 10, 1143a8–10).

56. *Eth. Nic.*, II, 4, 1105a32; VI, 5, 1140b7. Aristotle attributes much importance to the intention that animates man's behavior. In Stoic perspective the relevance of an intention is still considerably greater; the course of history is not determined by man but by the Divine Logos. Man should accept the development of history, as it is ultimately the work of God. This is the basic maxim of Stoic ethics.

individual acting in this way is not moved by personal interest; he is not pushed by egoistic feelings; he totally devotes himself to the search for what is good. Such an internal attitude implies moral wisdom: an agent will only be animated by such intention when he knows that his action performed in the concrete context of life and assessed after careful deliberation is truly good.[57] To do what is good because it is good supposes that the agent has seriously reflected on the ethical value of his action; when he has discovered what is to be done, even if it is difficult, he will decide to accomplish it, being motivated by the ethical worth of the act.

After these considerations we now turn to a closer examination of the possibility and nature of moral faults. This issue played an important part in Greek literature, particularly in tragedy and epic poetry. There are several famous examples of characters being severely punished after some tragic mistake that may hardly be regarded as a moral fault in the proper sense of the term. When Polycrates, king of Samos, received the king of Egypt, Amasis, in his palace and told him how wealthy he was and how successful in all his initiatives, the latter expressed his fear and anguish about this situation. He finally suggested that his friend freely renounce the most precious thing he possessed. Polycrates followed this advice: that most precious thing was a ring and he gave it to fishermen to be thrown into the sea. But the ring returned to the king's palace: it was found in the stomach of a fish, prepared for a royal banquet. At this stage Amasis leaves his friend and returns to Egypt: he is persuaded that grave disasters will destroy all the achievements of Polycrates. The gods do not tolerate humans being too successful, yet the conduct of Polycrates could hardly be called a moral fault.[58] The same obtains in the case of Oedipus: he killed his father and married his mother, but he did not know that the man he killed in a struggle in which he tried to save his own life was his father. When

57. *Eth. Nic.*, II, 4, 1105a31; III, 2, 1112a15.
58. Herodotus, *Historiae*, III, 40–43. Manifestly the story of Polycrates is an illustration of the ancient Greek maxim "Nothing too much." The wealth and power of the king of Samos were regarded as being too great for a human and mortal being: the gods could not tolerate humans going beyond the borders of their finite existence. Man has to avoid pride. Was Polycrates guilty of moral faults? In the context of this ancient religious belief the question asked is not entirely appropriate: Polycrates did not intend to provoke the jealousy of the gods; on the contrary he wanted to prevent it. In a sense he was a victim of his own successes: what is stressed is certainly not personal responsibility.

he married the queen of Thebes, Jocasta, he did not realize that she was his mother.[59] This way of behaving may be called a material fault, but it can hardly be regarded as a formal mistake, and yet Oedipus has been terribly punished. In popular opinion there was not a clear distinction between sheerly material culpability and formal responsibility, in which man fully assumes what he has done. On the other hand, the notion of the tragic is not the same in Greek thought as it was later: a tragic event in ancient culture is one in which a man falls victim of blind fate. The blows of fate are not intelligible, they are not the consequence of some misconduct, they are not justified as a result of previous behavior: they are blows proceeding from a power that lacks discernment. Some characters are tragic, not because they committed grave mistakes but because they were victims of this arbitrary and blind power.[60]

Being confronted with these popular opinions, Aristotle wonders whether a truly moral fault is possible and in which way. Are all moral faults to be reduced to errors in judgment? Can somebody ever accomplish an act clearly knowing that it is evil? Aristotle's answer is neither merely positive nor merely negative: the author introduces a distinction between various kinds of knowledge. There is first a distinction to be made between habitual and actual knowing: the first is knowledge that has been assimilated in the past and remains present in the mind, even if it is not exercised. If somebody has learned a foreign language, it remains in the mind even if that person does not use it in speaking or writing. Actual knowledge, on the contrary, is the type that is exercised: the object of knowledge is effectively grasped by the intellect, so a language may be used in the present in speaking, thinking, or writing. Somebody who knows in a habitual way that a planned action is wrong can perform it

59. Sophocles, *King Oedipus.* This work is a real tragedy. The parents of Oedipus did whatever they could to avoid the forecast of the oracle about their child. Oedipus himself, not knowing his true identity, was drawn into all kinds of situations he could not understand.

60. The ancient notion of "tragic" is closely connected with a widespread belief in the power of fate. In this respect tragedies of Shakespeare, Racine, Corneille, Goethe, Schiller, and others strongly differ from Greek tragedies: in these modern works misfortunes and all kinds of catastrophes are regarded as the result of some grave fault. Man is considered to be the author of his own life: he has to bear the consequences of his former conduct and remains responsible for what he has done. Tragic events are not dictated by a blind destiny; they are the result of human behavior, which in some cases is dominated by irrational passions and emotions.

despite this knowledge; when some knowledge is only habitual, it is not active and the object is not effectively taken into consideration. In Aristotle's view it is impossible to perform an evil action if the agent effectively knows that it is wrong.[61]

Moreover the author distinguishes between universal and particular knowing: with respect to ethical behavior the first refers to general rules and norms of conduct; somebody may know in general that robbery is to be censured and avoided. Particular knowledge is related to concrete behavior that is envisaged or performed in the changing circumstances of life. If somebody knows in general that robbery is evil, he still has to realize that a concrete act is unjust.[62] A particular moral judgment is considered to be difficult because the circumstances of life are never the same, and each action is a unique event. Concrete ethical insight requires experience and practice.

Another factor that explains the possibility of immoral actions is the influence of irrational tendencies. In each individual there is a permanent conflict between reason and passions: the latter should not be eradicated, but they ought to be ruled by the rational faculty. Only when irrational emotions are governed and dominated by the intellect will it be possible to attain a status of true equilibrium and harmony. But the power of passions is very strong: they are able in some cases to block and paralyze the normal activity of the mind, as happens in sleeping, drunkenness, and madness. In such situations the functioning of the mind may be partially or totally inhibited, in which case evil actions may be performed. If passions are very violent and not ruled by reason, moral insight will be damaged.[63]

61. *Eth. Nic.*, VII, 3, 1146b31–35. Between knowing in act and knowing in potency Aristotle accepts an intermediary stage, which is habitual knowledge: it means that knowledge is present in the mind without being exercised. If someone has learned a discipline it remains present even if it is not used. The question remains why such knowledge is not exercised in situations in which one could normally expect it to be used. Presumably Aristotle is thinking of some irrational impulses preventing man from using the knowledge he has acquired.

62. *Eth. Nic.*, VII, 3, 1146b35–1147a7. It is not always easy to apply a general maxim to a particular case: for example, it may be difficult to decide whether a particular act is a robbery.

63. *Eth. Nic.*, VII, 3, 1147a14–24. In this context Aristotle formally mentions anger and sexual desires: they clearly influence the bodily organism and may even cause some mental deviations (μανίας ποιοῦσιν). In such cases the normal activity of the mind is blocked. Can man be responsible for such a situation? Aristotle firmly maintains that an individual may be responsible for his ignorance.

Yet Aristotle states that truly scientific knowledge can never be overcome or suppressed by passion; an irrational movement can only hamper moral insight regarding a particular act, since in this case sensible knowledge is involved.[64] If particular ethical intuitions are not impeded by passions, the agent will necessarily behave in conformity with his insight.

There is still another explanation of immoral conduct: in a practical syllogism there may be two contradictory premises included: for example, all sweets should be avoided and sweets are delightful. If someone is confronted with a sweet object he will apply one of the two premises: if he has recourse to the second, he will perform the act, and if he applies the first, no action will be accomplished.[65] In this case the conflict is located at the level of moral doctrine: some issues may be controversial, and in some periods there may be many of them, as a result of new discoveries and technical performances. In such cases everybody chooses the premise that will determine his behavior: this choice is quite obviously a responsible moral act.[66]

Does Aristotle side with ethical intellectualism? Yes and no: he firmly believes that human behavior is governed by concrete ethical insights, but he does not accept that universal moral knowledge or habitual insights are a determining factor with regard to ethical conduct.

64. *Eth. Nic.*, VII, 3, 1147b15–17.
65. *Eth. Nic.*, VII, 3, 1147a31–b5. Quite obviously the choice of one of the premises may be influenced by desire. According to Aristotle, irrational animals cannot be regarded as incontinent: they are devoid of universal insights; they have only imaginations and recollections.
66. *Eth. Nic.*, III, 5, 1114a31–b25. In Aristotle's view a moral choice is a responsible act even if it is largely dependent upon the whole ethical attitude of an individual: everybody chooses according to his dispositions, but man is at least partly responsible for his habits and character.

[6]

RESPONSIBLE CHOICE

THE topic of human responsibility is constantly present in Western thought, not only in ancient philosophy but also in the later development of philosophical reflection until the present day. Philosophy does not start from nothing: it is essentially a critical reflection on popular opinions and beliefs, which are frequently connected with religious convictions. The issue of man's responsibility was obviously present in Greek prephilosophical thought. As Socrates mentions in the *Gorgias* it was commonly accepted that people who die after a life devoted to justice and sanctity move to the Isles of the Blessed, where they are free of all evil and are perfectly happy; on the contrary, those who are guilty of injustice and impiety have to go to the Tartarus, a place of expiation and suffering.[1] In his discussion with Callicles Socrates stresses this responsibility: a soul charged with crimes will be extremely unhappy in Hades. The Greek Master endeavors by all means to protect his fellow-citizens against this supreme distress:

---

1. *Gorgias*, 523a–b. In Hebrew tradition the perspective was rather different: people who were faithful to the divine commandments and truly religious were believed to be rewarded during their life on earth. It was expected that they would be blessed in their daily labor and in their family with wealth and a great number of descendants. This tradition was embodied in a figure like Job: he was a faithful believer, a wealthy and powerful man. He is regarded as an example of the Jewish tradition: he remained faithful even when he became a victim of heavy misfortunes. The Greek tradition to which Socrates refers has a different content: moral conduct will be rewarded, but this reward will be bestowed on the souls in their life after death. The souls of individuals who lived morally will be rewarded with happiness, whereas the others will be punished. The essential factor of both traditions is the same: ethical conduct will not remain without being rewarded. In his commentary on the *Gorgias* E. R. Dodds declares that the belief in post mortem reward or punishment is older than Pythagoras and Orphism, and he refers to some passages of the *Iliad* (3, 278 f.; 19, 259 f.) and the *Odyssey* (11, 576 ff.). (Cf. Plato, *Gorgias,* A Revised Text with Introduction and Commentary by E. R. Dodds, Oxford, 1959, p.373.)

his message is not one of superficial rhetoric; he does not try to flatter and please the people. His concern is moral education, always attempting to persuade his countrymen to pursue justice and temperance. This was a difficult task: most of the people did not like this kind of discourse, constantly reminding them of their duty to pursue a life of virtue. Socrates was quite conscious of the danger that threatened him: he was like a physician wanting people to be cured of their illnesses and imposing on them a treatment that was far from being pleasant but was to be adopted for the purpose of recovery.[2] Socrates states that he might be brought to trial and condemned to death: in his view such a verdict would be comparable to the trial of a physician initiated by a cook before a court of children. The physician would be unable to defend himself: he knows very well that the treatment prescribed is not pleasant. Socrates believes that if he were brought to trial, he would find himself in the same condition.[3] There are two ways of life, the one proposed by superficial rhetoric, oriented toward indiscriminate pursuit of pleasure; the other taught by philosophy and exhorting people to what is truly good, a life devoted to virtue.

In Plato's view each individual is a responsible person: in the *Gorgias* there is a mythical narrative describing how humans are judged at the end of their life. In the time of Cronos, at the beginning of the reign of Zeus, the trial took place just before death, when humans were still alive. This situation, however, led to sentences that were not always right: Pluto and other inspectors of the Blessed Isles were disappointed because many individuals came to this place without deserving it. They informed Zeus, who quickly

2. *Gorgias*, 521d. Socrates is convinced that people bear within themselves hidden knowledge of true moral values: in addition he is persuaded that an individual who grasps these ethical ideals will endeavor to make his conduct conform to those higher standards. Hence the dedication of the Greek Master talking with his fellows, especially with young people, and trying to stimulate and actualize their moral intuitions.

3. *Gorgias*, 521e–522a. Socrates likes to compare his teaching to that of the Sophists: what the latter intend is to prepare young people so that they may be influential in a democratic society. In this context they have to learn the art of rhetoric in order to be capable of communicating to their fellows some convictions they want to be accepted by them. In any case, what matters is the art of persuading people. In a sense this art is also important for Socrates, and yet the perspective is profoundly different: he wants to educate people in the most authentic sense of the word; he endeavors to bring them to the discovery of the true moral values within their own consciousness. What matters for Socrates is moral education, even if it is painful.

discovered the origin of the erroneous sentences: wealthy people came to the court dressed in luxurious clothes, accompanied by a group of friends and servants; benefiting from a broad culture and fine education, they were able to answer all questions adequately and to defend themselves when it was necessary. Poor people, on the contrary, did not possess these privileges: they did not have servants at their disposal and lacking education they could hardly advocate their cause. Sentences were not impartial: judges could not avoid being influenced by the social condition of individuals they had to examine.[4] Finally the decision was taken to judge everybody after death: only the soul will be invited to the court, without body, without clothes, without friends or servants. Only naked souls will be judged. They bear the responsibility for their conduct and will be examined in the same way by judges without any prejudice or bias.[5] According to Plato the soul is the very center of each individual; thoughts and decisions do not proceed from the body, but from the psychic principle and in the first place from the mind. If all human souls are judged equally by an impartial court, the sentence will be right and cannot be blamed. The meaning of the myth is obvious: everybody is responsible for his moral conduct and will be rightly judged after death.

The mythical narrative in the *Gorgias* corresponds to another that is found at the end of the *Republic:* it is called the myth of Er, son of Armenios and originally from Pamphilia. He had been killed in a battle; after ten days he was found on the battlefield and brought home to be buried; amazingly his body was still in good condition: when it was put at the stake to be burnt, it came back to life and

4. *Gorgias*, 523b–c. It is noticeable that Plato in this narrative draws attention to some social injustice and inequality: at the final judgment poor people are in an inferior condition to wealthy individuals. The author, however, does not criticize these different social situations: he wants to prevent these different conditions from influencing the final sentence of the judges. Relying on Iamblichus (*De Vita Pythagorica* [*Vit. Pyth.*], 155, 179; cf. Diogenes Laertius (Diog. Laert.), 8, 35). E. R. Dodds maintains that the doctrine of Judgment was already taught by Pythagoras: "Whether it is older than Pythagoras remains an open question" (Plato, *Gorgias*, ed. E. R. Dodds, p.374).

5. *Gorgias*, 523d–524a. In Plato's view each individual is responsible for his moral behavior: decisions are taken and choices are made by the central principle of each person, the soul or the mind. The ethical behavior of each individual is assessed and the destiny of the souls is determined in conformity with this valuation. Prephilosophical opinions on human destiny are not repudiated, but they are brought into harmony with the moral teaching of Socrates and Plato.

then Er narrated what he had seen in the meantime, between his death and his revival. What he had noticed was mainly a joyful meeting of souls on a great meadow: some of them came from the earth, others from heaven; souls coming from the earth had to expiate rigorously the faults they had perpetrated, whereas others were rewarded for all the noble actions they had accomplished. As to the souls returning to mortal life, they were invited to proceed to a decisive choice: all kinds of life were available; everybody was able to make a fully free and responsible option. The hierophant unequivocally proclaimed: "Everybody is responsible for his choice; divinity is not involved."[6] It was stressed, however, that after having taken a decision, each individual was by necessity bound to his option. The souls were invited to ponder the various possibilities very carefully before proceeding to a definitive selection. If someone made a bad choice, he could not accuse somebody else: he should not blame fortune, demons, or any other power. The choice of a life's content is a personal matter; it is the responsibility of each individual.[7]

Of course, one may ask why Plato treats this important subject of human responsibility in mythical narratives: does it mean that the issue is a matter of mythical belief and cannot be solved in a rational way? It must be acknowledged that both narratives contain many mythical elements, which rather belong to the literary presentation of the doctrine. But the teaching itself is not a sheerly mythical

6. *Respublica (Respubl.)*, X, 618e. In this mythical narrative personal responsibility is strongly emphasized: the souls coming from earth are either rewarded or punished according to their moral conduct. As to the souls returning to life on earth, they are fully responsible for their choice, since all patterns of life are available to everybody. Within the context of the myth the choice is made by the soul before entering into existence on earth. Why this previous option? It might be understood in the light of Plato's psychological doctrine: being the responsible principle of a human person, the soul will be judged after death. In this context each human soul chooses the way of life it wants to develop.

7. *Respubl.*, X, 617e. Instead of being dominated by all kinds of higher powers, human life in Plato's view is the result of personal decisions and choices. This doctrine was already professed by Socrates and was further developed by Aristotle. It influenced in a decisive manner the evolution of Western civilization: in this context the concept of man as a creative and responsible individual is at the very center. The idea that human life is in the hands of man himself, instead of being determined by some higher powers, represents a dynamic viewpoint in the evolution of culture. In Stoic thought and in Neoplatonic philosophy the personal freedom of each individual was again put into question and jeopardized. In this respect the teaching of Socrates and Plato was a stimulating factor and a starting point.

belief: in Plato's view man is truly responsible for his own destiny: as we already declared, the soul, and particularly the mind, is the center of a human being. This soul is spiritual and immortal: it preexisted before the body and it will never pass away. It is able to contemplate the immutable transcendent Forms and to make its life in this sensible world conform to these eternal patterns. A life of virtue is a growing process of assimilation to the Ideas: a man may decline to the level of the body and indulge in all kinds of irrational propensities; he may also lift himself to the level of the ideal exemplars. Everybody bears within himself a treasure of authentic knowledge: thus everybody has the capacity of attaining true wisdom and of participating in happiness.[8] What Plato represents in a beautiful narrative is actually a profound philosophical conviction, mainly based on a rational inquiry concerning the nature of human soul. Human mind is a principle of thinking and responsible choice.

This teaching of Plato is the outcome of a careful philosophical analysis and reflection: it is coherently connected with his whole philosophical system. On the other hand, it is very different from some traditional opinions and also from other philosophical theories. In the area of Greek culture fatalism was a widely spread opinion; it is not easy to elucidate its meaning adequately. Nemesius of Emesa, a Christian author living at the end of the fourth century, was still very much concerned with this trend. In his book *On the Nature of Man,* which was influential in the West, he deals carefully and extensively with this popular belief and he develops mostly Aristotelian arguments to criticize it.[9] It is striking that at the end of the fourth century A.D. fatalism was still influential and was considered to be the main opponent of human freedom and respon-

---

8. A mythical narrative like that of the *Gorgias* is a link with the religious and cultural tradition of the Greek world; this aspect is not unimportant. Mythology was a kind of prephilosophical attempt to interpret the universe and human existence. It was not based on rational arguing and scientific research; it was rather the outcome of an immediate intuition and poetical feeling. In a sense philosophy is a continuation of mythology: it pursues the same effort with a view to fully understanding the world.

9. The work of Nemesius was translated into Latin twice during the Middle Ages and three times in the Renaissance period: cf. *Némésius d'Emèse, De natura hominis.* Traduction de Burgundio de Pise, ed. G. Verbeke et J. R. Moncho, Leyden, 1975, p. LXXXVI–C. The first Latin version was elaborated by Nicholas Alfanus, archbishop of Salerno (d. 1085). In addition to the Latin versions, the treatise has been translated into Armenian, Arabic, and Georgian.

sibility. According to Nemesius five different notions of fate could be distinguished in ancient civilization. The most radical fatalism teaches that whatever happens in the world is determined and necessitated by the movements of the heavenly bodies.[10] Nemesius immediately dismisses this theory because it is contrary to common opinions; moreover, if this viewpoint is accepted, political society becomes useless, praise and blame lose their significance, even prayer becomes meaningless; this view finally denies any idea of contingency and freedom. In this opinion nobody can be guilty of wrongdoing: acts of injustice, murder, or adultery should be imputed to the celestial bodies, and ultimately to God himself. All these criticisms spring from Carneades and have been developed many times by pagan and Christian writers.[11]

A second and more mitigated type of fatalism is connected with two representatives of Stoic philosophy, Chrysippus and Philopater. According to these thinkers fate is not incompatible with human freedom. All beings have some characteristic features that stem from fate: water is cold, plants produce some specific fruits, stones are inclined to fall and flames to rise. The same obtains with respect to living beings: they are able to give their assent to what they perceive and to move by themselves. Hence such beings may come near to some objects, provided there is no external obstacle or impediment stemming from another fate.[12] According to Nemesius this view actually coincides with radical fatalism: human action, like every-

10. *De natura hominis*, XXXIV, p.133, 59–60. One of the doctrines censured by the bishop of Paris in 1270 is related to the same issue: at that time again human freedom and responsibility were questioned. The fourth sentence condemned in 1270 is formulated as follows: "Quod omnia que hic in inferioribus aguntur, subsunt necessitati corporum celestium."

11. *De natura hominis*, XXXIV, p.133, 60–77. Cf. D. Amand, *Fatalisme et liberté dans l'antiquité grecque*, Louvain, 1945, p.41–68. At the beginning of chapter XXXIV Nemesius writes: "Qui circulari motui astrorum causam omnium quae fiunt ascribunt, non solum communibus intelligentiis adversantur, sed et omnem civilitatem inutilem ostendunt." In an Aristotelian as well as a Stoic perspective common opinions could not be disregarded.

12. *De natura hominis*, XXXIV, p.133, 78–134, 86: "Hi vero dicunt quoniam et quod in nobis est et quod secundum fortunam est servatur." Within the context of Stoic philosophy fate coincides with Divine Reason and Providence: the Divine Logos is the immanent cause of everything that happens in the world. Is this viewpoint compatible with human freedom? According to the Stoics human freedom is only internal: man is unable to change the course of events in any way. Despite this qualification, it remains difficult to interpret a free choice within this context coherently.

thing, is necessitated by fate, since all constituents of an act, even judgment and assent, are determined by this higher power. The whole evolution of the world is an irrefragable concatenation of causes and effects, leaving no room for free decisions.[13]

The third kind of fatalism is attributed to some sages of Egypt. In their opinion what happens in the world is ruled by the movement of heavenly bodies. However, events are not totally unchangeable: some modifications in their development may be introduced as a result of prayers and sacrifices. These may be addressed either to the celestial bodies themselves or to some divine powers in view of propitiating them. In this way religious worship is justified and efficacious.[14] Regarding this opinion Nemesius declares that the meaning of fate has been thoroughly transformed: the term now refers to events that are undetermined, contingent, and unpredictable[15]; whatever has been determined by fate may possibly be changed through prayers or sacrifices. Moreover, divination and astrology become unpracticable: this objection is rather ad hominem, since the sages of Egypt attached much importance to the cast of someone's horoscope.[16] Nemesius also wonders why among human acts only prayers depend on personal initiatives and decisions: if religious acts are initiated by free choice, why cannot other actions also originate from some personal option?[17] If, on the contrary, the acts of prayer are necessitated by fate, then nothing escapes from the ruling of this blind power and this opinion also emerges into radical fatalism.[18]

The fourth theory related to fate is professed by the wisest men among the Greeks; these again belong to the Stoic school.[19] According to these thinkers human choice is to be considered as a free

13. *De natura hominis*, XXXIV, p.134, 86–135, 11: "Si enim et impetus nostros a fortuna nobis datos esse aiunt et hos quandoque quidem a fortuna impediri, quandoque vero non, manifestum quod omnia secundum fortunam fiunt, etiam ipsa quae videntur in nobis esse."

14. *De natura hominis*, XXXV, p.135, 14–19.

15. *De natura hominis*, XXXV, p.135, 19–21: "dicemus quoniam contingentium et non necessariorum faciunt esse fortunam; contingens autem est indeterminatum, quod vero est indeterminatum, est ignotum."

16. *De natura hominis*, XXXV, p.135, 21–136, 24.

17. *De natura hominis*, XXXV, p.135, 28–30: "Deinde altercabitur cum eis, qualiter omnibus aliis humanis gestionibus et electionibus in tali habitudine astrorum iacentibus, oratio sola in nobis est."

18. *De natura hominis*, XXXV, p.136, 31–39.

19. *De natura hominis*, XXXVI, p.137, 60–61.

initiative, but the outcome of man's activity is ruled by fate. As a matter of fact, this interpretation fits into the Stoic system: these philosophers believe that humans are unable to change the course of external events, to transform sensible reality; their activity is confined to their internal attitude regarding happy or unfortunate events of life. One may accept or refuse the course of history, but he is totally unable to change anything in it, since it depends in all respects upon Divine Reason. Nemesius partly agrees on this view, insofar as it recognizes freedom of human conduct. In a sense he also accepts the conclusion that the outcome of man's decisions does not entirely depend on his will.[20] And yet according to the Christian author the result of our activity is not fixed by fate, but by divine providence[21]; in his view there is an essential difference between the two. Fate is an invariable concatenation of causes and effects, whereas divine providence allows to everybody what is profitable and beneficial.[22] Some people suffer from mental illnesses and are unable to make free choices. In the Stoic view this mental illness is also caused by fate, so even the capacity of free choice depends upon fate and this again inevitably leads to complete fatalism.[23]

Finally, Nemesius deals with the theory of Plato, a teaching that deeply influenced the development of Christian theology. According to this doctrine the notion of fate has two different meanings: as a substance it refers to the worldsoul, and as an activity it indicates an immutable divine law that proceeds from an inescapable cause.[24] This law was given to the worldsoul by the Supreme God for the purpose of creation and government of the cosmos. Fate rules everything, but it is included in divine providence as a part of it.

---

20. *De natura hominis*, XXXVI, p.137, 62–64: "Nam hoc quidem quod in nobis ponunt electiones gestionum, non omnino vero et proventus, rectissime dicunt; fortunae vero imponere hos, non recte."

21. *De natura hominis*, XXXVI, p.137, 68–71.

22. *De natura hominis*, XXXVI, p.137, 71–78: "Fortuna vero, cum apud Graecos heimarmene dicatur ex eo quod est heirmos (id est ordo) quidam causarum intransgressibilis (ita enim eam Stoici determinant, hoc est ordinem et supercolligationem intransgressibilem), non secundum id quod confert, sed secundum proprium motum et necessitatem inducit fines."

23. *De natura hominis*, XXXVI, p.138, 78–84. If fate is at the origin of all things that happen in the world, it must also be the cause of mental illnesses: even the capacity for making choices will not be without the influence of fate.

24. *De natura hominis*, XXXVII, p.139, 96–100.

Whatever happens according to the laws of fate belongs also to divine providence. But the reverse is not always true: what occurs according to divine providence does not always coincide with the ruling of fate.[25] As a matter of fact, the governing of divine law depends upon the things that are concerned. Some matters have an immediate relationship with the divine law, for example, our assents, judgments, and impulses. These are a starting point of further events, which necessarily arise from our activity.[26] The choice of our acts depends upon our free initiative, but the results are effected (i.e., caused) by fate, which partly coincides with providence. Hence God is not involved in any wrongdoing, whereas moral conduct remains free and the possibility of divination is secured.[27] Nemesius criticizes only one aspect of this doctrine: the result of human decisions does not belong to the area of necessity. The outcome of human activity, which is subject to the rule of divine providence, can only be contingent.[28]

This survey of Nemesius gives an idea of what fatalism represented in classical culture: it was present in popular opinions, in religious cults, as well as in philosophical doctrines. Expounding his own theory on human freedom and responsibility, Nemesius relies most on Aristotelian arguments. According to Aristotle each individual is the author of his own destiny: fatalism is decidedly rejected.[29] In this respect the Aristotelian ethical treatises represent an important step in the growth of individual consciousness, personal responsibility, and human dignity. The teaching of the Greek

25. *De natura hominis*, XXXVII, p.139, 100–6: "Omne enim quod secundum fortunam est, et secundum providentiam fieri; non tamen omne quod secundum providentiam est, et secundum fortunam esse."

26. *De natura hominis*, XXXVII, p.139, 6–12.

27. *De natura hominis*, XXXVII, p.140, 20–27: "Contendit autem ipse in omni hoc sermone ostendere, quod electiones et quaedam earum quae secundum electionem sunt gestionum in nobis sunt, quae vero sequuntur has et fines, in fortuna sunt ex necessitate."

28. *De natura hominis*, XXXVII, p.140, 33–34: "Nos enim non secundum necessitatem sequi ea quae sunt providentiae inquimus, sed contingenter." In Nemesius' view Divine Providence and fate are not identical: God is regarded as an almighty principle of free initiatives.

29. According to Aristotle happiness ($\varepsilon\dot{v}\delta\alpha\iota\mu o\nu\acute{\iota}\alpha$) is the result of man's activity (*Eth. Nic.*, I, 6, 1097b24–25). A competent and constant accomplishment of the noblest activity of which man is capable, namely intellectual speculation, represents the highest degree of perfection and the supreme level of happiness. In any case, man himself is at the origin of his destiny.

Master on this subject is still incomplete, yet it is a decisive approach to something very different from current trends and widespread opinions: in this respect Aristotle was again a physician of his culture and he prepared what may be called "the image of Western man." However, Aristotle does not provide a metaphysical justification of human freedom: in his perspective God is not the creator of the cosmos; he is not the ontological source of whatever exists; and for that very reason he can not even know what happens in the world. Not being the creative cause of man, God is not involved in man's behavior and is not directly aware of individual conduct. From this viewpoint the teaching of our author shows an important difference from the doctrine of some medieval Christian theologians: according to Aquinas God created the world from nothing in a perfectly free initiative. Creation is not some event of the past, something completed that may be commemorated, belonging to a former period; creation as a producing of being in all its aspects can never be interrupted. It goes on in the course of time as a constant activity proceeding from the divine cause and entailing the permanent dependence of finite beings. The world is not necessarily derived from its divine source: it is the result of a free decision, and so human acts are not determined but involve finite participation in divine freedom.[30] This perspective is not present in Aristotle: God is considered to be Pure Act, an immutable substance, a closed consciousness, final cause of the cosmic evolution. The world always strives toward divine perfection, but it will never attain it: the universe loves that divine consciousness, but it is locked within itself. Does this lead to a cosmic tragedy? Not in Aristotle's view, since the relationship between God and world does not prevent man from reaching limited happiness.

A question frequently treated in contemporary thought is concerned with the coexistence of an infinite creator and finite beings

30. Thomas Aquinas, *De Potentia*, q. 3, a.15. In the writings of Aquinas there are many texts expounding and supporting the freedom of divine creation. The author is quite conscious of the difficulty: the creative act coincides with the essence of God; it is not an accidental perfection of the Divine Substance. Nevertheless creation is regarded as a free act of the will, as the divine will has no necessary relationship with any creature: "unde cum per modum intelligendi, actionis divinae principium, prout respicit creaturam, consideretur divina voluntas quae ad creaturam non habet necessariam habitudinem, non oportet quod creatura procedat a Deo per necessitatem naturae, licet ipsa actio sit Dei essentia vel natura" (ad 18).

that are totally dependent upon their cause. What happens to finite beings if there is an infinite cause of their existence? If all finite beings depend entirely upon an infinite creator, in what they are and what they do, can they ever possess any density or individual consistency? How can a finite being be the author of its own destiny if it is totally dependent upon its creative principle in whatever it undertakes? Some contemporary authors maintain such coexistence to be impossible[31]; others, on the contrary, accept it and emphasize that human freedom and responsibility are intended and constituted by the Divine Creator. There is neither conflict nor opposition: in his creative act God shapes man as a free and responsible person.[32] Aristotle does not handle this issue: it does not fit into his metaphysical thought; God is Pure Act, man is both act and potency. Man strives to the perfection of the Divine Substance, but he can only gradually actualize his hidden capacities.

Finally Aristotle does not endeavor to demonstrate freedom of human activity: he rather proceeds to a careful analysis of our decisions and he tries to distinguish the essential factors included in the process of deliberation.[33] In this way he does not prove freedom of action, but he shows how it is possible to recognize it in the development of human behavior. Later philosophers who endeavored to argue freedom of decision started from the formal object of volitive activity: this object is the good without any restriction, the good or valuable in its full extension, an extension that, like that of being, is transcendental or all-embracing. All particular values pursued by an individual are assessed in the light of the transcendental good. When a particular object is intended, the agent

31. M. Merleau-Ponty, *Sens et non-sens,* Paris, 1948, p.356: "Il y a toujours, dans l'idée de Dieu, une composante stoïcienne: si Dieu est, la perfection est déjà réalisée en deça du monde, elle ne saurait être accrue, il n'y a, à la lettre, rien à faire." Cf. P. Masterson, *Atheism and Alienation,* Dublin, 1971, p. X: "What emerges in the course of this study is the elaboration of a humanism of liberty which calls in question the possibility of the coexistence of finite and infinite being—or, more concretely, the coexistence of man and God."

32. If creation is considered to be a necessary process, it is difficult to explain free human initiatives: these must also be included in the process by which finite reality comes to be. If the creative act is interpreted as a free decision, human freedom will be a participation in the Divine Causation.

33. According to Aristotle everybody deliberates on things that he may achieve (*Eth. Nic.*, III, 3, 1112a33). Deliberation is meaningful only when it is performed in relation to some personal activity: it makes no sense to deliberate on things that occur independently of our will.

is normally aware of the limited character of what he intends and his acts cannot be necessitated by this finite perfection, because it does not fully correspond to what he desires. If the object were regarded as good and perfect in all respects and without restriction, then the agent would be irresistibly pushed to pursue it. Consciousness of limitation involves the twofold capacity of pursuing a good or of withdrawing from it.[34]

Examining the process of deliberation Aristotle penetrates into the heart of free decision. In his view deliberation is an internal discourse, which means that it is a temporal process[35]: each human act is a unique event, taking place in a constantly changing network of circumstances. It is certainly not easy to discover the best way of behaving in the variable situations of life. When important decisions are at stake, some individuals are almost unable to stop their reflection and to come to a conclusion.[36] In any case, a man who deliberates considers successively the various aspects and factors of a planned action and tries to disclose the possible consequences of various ways of acting. Deliberation is not an immediate and sudden intuition; it is a slow and gradual process, based on former experience and practice, with a view to uncovering and valuating the components of a project.[37] After having concentrated attention on one aspect of an action, an agent is already prepared to consider and weigh the other factors. A man who deliberates does not remain on the same spot: each stage of the deliberating process brings something new, a better insight, a more adequate understanding.

34. Thomas Aquinas, *De Malo*, q. 6, a. un. "Si autem sit tale bonum quod non inveniatur esse bonum secundum omnia particularia quae considerari possunt, non ex necessitate movebit etiam quantum ad determinationem actus, poterit enim aliquis velle eius oppositum, etiam de eo cogitans, quia forte est bonum et conveniens secundum aliquod aliud particulare consideratum, sicut quod est bonum sanitati, non est bonum delectationi, et sic de aliis."

35. *Eth. Nic.*, III, 2, 1111b9–10. In Aristotle's opinion children and irrational animals are unable to make a free choice although their activity may be spontaneous (ἐκούσιον): a choice is prepared by a process of deliberation; it does not occur suddenly. An agent successively considers several aspects and components of a possible action; this allows him to compare them and in this way to reach a final decision.

36. Shakespeare, *Hamlet*, Act III, 1: "Thus conscience does make cowards of us all."

37. *Eth. Nic.*, III, 3, 1112b21–23; b28–30; 1113a5–7. According to Aristotle decisions are taken by the leading principle of the soul (τὸ ἡγούμενον). A deliberation will come to an end when an agent, after a process of reflection, returns to himself the authority or power of deciding. As long as the deliberation continues, the agent is in a state of hesitation and uncertainty.

Dealing with soundness of judgment in deliberation, Aristotle distinguishes a deliberative process from scientific knowledge as well as from conjecture and opinion. In his view deliberation is far from being a sudden intuition: it extends over a long time (πολὺν χρόνον); various aspects of a future action are taken into consideration.[38] Of course, this action may be virtuous or evil. A vicious individual may also be competent in deliberating on his future behavior, yet what Aristotle properly intends when speaking of excellence in deliberation is the ability to elaborate sound judgments in view of moral actions.[39] In this context the author stresses the fact that deliberation is concerned with means, not properly with the final end of human activity. This end is settled by nature; everybody strives toward the good.[40] Yet there are many intermediary ends, which are at once means and ends: these are obviously objects of deliberation; they are decided as a result of due reflection. Each individual has to choose his own way in order to reach the final goal of his life.[41] According to Aristotle a deliberative process may be expressed in the shape of a practical syllogism[42]: true, human life is not a series of syllogistic arguments. What the author has in mind is something different: when the process of deliberation is completed and the agent has reached a decision, then the whole evolution may be summarized in a practical syllogism, although the actual way of proceeding is different. A scientific discovery may also be expressed in a syllogism. This again does not mean that the scientist follows this line of making progress. Moreover, when moral insight is concerned, as we already mentioned, the ethical behavior of an agent plays an important part: moral judgments are always

38. *Eth. Nic.*, VI, 9, 1142b2–5.

39. *Eth. Nic.*, VI, 9, 1142b20–22.

40. *Eth. Nic.*, III, 3, 1112b11–20; b33–34; 5, 1113b3–5; *Eth. Eud.*, II, 10, 1226a8; II, 11, 1227b38–40.

41. *Eth. Nic.*, I, 5, 1097b2–5: virtue is at once a goal that is chosen for itself and in respect to happiness. This teaching on intermediary ends is quite consistent with Aristotle's doctrine on the analogy of the good (*Eth. Nic.*, I, 4, 1096a23–27; cf. J. R. Moncho, *La unidad de la vida moral*, p.300). In dealing with human conduct, Aristotle makes a clear distinction between setting a goal and choosing the means. This latter is not only a technical matter; it is also invested with an ethical meaning (*Eth. Nic.*, VI, 10, 1142b33; *Politica*, VII, 13, 1331b26–34; cf. P. Aubenque, *La Prudence chez Aristote*, p.121–122).

42. *Eth. Nic.*, VI, 12, 1144a31–33. Practical syllogisms leading to a particular action or behavior are founded on some insight into what is good or what is the end to be reached. This insight is not merely theoretical and speculative: it refers to human action and is also dependent upon the moral conduct of a particular agent.

influenced by the ethical attitude and conduct of the agent; this is not the case in theoretical knowing.[43]

According to the syllogistic pattern deliberation is a passage from universal knowledge to a particular intuition: it is not enough to realize the moral value of a way of behaving; one has to apply this general insight to a concrete act.[44] At first glance such passage seems to be easy, since universal knowledge actually proceeds from sensible experience. In Aristotle's view universal concepts always stem from sense perception. This obtains also with respect to moral knowledge: it is not inborn; it grows and develops through experience and practice. The aim is to disclose the truly good in the variable conditions of life. There is always a reciprocal relationship between universal moral insights and concrete experience: general intuitions proceed from particular experiences and at the same time contribute to clarifying them; as to the concrete views, they are the origin of general insights, but on the other hand they need universal norms that can be applied to changing situations of life. In any case, concrete ethical judgments are justified in the light of some universal rules, but they are not deduced from them: a syllogistic formulation is not a description of the agent's actual proceeding.[45] The starting point of a deliberation may very well be a provisional intuition of the practical conclusion; a further justification on the basis of some general principles may be a later construction.

In the process of deliberation there is also a passage from habitual knowing to actual knowing: habitual knowledge is one that is present in the mind without being exercised.[46] Is it a natural presence? Not in Aristotle's view: habitual knowledge does not belong

43. *Eth. Nic.*, VI, 12, 1144a34–36. In this context Aristotle is quite categorical: it is impossible to be a wise or prudent person if one's behavior is not virtuous. Moral virtue protects the agent against the influence of irrational tendencies.

44. *Eth. Nic.*, VII, 3, 1146b35–1147a4. Aristotle points to the fact that human behavior always involves particular actions. Hence moral knowledge is only efficacious when it is concerned with concrete deeds: it is one of the essential functions of deliberation to pass from general knowledge to concrete moral assessments. It is not always easy to decide whether a particular act does or does not conform to the virtue of justice or temperance.

45. According to P. Aubenque deliberation in Aristotle's view is primarily concerned with choosing means to an end; it is not primarily a transition from universal knowledge to a particular assessment. In this respect the author criticizes the viewpoint of D. Allan (*La prudence chez Aristote*, p.140–142).

46. *Eth. Nic.*, VII, 3, 1146b31–35. The notion of habitual knowledge plays an important part in Aristotle's theory of education: any process of learning aims at

to the inborn equipment of an individual; it has been acquired, being the result of many previous acts. Virtues also are habits or abiding dispositions, the outcome of prior activities. As a result of antecedent acts of knowing, man possesses in a habitual way some hidden intuitions, not only in the field of theoretical sciences but also with respect to practical performance.[47] Through his education an individual knows in a habitual way that it is wrong to lie, but he has to face particular situations. It is not always easy to actualize the right habitual insight that is able to clarify the case. In a human mind there are many habitual intuitions; in a concrete situation an agent has to appeal to the one that is able to solve the question asked and to carry on the deliberative process to a conclusion.[48] Here again the starting point will certainly not be the recalling of a general rule, from which a concrete insight is derived. The point of departure will be a particular situation that is to be elucidated: the actualization of a habitual knowing is effected to solve an ethical problem. The syllogistic formulation is again a *post factum* schematic summary of a procedure that has developed in its own way. Deliberation as an actual process is a living discourse in which man slowly attempts to solve a problem by analyzing its various components.[49]

The deliberative discourse is teleological; it is oriented toward the discovery of the really good in a concrete situation. In this respect the dynamism that animates deliberation is a striving toward

---

acquiring a habitual knowledge of some discipline; studying geometry a pupil will progressively acquire an abiding knowledge of this branch of learning. In Aristotle's view man is a being able to be educated.

47. Practical wisdom is an intellectual virtue (*Eth. Nic.*, VI, 5, 1140a24–28; 1140b4–6). It is concerned with human actions and behavior and aims at disclosing what is really good for man; in this sense, it is called a habit that, with the help of reason, allows one to discover what is truly valuable ($\xi\xi\iota\nu$ $\dot\alpha\lambda\eta\theta\dot\eta$) in the various circumstances of life.

48. The truth of practical wisdom resides in the correspondence of its judgment with right desire, as this tendency is oriented toward the good (*Eth. Nic.*, VI, 2, 1139a29–31).

49. One may object that Aristotle's interpretation of a free decision remains intellectualistic: after all, everybody acts according to his insights. Seemingly this position conforms to the teaching of Socrates. Yet there is a considerable difference: in Aristotle's view moral insights are dependent upon ethical behavior; these insights are practical not only because they refer to actions but also because they are constantly influenced by human conduct. Moreover, man's actions are not determined by universal intuitions: they proceed from knowledge that is immediately related to concrete particular situations. Such knowledge is not exclusively intellectual; it is also sensitive and linked to the emotional propensities of human beings.

the good that is present in all humans as it is present in the whole universe.[50] Man can never accomplish what he actually believes to be wrong, so the danger that threatens deliberation is not that an agent may finally choose what he thinks to be wrong but that he may be deceived, that he may go astray in his search and reach a mistaken conclusion. The danger of erroneous opinions, particularly in moral matters, is rather high[51]: first of all, human insights spring from sensible experience. The objects of intellectual understanding are not immediately grasped by the mind. They are the result of an operation in which the active intellect plays a decisive part. In this process mistakes are always possible: an individual may be misled in his moral judgment by what is immediately given, the sensible world. All human knowledge is fallible, since intellectual under-standing is only reached on the basis of sensible experience, which is immediate but rather subjective; moral knowledge is probably more vulnerable than any other, because it depends on ethical conduct and is related to future behavior.[52] When an envisaged action is involved, man can easily be prejudiced and influenced by irrational inclinations and movements. Only a moral man, a man who dominates his passions and emotions, is able to elaborate correct ethical judgments and assessments; other people are frequently misled. They believe they grasp what is really good, but they cling to some apparent value, being deceived by their desires and emotions.[53]

50. In Aristotle's opinion deliberation leads to a choice (προαίρεσις). This Greek term does not always have the same meaning: in book III of the *Nicomachean Ethics* it refers to a personal decision, a choice of means to an end. In other books of the same treatise (II, VI, VII) the term designates the moral intention of an agent.

51. *Eth. Nic.*, VI, 5, 1140b25–28. Aristotle is deeply concerned with describing accurately the nature of moral wisdom: it does not deal with static reality but with human conduct in situations that are constantly changing. Hence moral wisdom does not coincide with scientific knowledge: it belongs to the opinative part of the soul (τοῦ δοξαστικοῦ). In Aristotle's teaching ethical wisdom is a virtue; it is an abiding habit allowing an individual to formulate right judgments about the way to behave in concrete situations. Is it merely a habit that works with the help of reason? Not exactly, since there is no oblivion with respect to moral wisdom, whereas forgetting may always occur in habits relying on reason.

52. *Eth. Nic.*, VI, 2, 1139b7–9. Deliberation is always concerned with a possible future way of behaving (περὶ τοῦ ἐσομένου καὶ ἐνδεχομένου). An agent has to make a choice among various possibilities, relying mostly on his experience of similar situations in the past.

53. *Eth. Nic.*, VI, 5, 1140b13–20. Pleasure and pain have no impact on purely theoretical knowledge, for example, geometrical matters. Their influence, however, is very strong when human behavior is at stake: according to Aristotle they can disturb the basic ethical insights of an agent.

Deliberation is always concerned with human action that is integrated into the all-embracing becoming of the universe. Man's behavior is a constant development: each action is an element in the evolution of an individual. Deliberating on his activity, man reflects on himself and his future.[54] The constant change of individual conditions occurs in a world that is not unmoved but evolving together with man toward a new horizon. In Aristotle's view the ceaseless change of the world is not a deceiving appearance; it is truly real. Man is not an exception: his own becoming is part of the movement of the universe. Both evolutions are real; they are considered to be passages from potency to act. An individual deliberates on the future, on what is to be done; he does not deliberate on the past, which can no longer be changed. Being concerned with the future, an agent takes into account the past and the present: he bears within his mind the memory of the past, he is conscious of his present situation and activity, and he looks at the future perhaps with anguish and uncertainty.[55] The future of a person is not unlimited: like other things in the world, man is able to develop within the limits of his potency; the trouble is that he has to disclose the possibilities and frontiers of his potency gradually. According to the Megarians the extent of a potency can only be grasped when it has been actualized. This view is not accepted by Aristotle, but it remains true that the hidden possibilities of a being are not revealed at once, but progressively in relationship with the evolution of the surrounding world.[56] It is a privilege of man to create to some extent his own future, remaining always within the area of his potency.

The becoming of human existence in the world is contingent: it is neither determined nor necessitated beforehand. Man's behavior

54. *Eth. Nic.*, VI, 5, 1140a24–31. Moral wisdom does not deal with a particular area of human life, such as health, but with human life as a whole. In the light of this basic insight a wise man is able to formulate right judgments on what is to be done for the purpose of attaining happiness.

55. *Eth. Nic.*, VI, 5, 1140a31–b6. In this context Aristotle points to the difference between moral wisdom and technical skill, which aims at producing something different from the act itself. In his ethical treatise Aristotle frequently refers to technical skills in order to illustrate the way in which moral virtues are gradually developed: when a habit has been acquired, the action that proceeds from it will be performed in an easy, steady, and effective way.

56. G. Verbeke, *The Meaning of Potency in Aristotle*, in: *Graceful Reason*, Essays in Ancient and Medieval Philosophy presented to Joseph Owens, CSSR, on the Occasion of his Seventy-fifth Birthday and the Fiftieth Anniversary of His Ordination, Toronto, 1983, p.55–73.

is the result of a personal choice: if everything were necessitated, even our future actions, deliberation would be useless. On the contrary, Aristotle stresses the importance of deliberation in view of moral conduct: man does not behave like irrational animals, moved by spontaneous impulses. Apparently animals do not reflect before proceeding to an act; they do not contemplate various possible ways of behaving with their advantages and disadvantages; there is no real deliberation. Hence the life of animals proceeds roughly according to the same pattern. Among animals there is no distinction between good and bad agents. On the contrary, man reflects and hesitates, he ponders over what he is going to do, and when he reaches a decision, he does so in a climate of uncertainty.[57] He should like to scrutinize the future, to uncover what is still hidden. He is unable to predict everything; he cannot foresee his own future. And yet each decision is a contribution to that contingent future: man ought to deliberate, because what is to be done is not immediately obvious.[58] One always lives in uncertainty: he partly creates his future, but at the same time he constantly has to face new events and circumstances that he did not expect or voluntarily cause. Aristotle also accepts some contingency in the physical world: nature is oriented toward the good and attains its goal in most cases[59]; in this way the future of the cosmos is always secured. The universe will not collapse but will continue to exist indefinitely. Second to nature the author accepts the impact of chance and fortune: consequently the course of events is not always predictable.[60] For all these reasons deliberation is both indispensable and difficult.

What are the origin and principle of this deliberative activity? In

57. *Eth. Nic.*, III, 3, 1112a30–34; b8–11. Everybody deliberates on things that he is able to achieve and that involve some uncertainty, such as matters of medicine, economy, gymnastics, or pilotage. In these matters there is much uncertainty: the result of an action is undetermined; nobody knows exactly what the outcome will be. The agent can only take into account what happens in most cases. In some circumstances, when an important decision is to be taken he will even appeal to the advice of other people.

58. *Eth. Nic.*, III, 3, 1112b11–12: deliberation is not concerned with the end but with the means to be used in order to reach the goal that is pursued.

59. Many texts in Aristotle declare that nature always pursues what is best or most perfect; moreover, nature never makes anything superfluous. All these texts illustrate Aristotle's teleological view of the universe.

60. *Physics*, II, 5, 196b10–197a8. The fact that there are unexpected and unpredictable events increases the uncertainty of human action: man cannot deliberate about these exceptional events, but he should be aware of their possibility.

Aristotle's view thinking cannot be the principle of thinking, nor can deliberation be the ultimate cause of deliberative reasoning. The author is quite convinced that there must be a principle of thinking and deliberation: if it were thinking itself, the questioning would continue indefinitely and there would be no final explanation.[61] Hence the principle that is looked for must belong to a higher level: it cannot be fortune; it must be more perfect than reasoning itself. According to Aristotle this highest cause is the Divine Substance: God moves everything, including human thinking.[62] Yet if human deliberation is moved by the divine principle, can it be the origin of a free and responsible choice? In the *Eudemian Ethics* where the Stagirite treats this question, man's responsibility is unambiguously asserted: man is the responsible author of his moral conduct.[63] God is considered to be the final cause of man's aspiration: each individual naturally and spontaneously strives toward the supreme perfection of Pure Act. This tendency is at the origin of all particular acts of reasoning and thinking. Are these concrete acts prevented from being free and autonomous? By no means; man is constantly concerned with particular ways of behaving in the changing circumstances of life. These acts are the result of deliberative reflection: man will try to discover whether a possible mode of conduct is really valuable and good. In this sense his deliberation and the decision that follows will reflect a responsible choice.

The internal discourse of deliberation will be closed when the agent decides to complete it.[64] This aspect of the deliberative process is not unimportant: it may go on indefinitely, since each concrete situation is unique and may be very complex; an agent may ceaselessly turn to the contemplation of new aspects and never reach a conclusion. If somebody wants absolute certainty, he will never stop pondering his planned activity: according to our author we choose what we best know to be valuable.[65] An agent has to be satisfied

61. *Eth. Eud.*, VIII, 2, 1248a15–21.
62. *Eth. Eud.*, VIII, 2, 1248a22–29.
63. *Eth. Eud.*, II, 6, 1223a2–15.
64. *Eth. Nic.*, III, 3, 1112b24–27. When an agent is confronted with something impossible, he will stop his deliberation; on the contrary, when he sees the possibility of achieving what he wants, he will start his action.
65. *Eth. Nic.*, III, 2, 1112a7–8. The author makes a distinction between εἰδέναι and δοξάζειν: this latter term refers to an opinative knowledge; choice is not always consonant with this lower degree of knowing.

with some degree of uncertainty: this aspect should not prevent him from taking decisions regarding his way of conduct. What matters is that a choice be made after careful consideration and reflection.[66] Man should not hesitate too much: he has to achieve the full development of his capacities in a short period of time. In any case, a decision taken at the end of a careful deliberation will be a personal and responsible choice. Man is not a merely physical being: intellective activity, although it constantly depends upon sensible experience, cannot be material; it belongs to the level of the spiritual and involves a moment of creativity (the active intellect), by which it transcends physical reality.[67]

An objection to this doctrine is that everybody chooses his way of behaving according to his character and his dispositions.[68] As a matter of fact, everybody aims at the good and chooses what seems to be valuable. However, some things are regarded to be worthwhile by one individual and not by another; considering this situation, one may be inclined to maintain that everybody acts according to his own opinion and that he is not responsible for what he believes to be valuable. Nobody may be blamed for pursuing what he sincerely thinks is good.[69] Aristotle's answer shows a profound understanding of human behavior and manifests the reason why he disagrees with moral intellectualism. In his view everybody is to some degree responsible for his dispositions: habits are the outcome of previous acts. Insofar as acquired habits are concerned, man is really at the origin of these dispositions.[70] But Aristotle is cautious in the formulation of his teaching: he states that man to some extent is the cause of his dispositions.[71] There are also dispositions that do

66. *Eth. Nic.*, III, 2, 1112a15.

67. *De anima*, III, 5, 430a12. This intellective principle is called τὸ αἴτιον καὶ ποιητικόν, τῷ ποιεῖν πάντα. Whatever is intelligible in potency is made intelligible in act; only after this transformation can an object be assimilated by the mind.

68. *Eth. Nic.*, III, 5, 1114a31–1114b1. The objection points to the fact that everybody chooses what he believes to be good and that he is not responsible for this opinion(τῆς δὲ φαντασίας οὐ κύριοι).

69. *Eth. Nic.*, III, 5, 1114b3–12. The essential question is whether particular moral judgments are determined by an individual's natural abilities or not: some individuals have excellent eyes and observe quite precisely, whereas others do not.

70. *Eth. Nic.*, III, 5, 1114b1–3. In Aristotle's view particular moral judgments are not merely a matter of natural disposition. They are mainly dependent upon the moral habits of a particular agent.

71. *Eth. Nic.*, III, 5, 1114b21–25. The author explains that each person is to some extent (πως αἴτιος) at the origin of his habits and therefore is to some degree the principle of his moral assessments.

not depend on former activity: intellectual and physical capacities are not the same in each individual and they are not the result of a free choice. Everybody is the outcome of two kinds of dispositions: some have been deliberately acquired by previous acts; others are innate and belong to a person without his former choice. If an agent is responsible for his dispositions, he will also be responsible for what he believes to be good. What a virtuous individual judges to be valuable will be truly good; an immoral agent will also assess things in conformity with his dispositions; hence what he will regard as good will be contrary to moral behavior.[72] Everybody chooses the concrete goals and objectives of his life and activity. Aristotle does not deny that these options are made according to the dispositions of an individual; what he stresses is that these dispositions do not entirely exclude personal responsibility. Everybody is the author of his choices because he is at least partly at the origin of his dispositions.

Moreover, an agent may be responsible for his ignorance[73]: Aristotle acknowledges that somebody may perform some actions as a result of inevitable ignorance; in this case he will not be responsible for what he does. The Stagirite, however, is convinced that ignorance does not always suppress personal responsibility: ignorance may be the consequence of a lack of reflection, of some negligence in the deliberative process. In a sense man is responsible for his mistakes and his ignorance. Finally, Aristotle wonders whether some individuals are not totally irresponsible, since they are morally degenerate and are no longer capable of changing their conduct. If somebody as a result of previous behavior has become unjust and intemperate, he certainly cannot change his conduct whenever he wants.[74] When somebody acts under the impulse of such inveterate habits, one may believe that he is not responsible for what he is doing. In a sense this is true, but Aristotle maintains that these actions are voluntary in their cause: immoral habits were gradually

72. *Eth. Nic.*, VI, 12, 1144a34–36.

73. *Eth. Nic.*, III, 5, 1113b30–33. The author mentions the example of drunkenness: being responsible for this situation, an individual bears the responsibility for ignorance that is caused by it.

74. *Eth. Nic.*, III, 5, 1114a13–16. It is impossible for an agent to change his moral behavior suddenly: ethical virtues are the result of many previous acts. As to people who generally behave in an immoral way, they will gradually acquire vicious habits; in their case a sudden passage to moral conduct will be impossible.

acquired as a result of an activity for which an agent is responsible. If somebody stands on the top of a tower, he may or may not throw a stone downward, but when he has launched the stone, he cannot seize it again.[75] Even if an individual finds himself unable to change his conduct, he remains responsible for the dispositions he has gradually acquired.

Man is a responsible person: this viewpoint had already been accepted by Socrates and Plato; both philosophers opposed fatalism, which is incompatible with free choice and moral responsibility. In Plato's view man is the author of his destiny, both in his present life and in his life after death. Aristotle does not accept the immortality of human soul: the world has no beginning and will never end. Humans, however, come to be and pass away: within their short period of life they are able to attain a limited happiness. Aristotle did something more than his predecessors: through his analysis of deliberation, he showed that everybody is responsible for his moral conduct. So he not only rejected fatalism but elaborated a rational argument showing that human behavior is not necessitated by some blind power but is the result of free initiatives and responsible choices. Man is not simply pushed by irrational impulses; he is an animal that deliberates and chooses its own way of life.

75. *Eth. Nic.*, III, 5, 1114a16–21. People who have acquired vicious habits are responsible for what they do under the influence of this disposition. As to the future, Aristotle simply states that they cannot change their attitude whenever they want (ἐάν γε βούληται); he does not deny that a gradual change is possible.

REASON AND PASSIONS

THE *Iliad* played an important part in Greek education: as an early and outstanding literary work it was constantly read and explained; it gradually penetrated into the mind of young people and was assimilated as a reliable expression of an old tradition.[1] This remarkable poem not only shows exceptional literary qualities but contains a considerable amount of information regarding ancient religion and moral behavior. The narrative displays a series of human conflicts, tensions, and sharp oppositions; divinities also interfere in human affairs, siding with some individuals and struggling against others. In this respect the poem tells us a drama of heaven and earth: the Trojan War is invested with a universal dimension. It is not presented as an occasional battle between two cities, a conflict that had to be settled as soon as possible; it is both a human and a divine struggle. In this way the *Iliad* shows not only human characters in their relationships with each other but also divine beings deeply involved in earthly affairs: gods are not indifferent to events in this world; they participate in them almost like humans. Religious anthropomorphism permeates the whole drama: the Trojan War becomes an event that has been divinized.[2]

What exactly was the origin of the conflict? Did Sparta want to conquer Troy, to subdue the population and to increase its eco-

---

1. W. Jaeger, *Paideia: The Ideals of Greek Culture* (transl. Gilbert Highet), Oxford, 1946, vol. I, p.36. "He (Homer) is the first and the greatest creator and shaper of Greek life and the Greek character"; p.39: "Homer, who stands on the threshold of Greek history, became the teacher of all humanity."

2. R. Schaerer, *L'homme antique et la structure du monde intérieur d'Homère à Socrate*, Paris, 1958, p.14: "La colère qui fait le sujet de l'*Iliade* n'est donc ni la vraie colère humaine, qui s'est estompée dans le passé, ni une colère divine, puisqu'elle est colère d'Achille: elle est colère humaine divinisée."

nomic wealth and power? This is unlikely: the two cities were far
away from each other; it was quite an expedition to travel from the
Peloponnesus to the Asian coast. As a matter of fact, Troy was not
an unimportant town; it had been frequently destroyed and rebuilt.
It was located on the hill Hissarlik, at the right side of the river
Menderes, not far from the Dardanelles, excavations have shown
that some remains date back to about 3000 B.C. If Sparta wanted to
extend its territory and increase its power, it could have undertaken
much more easily an expedition to a nearer country. The reason for
the Trojan war was of a different kind: Sparta did not want to
conquer a new colony nor to extend its political power and influence. The true reason for the conflict was passion; the origin of the
war was a drama of love; what Sparta wanted to conquer was a
beautiful woman.[3] Helen had married Menelaos, king of Sparta;
during an absence of her husband, she had been raped by Paris, the
son of Priam, King of Troy. Paris is described as a rather weak
character, who had repudiated his own wife; Menelaos had been
several times to Troy in order to meet Paris and to persuade him to
return Helen, but without success. Finally he decided, in agreement
with his brother Agamemnon, to undertake a military expedition
against Troy in order to recover Helen and to bring her back to
Sparta. The war lasted ten years: we do not know how many people
were killed; two famous warriors, Hector and Patroclos, lost their
lives. Finally the Trojans lost the war and their town was destroyed.
Is the meaning of this narrative a moral one? Was the victory of the
Greeks due to the fact that their cause was the right one, since they
wanted to return Helen to her husband?

There is certainly an implicit moral teaching in the epic poem:
some general moral principles are in the background of the story.[4]
Lying is clearly censured; wrongdoing, particularly with respect to
people who are helpless or aged or strangers, is disapproved; courage is highly praised, whereas cowardice is condemned. Yet the

3. Apparently the Greek cause was fully justified: Helen had been raped and
Menelaos, her husband, wanted to bring her back to Sparta. Yet the moral aspect of
the issue is not emphasized: the *Iliad* cannot be regarded as a poem that endeavors
to show the ethical superiority of the Greeks to the Trojans. W. Jaeger rightly
remarks, "What interests the poet in the Achaean army is not the justice of its cause,
but the brilliance of its heroes" (*Paideia*, I, p.45).

4. Cf. W. Jaeger, *Paideia*, I, p.47: "We must therefore conclude that the *Iliad* has
an ethical design."

meaning of the Homeric poem is not to recommend faithfulness in marriage: the Greeks are not depicted as the protagonists of marriage against the Trojans, who would tolerate rape and unfaithfulness. Menalaos loved his wife and wanted to get her back to Sparta. As to the gods, they sided with the two parties according to their preference: those who supported the Greeks in their battle did not justify their attitude on moral grounds; obviously they were not concerned with protecting the dignity of marriage. When they sided with the Greeks against other divinities they did so because of personal sympathy.[5]

The *Iliad* is a drama of passion in many ways: the very first term of the whole poem refers to passion, a very violent passion of anger and revenge ($\mu\tilde{\eta}\nu\iota\nu$). The opening sentence indicates the topic that will be treated and the whole poem is concentrated on this particular issue, the anger of the most outstanding warrior in the Greek army, Achilles.[6] So the subject dealt with is not the unfaithfulness of Helen or the sorrow of Menelaos: we are not informed of the feelings of Helen and we do not know whether she was happy in her new condition or wanted to return to Sparta. At the beginning of his poem the author invokes the help of the divine Muse in order to compose his song: this is quite understandable, since the song does not only deal with human affairs but also with conflicts among the gods. On the other hand, one may wonder whether the subject matter of this narrative is worthy of being developed with the help of a divine Muse; should divine beings not rather support a song on virtue than one on passion? Yet the author recognizes that the anger of Achilles was the cause of much suffering, of many killings, of the death of many heroes among the Greeks. But he immediately

5. Divinities in Greek religion may hardly be regarded as models of moral conduct; this factor is an inevitable consequence of religious anthropomorphism. Gods are presented like humans, in their external appearance, behavior, and emotional reactions. Moral faults and weaknesses occur not only in the life of humans but also in the conduct of gods.

6. From the very beginning of the poem this violent passion of anger is blamed: it is considered to be accursed, execrable, detestable ($o\dot{v}\lambda o\mu\acute{\epsilon}\nu\eta\nu$). It was the origin of much harm to the Greeks: there was no longer any agreement between the two responsible leaders of the expedition. Achilles stubbornly refused to take part in the battle and many Greeks were killed. Yet in the poem the anger of Achilles is not blamed for moral reasons: as a matter of fact, the warrior had some good motives for being angry, since he had been deprived of a girl slave to whom he was very attached. The behavior of Agamemnon was the cause of Achilles' anger.

adds that all these misfortunes inflicted on the Greeks were in agreement with the plan of Zeus, who, at the request of Thetis, had decided to sacrifice the Greeks to the Trojans till the insult of Achilles had been revenged.[7]

The conflict between Agamemnon and Achilles was again a matter of passion. Chryses, a priest of Apollo, came to the Greeks with an important ransom in order to get back his daughter Chryseis, who had been captured. He respectfully and kindly turned to Agamemnon, addressed to him his best wishes in the war, and asked him on behalf of the gods to get his daughter.[8] Agamemnon immediately refused this request with brutality, but the divine Apollo sided with the priest and, coming down from Olympus, sent his arrows on the Greek army.[9] After nine days an assembly is convened and Achilles proposes to consult a diviner. Calchas explains why Apollo is angry and finally persuades Agamemnon to return his beloved Chryseis. But there is a condition: instead of Chryseis, Agememnon wants to take Bryseis, the slave of Achilles, to whom the warrior is very attached.[10] Achilles becomes so upset that he wants to kill Agamemnon on the spot: then Athena interferes and prevents Achilles from killing.[11] Finally Achilles obeys the divine command: he is deeply hurt but refrains from killing. On the contrary, Aegisthos, the lover of Clytemnestra, was also driven by strong passion; he wanted to suppress Agamemnon. He received a divine warning but refused to listen and yielded to his passion.[12]

The whole conflict between Agamemnon and Achilles was a matter of passion: thus the origin of the drama, the cause of Achilles'

---

7. *Iliad*, I, 503–528. Zeus promises to support the Trojans as a result of an intervention by Thetis: neither Zeus nor Thetis asks whether the cause of the Trojans is right or wrong. The rape of Helen is not even mentioned.

8. *Iliad*, I, 17–21. There is a contrast between the reaction of Agamemnon and the attitude of the people, who spontaneously are ready to yield to the request of Apollo's priest.

9. *Iliad*, I, 43–52. The intervention of Apollo against the Greek army is motivated only by the request of his priest: it does not mean that the god approves of the Trojans in their battle against the Greeks.

10. *Iliad*, I, 182–187. The attitude of Agamemnon is one of pride: he does not accept being put on the same level as the other members of the assembly.

11. *Iliad*, I, 207–214. The intervention of Athena involves no compulsion: she formally asks Achilles to obey; she does not constrain him.

12. *Odyssey*, I, 32–43. Zeus sent Hermes to Aegisthes to persuade him to refrain from killing Agamemnon; the intervention, however, was without result, although it was initiated by the highest divinity.

anger, of his stubborn withdrawal from the battle, was his conflict with Agamemnon, who had taken away from him a slave he loved. In a sense both Agamemnon and Achilles finally accepted a reasonable solution: the first returned Chryseis, the later did not kill, but the whole story shows the dangerous power of unrestrained passion.

Next to these two characters there is also the more balanced, less passionate temperament of Hector: he is the most noble character of the poem. He was the oldest son of Priam and Hecuba; he married Andromache and was the father of Scamandrius. Being a very courageous warrior, he was always ready to defend his country; in a battle he killed the friend of Achilles, Patroclus. In the development of the Trojan War the death of Patroclus was a decisive event, since it caused a radical transformation in the attitude and behavior of the Greek hero. Andromache was quite conscious of the danger that threatened the life of her husband: she was full of anguish for herself and her child. In a meeting with Hector she told him that his passion ($\mu\acute{\epsilon}\nu o\varsigma$) would drag him down,[13] but what she called an impulse was in the mind of Hector a deliberated and firm decision. Talking with Hector Andromache recalled all the sufferings and hardships of her life. Her father had been killed by Achilles, when the city of Thebes had been captured. She had seven brothers: all were killed by Achilles the same day. Even the mother of Andromache had been captured by the Greek warrior: she had been freed only by payment of a large ransom.[14] The poor woman urges Hector not to stay outside the walls of the town. Hector's answer is motivated by a deep sense of *aidōs*, of honor, which plays an important part in the morality of the *Iliad*. What he wants to avoid above all is to stay far away from the battle, like a coward. He has always been a courageous warrior, fighting in the first ranks in front of the

13. *Iliad*, VI, 407: $\phi\theta\acute{\iota}\sigma\epsilon\iota$ $\sigma\epsilon$ $\tau\grave{o}$ $\sigma\grave{o}\nu$ $\mu\acute{\epsilon}\nu o\varsigma$. Hector is in a very difficult situation: he is deeply attached to his wife and his child. He loves his city, which is threatened by the Greek army; he also loves the royal family to which he belongs: does he approve of his brother, who raped Helen and brought her to Troy? This aspect of the war is hardly taken into account and apparently plays no part in the decisions taken by Hector. The Trojan hero fights for his country: he does not consider the possibility of ending the war by returning Helen to her husband.

14. *Iliad*, VI, 413–428. The reasons put forward by Andromache are very impressive: they are related to the dramatic misfortunes of her life and to the future destiny of her and her child, if Hector is killed. She does not question the cause of the Trojans: she wants to save Hector from the dangers that threaten his life.

enemy: he knows the unfortunate destiny of his poor country, he knows that sacred Ilium will be destroyed, and yet he will endeavor to attain a great honor for his father and for himself. Certainly he deeply loves Andromache and his child and he is profoundly concerned with her future: she will be a captive and compelled to work for the Greeks.[15] A similar supplication is addressed to Hector by his parents: they also urge him to stay inside the walls of Troy. After this intervention Hector hesitates; at some stage he is pondering the possibility of going unarmed to Achilles and offering whatever he wants, Helen and the treasures of Troy.[16] But this hesitation does not last long: again the sense of honor plays a crucial part; he decides to stay outside the walls and to meet Achilles in a definitive battle. In this confrontation Hector is killed.

As a book of education the *Iliad* shows at once the dreadful consequences of violent passions and the harmonizing influence of reason and reflection. The stubborn anger of Achilles was the cause of many misfortunes: many people died as a result of this attitude. As to Agamemnon he stated that he was not guilty because he had been blinded by some irresistible powers; he believed himself to be a victim of Ate, which means blindness and is the name of a daughter of Zeus.[17] But the blindness of Agamemnon is in fact the blindness of irrational passion. Hector is not blinded by passion: he loves his parents, he is deeply attached to his wife and his child, but he is animated by a profound sense of honor. He does not fail to deliberate about his conduct; he carefully considers the situation of his country and his family; he wants to be courageous and to fight in the first rank, outside the walls of Troy. The conflict of reason and passion is a central issue in Greek morality; it is at the very heart of philosophical studies on moral behavior. According to Heraclitus

15. *Iliad*, VI, 441–463. Hector foresees the tragic end of his city: this knowledge, however, does not prevent him from fighting with bravery and defending his country against the enemy. What matters in his view is preserving the honor of his father and of himself.

16. *Iliad*, XXII, 38–89. The possibility of returning Helen to the Greeks is hardly taken into consideration; what brings Hector to consider this solution is certainly not that raping Helen was wrong and that returning her would redress the evil.

17. *Iliad*, XIX, 86–89. Agamemnon acknowledges that he acted wrongly, yet he believes he is not guilty ($\dot{\epsilon}\gamma\grave{\omega}$ δ'$o\dot{\upsilon}\kappa$ $\alpha\ddot{\iota}\tau\iota\acute{o}\varsigma$ $\epsilon\grave{\iota}\mu\iota$). The origin of his fault was blindness: this lack of insight is attributed to the influence of some higher powers, not to the responsibility of man himself. But if it was not right to take away Achilles' girl slave, what about Paris, who raped the wife of Menelaos?

conflict is the father of everything[18]: there are all kinds of conflicts that may daily be noticed: the conflict between day and night, between light and darkness, between life and death, between war and peace. Hence the philosopher wonders in which way all these changes are possible: in his view what something becomes is already present in it before the process begins; if light follows upon darkness, it is because light is already present in darkness. Change is possible because everything is in everything: all things involve conflict, since they contain within themselves opposing components.[19] Change is the manifestation of what was already there: in a sense everything constantly changes, but one can also state that nothing changes: nothing new comes to be, but hidden elements show themselves. According to Heraclitus the whole process is governed by a supreme principle, Logos or Reason: this powerful cause brings all things to order and harmony; things evolve in conformity with what they already are: out of the evolving diversity a cosmos comes to be.[20] In Heraclitus' view there is already a link between logos and cosmos: the latter term primarily means order, harmony, beauty; the cause of this harmony is logos. Reason is considered to be a factor that creates orderly arrangements. Heraclitus emphasizes the instability of reality, but at the same time he insists on its harmony. This harmony is not the result of chance, but of a rational principle.

In dealing with the notions of reason and passion in moral thought, we have to examine the original meaning of these terms more precisely. According to an ancient axiom man should carefully avoid all kinds of excesses: nothing too much[21]; the sentence is very brief and may be interpreted in many ways. We have to look at it

18. Heraclitus, Fr. 53 (Hippolytus, *Refutatio omnium haeresium (Ref.)*, IX, 9, 4): πόλεμος πάντων μὲν πατήρ ἐστι, πάντων δὲ βασιλεύς. Cf. *The Presocratic Philosophers: A Critical History with a Selection of Texts*, by G. S. Kirk and J. E. Raven, Cambridge, 1957, p.195: "Strife or war is Heraclitus' metaphor for the dominance of change in the world. It is obviously related to the reaction between opposites."

19. Heraclitus, Fr. 10 (Aristotle, *De mundo*, 5, 396b20): "Out of all things there comes a unity, and out of a unity all things" (*The Presocratic Philosophers*, p.191). According to the interpretation of Kirk and Raven, "The unity of things lies beneath the surface; it depends upon a balanced reaction between opposites" (p.193).

20. Heraclitus, Fr. 50 (Hippolytus, *Ref.*, IX, 9, 1): "Listening not to me but to the Logos it is wise to agree that all things are one" (*The Presocratic Philosophers*, p.188).

21. Μηδὲν ἄγαν. This axiom is very condensed; the question inevitably arises as to what exactly belongs to the area of things that are considered to be too much. These things have been determined within the framework of Greek religious tradition: man should know himself and be conscious of his mortal nature.

in the context of a religious background: the gods are jealous, they do not tolerate humans who endeavor to be their equals; man has to be moderate in whatever he wants and undertakes. He is mortal, whereas the divine beings are immortal; man has the capacity of knowing himself; he should always be aware of his limits.

In his *Introduction to Metaphysics* Martin Heidegger tries to disclose the original meaning of logos; he immediately points to the link between *logos* and *legein:* the verb means to speak, but it basically signifies to gather, to join, to bring together, to unite.[22] In Greek thought there is a close connection between speaking and reasoning or thinking: articulate language not only aims at communicating with other individuals but is also linked to the act of thinking. Terms correspond to universal notions, which are formed in the mind: in Aristotle's view the passage from sensible experience to intellectual understanding is implemented through a process of universalization; the starting point is a concrete and particular perception, whereas the final achievement is universal knowledge. Such universal concepts correspond to linguistic terms, which may be predicated of particular things and which put each of them into a larger context. The whole process shows the proper character of thinking activity: the mind operates with universal categories, which derive from sensible experience; in this way particular things are related to universal ideas. Because man is a unitary being, sensible perception and intellectual activity are not separated: the mind grasps both particular objects and general notions. According to Heidegger the activity of the mind is one of bringing together, of gathering and unifying: the intellect always endeavors to unify in a coherent way things that are different and changing.[23] At the beginning of Greek philosophy Ionian thinkers already wanted to find a principle able to unify the variety of things in the sensible universe, and they searched for some primordial element that could be the origin of everything else. Whether this element be water, air, or fire does not matter in this context: what matters is the fundamental

22. M. Heidegger, *Einführung in die Metaphysik*, Tübingen, 1953, p.95. Referring to Heraclitus, the author writes: "Was hier vom λόγος gesagt wird, entspricht genau der eigentlichen Bedeutung des Wortes: Sammlung" (p.98).

23. M. Heidegger, *Einführung in die Metaphysik*, p.102: "Wenn wir die Grundbedeutung von λόγος als Sammlung und Gesammeltheit begreifen, so ist dabei festzustellen und festzuhalten: Die Sammlung ist nie ein blosses Zusammentreiben und Anhäufen. Sie behält das Auseinander- und Gegenstrebige in eine Zusammengehörigkeit ein."

striving of the mind toward unifying various factors; reason brings together in a coherent manner and endeavors to reduce diversity to some unity.

There is also a connection between logos and cosmos. A cosmos is not a chaotic assemblage of different things; it is a well-ordered and harmonious whole. When this word was used to designate the world, it was because the Greeks were particularly impressed by the orderly disposition of the universe. In his *Physics* Aristotle wonders whether the cosmos may be composed of atoms, brought together as a result of their fortuitous encounters: this is the theory of Democritos, taken over by Epicurus. Atoms move in space and collide fortuitously: when many atoms have met in this way, a body comes to be. According to this theory, the cosmos is the outcome of mere chance. Aristotle firmly rejects this teaching: the cosmos is a perfectly arranged and harmonious whole; it can not be an effect of chance but must be the work of intellect.[24] Reason and mind are principles of order and harmony: they put things together in such a way that the whole is a work of art and beauty. Similar considerations have frequently been developed in order to demonstrate the existence of God: this proof is usually called the finality argument and is based on the conviction that order and harmony spring from reason.[25] In Greek tradition not only physical order but also moral harmony proceed from reason.

The term *passion* derives from the verb πάσχειν, to suffer, to undergo, to be passive; passion is considered to be an irrational impulse, some power that is present in man without being the outcome of a personal initiative. A passion is regarded as an emotional propensity that is undergone. Passions may be very violent and persistent: the anger of Achilles was a persistent passionate movement with serious consequences not only for the agent but for the other warriors of the Greek army; the passion of Phaedra with

24. *Physica*, II, 6, 198a5–13. In this context Aristotle mentions several possible causes of the universe; among them are fortune and chance. These latter are regarded as accidental causes (κατὰ συμβεβηκός) and are posterior to essential causes, which are intellect and nature. If the causality of chance is relevant with respect to heavenly bodies, that of intellect and nature must be more fundamental, not only with respect to heaven but also with respect to many other things and the universe itself.

25. Thomas Aquinas, *Summa Theologiae*, I, q.2, a.3: "Ergo est aliquid intelligens, a quo omnes res naturales ordinantur ad finem: et hoc dicimus Deum"; cf. *Summa contra Gentiles*, II, 24, n. 1005.

regard to Hippolytus was also a disturbing emotional impulse.[26] Being irrational, passions readily lead to excesses: if they are not sufficiently controlled and ruled they may irresistibly drive humans to a kind of madness. In Greek tradition there was a striking opposition between two divinities, Apollo and Dionysus: Apollo was the symbol of reason, of understanding and balanced behavior, whereas Dionysus was an example of irrational inspiration, of obsession and madness. In his *Bacchae* Euripides describes the emotional excesses of women during the celebration days of Dionysus: they show the disastrous results to which uncontrolled passions may lead.[27] In any case, in popular tradition passions are considered to be a source of disorder and disturbances, particularly when they are not governed and ruled by reason. One of the most dangerous human passions is that of hūbris: it drives man to an excessive desire for honor, power, and wealth; man forgets the limits of his capacities and possibilities; he wants to be equal to the gods, to be immortal.[28]

In the framework of Greek tradition, philosophers endeavoring to clarify ethical values and moral conduct could not avoid facing this conflict between reason and passion: they had to find a solution for this crucial aporia and had to indicate how man ought to behave in order to solve this problem in an appropriate way. In addition one may ask why this conflict exists: why is man a divided being, constantly disturbed by an internal opposition? Was there any ancient event that originated this condition, or was man always in this distorted situation? Seemingly Greek philosophers are not concerned with the origin of the internal conflict that is present in all humans: they do not try to discover some original fault or mistake that may explain the split in man's internal life. The structure of man is accepted as it stands without questioning its cause or origin.[29]

26. Phaedra was the stepmother of Hippolytus: she fell in love with him and since the young man did not yield to her passion, she was so deeply disappointed that she insulted him to his father Theseus, who cursed his son and asked Poseidon to punish him. Euripides dedicated two dramas to this topic; one of them is lost.

27. Euripides, *Bacchae*, ed. with Introduction and Commentary by E. R. Dodds, Oxford, 1953. In his introduction the editor writes: "Athenian public opinion is thus, as far as we happen to know, on the side of law and order" (cf. Plato, *Leges*, X, 910b–c).

28. Cf. B. Snell, *Die Entdeckung des Geistes*, Göttingen, 1974, p.158, 172.

29. It is the proper duty of moral education to assist man in bringing his internal conflict or split to a balanced and enduring solution, a coherence under the direction of reason (E. Fink, *Metaphysik der Erziehung im Weltverständnis von Plato und Aristoteles*, Frankfurt, 1970, p.246).

As to the practical handling of the conflict, various theories have been put forward. The most radical is the one proposed by the Stoics: this viewpoint has been very influential, since Stoicism dominated the civilized world during five centuries; in antiquity no other philosophical trend was so widespread and persistent. According to the Stoics passions are irrational by nature: nobody is able to change their essence; they always remain what they naturally are, irrational impulses.[30] Consequently the only way to deal with them adequately is to eradicate them. The wise man, the man who has reached the highest level of moral conduct, is an individual without passions, totally impassive; his life is not disturbed by irrational inclinations. As long as emotional disturbances are present, an individual cannot be fully moral: there is no intermediate way, no possibility of subduing them to reason.[31] Of course, one may ask whether these passions proceed from the Divine Logos: how can Divine Reason ever produce tendencies that are essentially irrational? Human soul is a particle of the Supreme Logos, and it has to free itself from irrational propensities, which belong to a lower level of perfection. Stoics strongly emphasize the unity of moral life: in their view it is impossible to possess one virtue without also having the others; all virtues are linked together—for example, a lack of temperance must have an impact on the other aspects of moral behavior—a moral person possesses all virtues.[32] The Stoic viewpoint implies that it is impossi-

---

30. Diogenes Laertius (VII, 110; SVF I, 205) quotes the definition elaborated by Zeno, the founder of the Stoic School. According to this text passion is a movement of the soul; what is intended is not a local movement but rather a qualitative change of the psychic principle. This change must be a profound one: in the framework of Stoic thought human soul is a particle of the Divine Reason. A passion, however, is an irrational movement that is further described as being against nature ($\pi\alpha\rho\grave{\alpha}$ $\phi\acute{\upsilon}\sigma\iota\nu$). In a Stoic context nature coincides with reason: the Divine Logos is present everywhere; it permeates the whole cosmos. In addition, passion is characterized as an excessive impulse. The various factors of this definition point to the same feature: passions by their very nature are irrational. As to Chrysippus, he rather believes that passions are judgments of the rational power of the soul. If human soul is essentially a particle of Divine Reason, how can it ever be irrational? Chrysippus tries to explain passions within the framework of rational activity (Galenus, *De placitis Hippocratis et Platonis (De plac. Hippocr. et Plat.)*, V, 1, p.405 M; SVF III, 461).

31. Seneca, *Epist.* 116, 1: "Utrum satius sit modicos habere adfectus an nullos, saepe quaesitum est: nostri illos expellunt, Peripatetici temperant"; Diog. Laert., VII, 117.

32. Stobaeus, *Eclogae (Ecl)*, II, p.63, 6 W; Cicero, *Academica Posteriora (Ac. post.)* I, 10, 38: "Cumque superiores non omnem virtutem in ratione esse dicerent, sed quasdam virtutes natura aut more perfectas, hic (scil. Zeno) omnes in ratione ponebat; cumque illi ea genera virtutum, quae supra dixi, seiungi posse arbitrarentur, hic nec id ullo modo fieri posse disserebat."

ble to educate passions; it is not possible to submit them to ethical rules, because they are essentially irrational. In the further development of the Stoic School some mitigation was introduced in this respect: Panaetius and Posidonius chiefly adopted a more flexible position; in their view, some moral progress can be effected. Mankind is not merely divided into two groups, a very small number of wise individuals and a mass of insane people. Later Stoics agreed that it is possible to achieve gradual improvement in moral conduct: the ideal of apatheia remains, but the way leading to this summit is long and slow. Individuals who accomplish real progress are no longer in the category of the insane, but in an intermediary group including those who advance.[33] According to the ancient Stoic position moral conduct is incompatible with the presence of passion; even in the view of later Stoics the full development of ethical life requires the elimination of passions.

The teaching of Socrates and Plato is less radical. According to the first, philosophy is a way leading to wisdom and truth; it is like a training through which man learns to die, an exercise of dying.[34] This elliptic definition refers to the life and death of Socrates: the death of this remarkable man was not a contingent event, something that happened as a result of unfortunate circumstances; this death is invested with a symbolic and dialectical meaning, since it is the expression of a profound conflict between the life and teaching of this Master and the society of his time. The death of Socrates was something logical and inevitable: it was not caused by the accidental presence of a hostile government; the philosopher was condemned by the society to which he belonged. Moreover, this death was a philosophical act: a philosopher has to withdraw from sensible reality and to join authentic truth, which cannot be found in the varying impressions of perception but in the understanding of reason. The whole life of Socrates was animated by a craving for truth. Moral conduct also entirely depends upon grasping true reality: if

33. Seneca, *Epist.* 75, 8: "Quid ergo? infra illum nulli gradus sunt? statim a sapientia praeceps est? Non, ut existimo: nam qui proficit, in numero quidem stultorum est, magno tamen intervallo ab illis diducitur. Inter ipsos quoque proficientes sunt magna discrimina"; (*Epist.* 71, 36ff.; Plutarch, *De profectibus in virtute (De prof. in virt.)*, 12, p.82ff.; SVF I, 234).

34. *Phaedo*, 81a: μελέτη θανάτου. In order to grasp transcendent reality, man should die: he should detach himself from the sensible things that are only a shadow of the Forms.

somebody knows the authentic moral values, he will certainly pursue them.[35] The conquest of truth is the main concern of Socrates, because he is persuaded that ethical behavior depends upon this knowledge. Logos or reason is at the very center of Socrates' thought.

In his *Republic* Plato develops a similar doctrine: his notion of the ideal city clearly shows the important part he attributes to reason. In his view passions should not be extirpated, but they are to be submitted to the rule of reason. According to Plato there are in a human soul three parts or levels, which are located in different bodily organs.[36] The supreme faculty, reason, is situated in the head; it should not acquire nor assimilate new objects of knowledge: the role of sensitive perception is not to extend the amount of knowledge but to stimulate the activity of the mind, so that it may discover within itself the truth it is looking for. In this way human intellect is able to contemplate the transcendent Forms or Ideas, the perfect patterns of moral behavior.[37] The virtue that corresponds to this part of the soul is wisdom: a philosopher is not like the prisoners in the cave looking at shadows and believing that they are true reality; through his virtue of wisdom he contemplates the transcendent exemplars; he seems to be estranged from the immediate reality, because he is fascinated by the higher world of true being.[38] The second part, situated in the breast, is called in the Latin tradition the irascible appetite; it represents an emotive power, oriented toward self-defense and self-affirmation. In Plato's ethics the proper virtue of this part is courage, which is an emotional impulse governed by reason: in this way harmony is secured and the impulse is kept within some limits. The third part is located in the belly and is called the concupiscible impulse or desire: its appropriate virtue

35. *Protagoras*, 352c–d. Nothing in man is more valuable and more powerful than true knowledge and wisdom. In Socrates' view nobody sins willingly.

36. *Respubl.*, IV, 441c; 442a–b. In Plato's teaching it is the role of reason to govern the lower parts of the soul: being gifted with wisdom, reason exercises a kind of providence on the other powers. What the philosopher-king should be in the ideal state reason ought to be at the level of each individual human soul.

37. *Respubl.*, VII, 518b–d; *Meno*, 81b; 81c–d. In this context Plato explains the true meaning of education: what is intended is not to put into a subject some knowledge brought from outside; true education consists in turning the eye of the soul to the contemplation of authentic reality.

38. *Respubl.*, V, 476b–d; 479e–480a. People who are unable to distinguish between true reality and some of its imperfect imitations are comparable to those who dream and are convinced to deal with real things.

is temperance. Sophrosyne is a typically Greek attitude: the name indicates that moderation in this area is dictated by the rational faculty.[39] Plato also recognizes the great importance of justice, which is not linked to one single power but safeguards the harmony of all. In this perspective the ideal relationship of reason and passions consists in the supremacy of the intellect over all irrational tendencies: the mind is able to contemplate the highest moral values and should rule the emotions in conformity with these perfect standards. Passions, when they are not governed by reason, drive man to excesses and wrongdoing.

According to Aristotle the conflict between reason and passion is brought to a harmonious solution in the life of a virtuous person. The position of Aristotle with regard to passions and emotions certainly is less negative than the Stoic doctrine: emotions may be submitted to the rule of reason and in this way contribute to the development of human life. Yet the author uses some expressions that recall the Stoic viewpoint: moral virtue is considered to be a kind of impassivity or tranquility with regard to pleasure and pain.[40] However, what the author means is not eradication of emotional impulses but moderation of possible excesses. Passions and emotions are not necessarily evil; some play an important role in the development of human existence. Let us look at some of those that are listed in the *Nicomachean Ethics*[41]; the following passions are mentioned: desire, anger, fear, audacity, envy, joy, friendship, hatred, regret, emulation, and compassion. The objects of desire are mainly food and sexual intercourse; in Aristotle's opinion these emotions should not be extirpated, because they may have a fruitful impact on the evolution of human life. As to friendship and love, they play an essential role in marriage, family life, and other communities, particularly in political societies, which are indispensable in view of man's moral development. Even passions such as anger, fear, and audacity can have a fruitful influence on man's conduct; the same obtains with respect to compassion. The most dangerous passions are jealousy and hatred: they are harmful in themselves and

39. *Respubl.*, IV, 442b–d. With respect to temperance and justice, Plato stresses the fact that they are the same in an individual and in a political community. Concerning justice, the author explains that through this virtue each part fulfills its function with respect to ruling and being ruled.

40. *Eth. Eud.*, II, 4, 1222a2–5.

41. *Eth. Nic.*, II, 5, 1105b21–23; cf. *Rhet.*, II, 2–11.

ought to be suppressed. All the other emotions may be subdued to reason and may contribute to the progress of moral behavior: in this sense passions are not totally irrational; they may be controlled and moderated by reason.[42]

Virtue is a central notion in the ethical treatises of our author: it corresponds to a natural capacity of each individual, and yet it is not merely a gift of nature; it is also the result of exercise and training.[43] Virtue really belongs to the equipment of a moral agent, as something he has conquered through his actions. Not everybody is virtuous: people have to be educated in a political community, under the rule of good laws, if they want to reach moral perfection. Let us look more closely at the proper characteristics of a virtuous individual.

According to Aristotle a virtuous man does not possess only one virtue, such as courage or temperance: he is an individual whose behavior is moral in the various circumstances of life. When technical skills are concerned, special abilities may belong to one craftsman, whereas other capacities belong to another: a good carpenter is not necessarily a skillful mason. This division and separation are not possible in ethical conduct: virtues do not exist independently of each other.[44] Of course, justice does not coincide with practical wisdom, and yet the two virtues may not be considered as totally autonomous attitudes. In the living unity of a particular person virtues are linked to each other, at least when the moral habits have been sufficiently developed. Aristotle distinguishes not only the four traditional virtues but also many subordinate dispositions that are further specifications of the traditional ethical habits. The author agrees that in an initial stage virtues may be separated: all virtues cannot be acquired at once. But in the further evolution and progress of moral life, virtues are connected with each other and cannot

42. *Eth. Nic.*, I, 13, 1102b13–29; 1103a2–4.

43. *Eth. Nic.*, II, 1, 1103a23–26: virtues are not merely present in man by nature, nor are they against nature or unnatural: man is able to acquire them, provided he has been educated by training. In this sense moral conduct is based on nature, yet it is more than nature.

44. *Eth. Nic.*, VI, 13, 1144b30–1145a2: at the level of natural virtues, separation of these habits is possible; not, however, when real moral virtues are concerned. Moral attitudes cannot be totally separated from each other: moral wisdom is implied in other virtues, and in its turn it presupposes the presence of the other ethical habits. With regard to magnanimity, Aristotle declares that it is like a cosmos of virtues (*Eth. Nic.*, IV, 1, 1124a1–3).

be separated.[45] As it has already been explained, moral insight cannot exist independently of the other ethical habits, such as temperance, justice, and courage. If these habits have not been acquired, ethical judgment will go astray under the impact of passions. On the other hand, practical wisdom is required in order to develop the other virtues; it is not possible to behave morally in the various circumstances of life without the guidance of practical wisdom. A prudent man will also be temperate and courageous: these moral habits prevent him from being disturbed in his judgment.[46] Aristotle's view of the connection of virtues is not as radical as it is in Stoic teaching; nevertheless, moral life is regarded as an organic whole, in which the various virtues are mutually dependent. In this context the Aristotelian teaching on magnanimity ought to be mentioned: magnanimity is not just one virtue next to some others; it is not simply one member in a series of moral habits. It actually involves all virtues: it is a cosmos, a harmonious synthesis of all ethical dispositions.[47] Moral life starts from a split, a conflict between reason and passions: through ethical conduct this duality is gradually overcome and brought to harmony and unity. Instead of being the theater of oppositions and struggles a virtuous man comes closer and closer to unity, the harmony of reason governing irrational propensities. This unity is not static but dynamic: it is constantly enhanced by persistent moral behavior. The highest level of this development is magnanimity: a magnanimous individual is characterized by self-affirmation and self-consciousness: he is aware of his ethical condition, since it is a personal conquest, the outcome of many efforts. Possessing all ethical virtues, he realizes the highest

45. In Aristotle's view virtues are gradually acquired by repeatedly performing the same acts (*Eth. Nic.*, II, 1, 1103b21). But how could someone perform an act of virtue without already possessing the habit concerned? According to our author it is possible to accomplish such actions at the suggestion of somebody else (*Eth. Nic.*, II, 4, 1105a23). Therefore, laws ought to be compulsory (*Eth. Nic.*, X, 9, 1180a21–22): through their guidance citizens progressively acquire moral habits.

46. Aristotle believes that the acquisition of moral virtues is in many respects similar to the acquisition of technical skills, yet there is also a basic difference. Technical skills are fully developed when they are able to execute an external performance or product correctly, whereas virtue requires some internal factors, such as knowledge, free choice for the sake of the good, and stability (*Eth. Nic.*, II, 4, 1105a26–b2). Moral virtue belongs to a higher level of perfection than the ability of a craftsman (*Eth. Nic.*, II, 6, 1106b14).

47. *Eth. Nic.*, IV, 3, 1124a1–5.

degree of unity of which humans are capable.[48] This moral unity will be the most adequate incentive for intellectual contemplation, true leisure, and self-sufficiency.

A virtuous individual is a steady person, an agent who does not change easily and without reason his way of behaving. In a sense it is possible to predict how he will behave in the future, because his conduct is in conformity with firmly established habits.[49] Each virtue is a steady disposition: it is not easily acquired, and when it has been achieved, it is not readily lost.[50] A virtuous person is equipped with a series of habits constantly present and yet developing in the course of life; a virtue may become more perfect through appropriate moral actions, but it may also happen that moral habits are weakened through lack of exercise or unethical conduct.[51] Aristotle believes that it is almost impossible to change an individual with inveterate immoral habits.[52] The reason is obvious: a habit is the outcome of many previous acts and is, as it were, part of the structure of an individual. The stability that characterizes a virtuous man has an undeniable ethical value: the conduct of a moral person is coherent; when he accomplishes a moral action, it is not accidentally or by chance, but as a result of an internal disposition that represents a permanent orientation.[53] Therefore, a moral action springing from a firm attitude is particularly worthy: it is not just the act of one moment, a precarious and fugitive intention, but the outcome of all previous conduct. The steadiness of virtue is the expression of a profound conviction: an individual who has acquired a stable moral habit has already performed many similar acts in the past, which

48. J. R. Moncho, *La Unidad de la vida moral según Aristóteles*, Valencia, 1972, p.200–215. Cf. R.-A. Gauthier, *Magnanimité: L'idéal de la grandeur dans la philosophie païenne et dans la théologie chrétienne*, Paris, 1951, p.86.

49. *Eth. Nic.*, II, 4, 1105a32–33: βεβαίως καὶ ἀμετακινήτως ἔχων. It may be noticed that a virtuous individual is at the origin of his own stability, as he is the author of his moral habits; IX, 4, 1166a29; *Eth. Eud.*, III, 1, 1228b30–38. In any case, a virtuous man is unfluctuating.

50. *Eth. Nic.*, II, 4, 1105b4: a moral habit is the outcome of repeatedly (πολλάκις) performed acts of justice, temperance, or other virtues (1105b9–10).

51. *Eth. Nic.*, II, 4, 1105b11–18: Aristotle always insists on the necessity of practice: mere speculation on virtue is not helpful for acquiring moral habits.

52. *Eth. Nic.*, III, 5, 1114a17: when a stone has been thrown, it is no longer possible to recover it. Yet Aristotle believes that an incontinent individual may be cured, although his recovery will be hard (*Eth. Nic.*, VII, 9, 1150b33; VII, 11, 1152a29–31).

53. A moral act implies that the good be chosen for its own sake (*Eth. Nic.*, II, 4, 1105a32).

manifest an intense desire and firm will to behave morally. A virtuous man takes pleasure in performing moral actions: through his training he has acquired abiding habits, which enhance the quality of his ethical conduct and make it more easy and pleasant. In Aristotle's opinion the pleasure that accompanies moral actions is a kind of criterion allowing assessment of the ethical level of an agent: if somebody enjoys refraining from bodily pleasures, he is temperate; if he abstains with reluctance, he is incontinent.[54] The same criterion may be applied in other fields of behavior: a virtuous man takes pleasure in accomplishing virtuous actions. Moral virtues mainly deal with pleasure and pain: if men behave wrongly, it is because they pursue pleasure and try to avoid pain. However, moral education is primarily concerned with pleasure and pain: youths should be educated in such a manner that they enjoy what is good and suffer pain when their conduct is evil.[55] From an early age the emotions of pleasure and pain are to be educated.

Besides, virtue manifests the temporal character of human existence as a whole: morality is not confined to some human actions, whereas others are neutral and amoral, without ethical relevance. On the contrary, morality animates the whole free activity of human beings: man's life is composed of a series of choices or options, which are at the origin of some permanent dispositions.[56] Virtue is not merely a gift of nature; it is the result of many options that have been made in a coherent way.[57] The shaping of a virtuous habit requires much time, because the resistance of irrational tendencies and inclinations is to be overcome in a steady way: hence a moral habit refers not only to an immediate past but to a large period of an individual's existence.[58] The whole past of a person is still active

54. *Eth. Nic.*, II, 3, 1104b3–8; cf. VII, 9, 1151b34–1152a6. With regard to temperance Aristotle distinguishes various degrees of virtue and vice: the highest level is represented by those who are temperate and wise ($\sigma\acute{\omega}\phi\rho\omega\nu$); then follow people who are self-controlled and self-disciplined ($\grave{\epsilon}\gamma\kappa\rho\alpha\tau\acute{\eta}s$). A similar distinction is made in the area of vice: some individuals know what is right but do not perform it because they are overwhelmed by their passions ($\grave{\alpha}\kappa\rho\alpha\tau\acute{\eta}s$), whereas others consciously and deliberately cling to their wrongdoing ($\grave{\alpha}\kappa\acute{o}\lambda\alpha\sigma\tau\sigma s$).

55. *Eth. Nic.*, II, 3, 1104b8–13; II, 3, 1105a10–13; *Eth. Eud.*, II, 4, 1221b37–39.

56. *Eth. Nic.*, II, 4, 1105a31–32. A virtuous action implies knowledge, free choice for the sake of moral virtue, and finally an abiding ethical attitude.

57. *Eth. Nic.*, II, 5, 1106a3: virtues are considered to be free choices, or at least they cannot be generated without free choice.

58. *Eth. Nic.*, II, 4, 1105b4: $\grave{\epsilon}\kappa$ $\tau o\hat{v}$ $\pi o\lambda\lambda\acute{a}\kappa\iota s$ $\pi\rho\acute{a}\tau\tau\epsilon\iota\nu$; II, 1, 1103b21; 1103a31–33.

in the present; in this sense moral life is comparable to the apprenticeship of a technical skill. But it is also different from it because moral behavior is a unitary whole; it requires not only external performances but also internal dispositions; a virtuous person accomplishes what is good because it is good.[59] Man is a temporal and historical being: according to E. Husserl a human subject at each moment experiences not only the present but also the immediate past and the immediate future (Retention, Protention).[60] In this way man is able to grasp a conversation or a musical phrase, a melody. In a conversation all words cannot be pronounced at once; the same obtains in a musical phrase, in which there is a combination and succession of sounds. Understanding a sentence composed of several words or a melody including a series of sounds implies that man is able to combine his knowledge of the present with that of the immediate past and of the nearest future. The act of knowing is not confined to the present; it joins the present to the past and the future; consciousness not only preserves the past but also tends to what will follow. It extends to the future. In the case of humans this extension of consciousness not only comprises the nearest past and future but also refers to more distant periods of time. An act of knowing is integrated into a chain of previous and future acts; it is not isolated as an autonomous unity.[61] The same situation is noticeable in ethical conduct: a virtuous act is the outcome of a present choice, but it involves in a sense the whole past of an agent. If the act were able to speak, it would state, "I am possible because many similar acts preceded me," and since it is an act stemming from a firm disposition it may add that many similar actions may be expected in the future.[62] Virtue manifests human existence as a constant synthesis of past and future with the present.

A virtuous individual is a balanced or harmonious person, an

---

59. *Eth. Nic.*, II, 4, 1105a32: προαιρούμενος δι ᾽αὐτά.

60. H. Spiegelberg, *The Phenomenological Movement; A Historical Introduction, I.* The Hague, 1960, p.148.

61. Man's knowing and willing always integrate a particular object into the background of an all-embracing basic notion and value: such integration ensures the unity of cognitive and volitive life in each individual. Cf. G. Verbeke, *Le développement de la connaissance humaine d'après saint Thomas*, in: *Revue philosophique de Louvain*, 47, 1949, p.437–457; *Le développement de la vie volitive d'après saint Thomas*, in: *Rev. philos. de Louvain*, 56, 1958, p.605–623.

62. Moral virtue is an expression of faithfulness: a virtuous individual, having acquired firm moral habits, demonstrates that he remains faithful to his ethical ideal.

agent who constantly discards excesses, extreme ways of behaving, according to the ancient maxim "Nothing too much." Aristotle focuses attention on the fact that in affections and actions, there can be excesses or deficiencies, as in fear, audacity, desire, anger, and, generally speaking, feelings of pleasure and pain.[63] He does not repudiate these affections; he blames only what is too much or too little.[64] Hence the question: how is it possible to know that a movement of anger or fear is excessive or deficient? The author only provides some general criteria: the mean that is intended is not a mathematical one; a mathematical mean refers to objects, whereas the mean envisaged by Aristotle is related to the agent and his moral conduct.[65] The mean ought to be determined by the mind, which will take into account the agent involved and the circumstances: what is too much for a particular person is not necessarily excessive for all, and what is excessive in certain circumstances is not necessarily excessive in others. It is the responsibility of the mind of the agent to formulate an adequate judgment on the basis of his experience and practice.[66] Let us take the example of courage. It is a balanced disposition located between two extreme attitudes: temerity is an excess that is characterized by too much confidence and too little fear. On the contrary, cowardice shows too much fear and too little confidence. Courage is a mean with regard to the agent and it is fixed by reason, which will not neglect to take into account the particular circumstances of an action. The definition of the mean is very flexible, since each human action is a unique event, inserted into a flowing course of time in which successive situations are never the same.[67] Aristotle's teaching on the mean as an ideal of moral excellence not only refers to Greek cultural tradition but is also related to physiological and medical doctrines. The well-being of

63. *Eth. Nic.*, II, 3, 1104b8–9; 1105a10–13.

64. *Eth. Nic.*, II, 6, 1106b8–14. Virtue always tries to avoid what is excessive or deficient; it constantly pursues what is balanced (1106b15: τοῦ μέσου ἂν εἴη στοχαστική).

65. *Eth. Nic.*, II, 6, 1106b36–1107a2. In this context Aristotle also refers to practical wisdom: in the changing situations of human behavior the mean ought to be determined by a wise person.

66. *Eth. Nic.*, II, 6, 1107a1–2. The mean as a criterion of moral behavior is already present in the work of Plato: *Respubl.*, 359a5–b1; 619a5–6; *Leges*, 792c9–d7; 728d7–729b1. Cf. T. Tracy, *Physiological Theory and the Doctrine of the Mean*, p.77–156.

67. *Eth. Nic.*, III, 6–9. Aristotle tries to describe the exact nature of courage as a mean between two extremes, audacity and cowardice.

the body is described as a blending of hot and cold in due proportion with respect to one another as well as to the surrounding area: opposite elements are brought together to a middle state, to a harmony or a mean. What is noticed in the bodily condition is extended to beauty, to strength, and to all kinds of excellences or deficiencies.[68] If the harmonious blending is disturbed, diseases and other bad consequences will follow. So what has been observed in the condition of the body is extended as a kind of universal law, and it is primarily applied to the field of moral virtue: ethical behavior is also a middle state located between excesses. Emotions quite obviously are inclined to go beyond the frontiers of order and harmony; it is the duty of reason to restore excesses to balance and stability.[69]

Being balanced and harmonious in a steady way, a virtuous individual is a happy person: of course, the future always remains more or less uncertain and unpredictable. But the great privilege of a virtuous agent is to be equipped with steady moral dispositions. In this way the future is secured insofar as possible: the internal conflict between reason and passion is solved in an appropriate way, and that is a warrant for the future. In Aristotle's perspective virtue and happiness are closely linked: happiness means the highest development and perfection of an individual[70]; being equipped with stable moral dispositions, an agent achieves his highest possible perfection. He has actualized in a permanent manner his most noble capacities. This moral attitude also makes it possible to dedicate time and energy to the highest activity of the mind, the contemplation of truth.[71] In Aristotle's view an immoral man cannot be happy: he is a victim of his passions. A virtuous man accomplishes what is good because it is good: his behavior is animated by firm dispositions acquired through previous acts; he is a balanced and reliable person. In the context of Aristotle's thought he represents the highest level of human perfection and happiness.

---

68. *Physica (Phys.)*, VII, 3, 246b4–8; *De Partibus Animalium (De Part. An.)*, I, 7, 652b17–19; *De Generatione Animalium (De Gen. An.)*, 4, 2, 767a16–20.

69. *Eth. Nic.*, II, 6, 1106b14–28.

70. *Eth. Nic.*, I, 7, 1098: Act is more perfect than potency; hence happiness will belong to an act rather than to a potency.

71. *Eth. Nic.*, X, 7, 1177a12–17. In this context Aristotle stresses that intellectual speculation is the most lasting (συνεχεστάτη) of all human activities: a man is able to contemplate in a more lasting way than he is to perform any other activity.

[8]

HUMAN RELATIONS

ONE OF the privileges of human existence is self-knowledge: man not only grasps the surrounding world but is also present to himself; he is constantly aware of his own being among other similar subjects, at a particular place and time in the universe. Being constantly in contact with the outside world, man is at once conscious of the impressions he receives and of his own reactions and activities. Yet self-knowledge is not the result of a direct intuition; if an individual tries to look directly into himself and to seize his internal reality and structure, he will discover nothing. Self-knowledge is the outcome of an indirect process: everybody discovers himself in the development of his activity and in the works he produces. When Aristotle wants to know whether human soul is immortal, he does not directly scrutinize the essence of this principle; he analyzes its activity. His conclusion is negative because there is not a single activity of the soul that is entirely independent of the corporeal organism.[1] The same obtains with respect to cultural activities: whether they are philosophical speculations, works of art or literature, scientific discoveries, or technical performances, they all uncover the distinctive nature and capacities of human individuals. Through the progress of science and culture, man more adequately realizes what he is and what he is able to achieve. Each

---

1. *De anima*, I, 1, 403a3–25. The question asked is whether human soul can continue to exist after death; in other words, can the soul ever exist without being linked to the body? The criterion used to answer this question has been invented by Aristotle: if the soul is able to perform some activity independently of the body, then it is able to exist without the body. If it is totally unable to exert any activity when separated from the body, then it must perish. The implicit background of this argument is quite clear: the existence of human soul is believed to be impossible if the soul is unable to perform any activity. In Aristotle's opinion the substantial form is regarded as a principle of an appropriate activity.

human performance contributes to a better knowledge of its author: man gradually discovers his specific capabilities in his own works.

According to Epicurus man is entirely the creator of his cultural achievements: progress is not a divine gift; it is effected through human efforts and ingenuity.[2] The author does not deny the existence of divine beings, but they stay far away from human affairs and are not concerned with them; prayers and offerings to gods are useless: gods never interfere in the activity and strivings of human beings; they are only concerned with their own quiet and undisturbed existence.[3] This viewpoint represents a denial of the Greek mythological tradition, according to which divinities frequently intervene in the affairs of man. Lucretius, in reproducing the teaching of Epicurus, extensively describes in his *De rerum natura* how civilization gradually developed from a very primitive stage to the situation of his own time, when a series of important discoveries had already been achieved. This general survey of the evolution as it is expounded is different from the Stoic interpretation[4]: according to the Stoics, the development as a whole is a gradual decline, starting from a kind of initial paradise; at the beginning of mankind humans lived in a much more happy and moral condition than they did in later periods. In their opinion moral decline is always continuing: when it has reached its lowest level, then the cosmic cycle will come to an end; the world will pass away and a new cycle will start, showing the same evolution from better to worse.[5] On the contrary, the interpretation of Epicurus is characterized by a gradual progress: primitive men were in a very poor condition; their life and behavior were almost as those of irrational animals.[6]

2. *De rerum natura*, V, 1448–1457.

3. C. Bailey, *The Greek Atomists and Epicurus*, Oxford, 1928, p.475–476. Epicureanism means an important step in the development of individual consciousness. The whole evolution of human civilization is fully attributed to man himself: he is considered to be the author of his destiny, he makes himself to what he is, he creates his own world. In this perspective civilization becomes gradually more and more perfect.

4. G. Verbeke, *Les Stoïciens et le progrès de l'histoire*, in: *Revue philosophique de Louvain*, 62(1964), p.5–38.

5. G. Verbeke, *Les Stoïciens et le progrès de l'histoire*, p.7–14. The Stoic interpretation of the development of mankind is closely connected with their moral system: if the great majority of the people live in a state of moral degradation or insanity, a gradual decline of civilization is inevitable. In this context the development of history cannot be viewed as a constant progression.

6. *De rerum natura*, V, 931–932. Within the same context humans are called "miserable mortal beings" (*miseris mortalibus*, V, 944).

They had no openness toward other individuals: they were, as it were, locked within themselves and were only concerned with themselves; there was no true communication between these primitive beings, who were unable to envisage common good and had no customs or laws regulating their mutual relations. In order to subsist, everybody seized the prey he could capture on his way and used it for himself, without taking into account the needs of others.[7] Similar behavior was demonstrated in sexual intercourse: women were driven to sexual relations either through their own desire, or through constraint by violence or passion of males, or through seduction by the promise of some reward.[8]

What is lacking according to this description is a fundamental feature of human existence, called in contemporary philosophy intersubjectivity or communication with other individuals. Man is able to understand other subjects, to talk with them, and to love them. According to Aristotle, as we have already mentioned, man is by nature a social being; he is naturally inclined to live in a community with other humans; he even needs such a community in order to reach his perfection, the actualization of his capacities.[9] The main arguments expounded by the Stagirite in order to support his view refer to language and moral sense: humans are able to speak with each other and possess a natural understanding of moral values; on the basis of an agreement on moral issues and rules a political community is possible.[10] The teaching of Epicurus is different; what he describes as the most primitive stage of civilization is in fact a prehuman condition: an animal living within itself and for itself, without communication with other animals, without concern with others, cannot be called a human being. True, the specifically human

7. *De rerum natura*, V, 958: "Nec commune bonum poterant spectare neque ullis moribus inter se scibant nec legibus uti." The sense of common good, expressed in laws regulating mutual relations, is considered to be the basis of political society.

8. *De rerum natura*, V, 962–965. What Lucretius (Epicurus) intends to stress is that sexual relations at this early stage were not invested with a specific human character or meaning.

9. *Politica*, I, 2, 1253a2. If somebody is asocial by nature, not merely by accident, he must be either less perfect or more perfect than a human being. Divine beings do not need the help of a political community in order to attain their perfection.

10. *Politica*, I, 2, 1253a14–18. Nature does nothing in vain; the works of nature are oriented toward an end, which is the good. If nature endowed man with the capacity of speaking and with moral insight, it must be to some end: man has been prepared to live in a political society; it is only in this social context that he is able to attain his full development.

characteristics will, according to Epicurus, develop later: are they already present in the primitive beings described by Lucretius? They can hardly be present if they do not manifest themselves in daily conduct, but if they are not present, how can they ever appear in a later stage of development? Apparently what Epicurus wants to show is that the whole process of growing civilization is an invention of man.

The next stage shows the dawn of human behavior: instead of living in forests as wild beasts, men started building houses; in this way humans were linked to a firm residence, where men lived with their wife and children. At this stage of evolution monogamy was introduced; instead of having sexual intercourse with several women, every man had his own wife. Monogamy means a special relationship between one man and one woman: it is a decisive step from prehuman conditions to a human way of life.[11] Hence the building of houses is not something contingent and unimportant: it represents considerable progress with respect to marriage and family life because husband and wife live together with their children, who are educated by both parents. In connection with this stage of evolution Epicurus further mentions the use of animal furs for clothing and the use of fire. In Greek tradition the invention of fire was connected with the myth of Prometheus, in the poem of Lucretius the story is demythologized; the use of fire has been discovered by man himself. Fire was utilized for heating and it was also the origin of important technical skills. As to clothing, it manifested a distinctive characteristic of man compared to other animals: man uses skins of other animals to protect himself, but also to manifest his own worth among other living beings. Progressively man becomes conscious of his prerogatives and proper dignity.[12]

At this stage humans became gradually less and less rude: living with their families in houses, they had some contacts with neighbors and initiated relations of friendship with them; they tried to avoid acts of violence among them and in this way endeavored to protect

---

11. *De rerum natura*, V, 1011–1018. According to the picture of Lucretius family life has been invented by man himself: he progressively brought himself from polygamy to monogamy. In this way man made his way of life more and more different from that of irrational animals; the building of houses and the introduction of monogamy are considered to be important steps in this respect.

12. The use of clothes in its turn manifests the distinctive nature of humans toward other animals: man gradually promotes himself to the master of the material world.

their wives and children. Thus instead of opposing and fighting
with their neighbors, they made agreements and carefully kept them.
In fact, this community of neighboring families was an extension
of each of them: these families living near to each other endeavored
to protect the most vulnerable individuals.[13] Language had not yet
been invented; nevertheless, people attempted to communicate with
each other through gestures and sounds, showing that it was right
to have pity for people who are weak. Lucretius states that such
agreements did not exist everywhere, but a great part of mankind
made such contracts and respected them. In this perspective communities were initiated by men belonging to neighboring families in
order to protect their wives and children: at this stage we already
notice a link of friendship, not only within the framework of a
particular family but also among several families. Yet not being able
to use language, humans could only communicate in a vague and
confused way: they could not express clearly what they desired
and even less adequately why they wanted an agreement among
families.[14]

The invention of language represented a decisive step in human
relations. According to Epicurus language originates both from
nature and from the needs of daily life: in each individual there is
a spontaneous propensity to utter some sounds, as there is in variable
circumstances of time a need to refer to particular objects. In his
everyday life man needs several kinds of things in his environment:
hence the tendency to designate them through particular names.
Epicurus firmly repudiates the view attributing the invention of
names to one individual, from whom all other people learned the

---

13. *De rerum natura*, V, 1019–1023:

> Tunc et amicitiem coeperunt iungere aventes
> finitimi inter se nec laedere nec violari,
> et pueros commendarunt muliebreque saeclum,
> vocibus et gestu cum balbe significarent
> imbecillorum esse aecum misererier omnis.

Friendship among neighbors and concerns with the weakest members of the families
are regarded as a development toward a more human way of life.

14. *De rerum natura*, V, 1024–1027. According to Lucretius humans were spontaneously driven to found communities larger than separate families: this need developed from a growing awareness that families were not always able to protect their
members adequately. Even before humans were able to speak with each other and
to express their needs in language, they had already started bringing families together
into a larger community.

vocabulary.[15] It could never be explained why one particular person had received the privilege of designating things by names: other people also are able to give names to concrete objects. Moreover, no single person could ever constrain others to use the names he had invented, nor could he ever teach them to other people against their will.[16] Therefore, language does not originate from a particular individual; it springs from mankind as a whole: a common creation of all humans. A kind of language is already noticeable at the level of irrational animals: the author mentions examples of dogs, horses, and birds. They utter some sounds in conformity with their sensations; different sounds refer to different sensations.[17] This corresponds on a lower level to what humans do: by using different names they refer to different things in the surrounding world.[18]

The use of language made larger communities possible; however, when people came together and founded political societies, everybody wanted to seize power and to rule over the others. This situation became unbearable. At that time a select group of people persuaded the others to elect responsible magistrates and to establish some principles of law.[19] In a political community laws are an important factor, ensuring stability, order, and harmony[20]: the formulation of laws is made possible by language. Laws also express agreement among members of a community on some basic moral maxims.

15. *De rerum natura*, V, 1041:

> Proinde putare aliquem tum nomina distribuisse
> rebus et inde homines didicisse vocabula prima,
> desiperest.

16. *De rerum natura*, V, 1043–1055. Lucretius strongly emphasizes that the invention of language was the result of a common effort and endeavor of all humans: they all felt the same needs and were gifted with the same capacities. Thus all humans were involved in the progressive creation of their civilization.

17. *De rerum natura*, V, 1059–1086. Lucretius does not suggest that human language was the result of a natural evolution from the sounds uttered by irrational animals: he only points to some degree of similarity between the sounds of animals and human speech. Humans are able to invent language as they are gifted with reason.

18. *De rerum natura*, V, 1087–1090. In Lucretius' view language was initially created in order to designate some objects of the sensible world.

19. *De rerum natura*, V, 1141–1144. At this stage the use of language becomes much more comprehensive and shaded: words refer not only to sensible things but to moral principles.

20. *De rerum natura*, V, 1152–1155. An agreement on laws is the basis of any political community: laws express the rules according to which society will be organized.

In this context the invention of religious worship is to be mentioned: according to Epicurus it was a deplorable and disastrous initiative. Religion is considered to be mainly a creation of imagination: people introduced divine beings, because they believed they observed them in their imagination, particularly in their dreams. They were convinced they perceived all kinds of higher beings more perfect than humans; impressed by their beauty and power, they regarded them as immortal.[21] On the other hand, people also observed the beauty of the heavenly bodies—their perfect and immutable harmony, their wonderful movements, the regular return of seasons—and they spontaneously believed that all those marvels of nature could not be attributed to accident; in their opinion they were caused and governed by divine beings, living in heaven.[22] In fact, divine beings were invented because people ignored the real causes of things: religion was the result of ignorance. When gods had been introduced, people started worshipping them; in this way religious cult was created. It was a calamity[23]: true piety has no relation to the veneration of gods; it is the capacity of considering everything with an undisturbed mind.[24] Instead of peace and quietness, religion originated constant anguish and fear: ignoring the true causes of things, humans were always disturbed and disquiet; they were full of anxiety with respect to their behavior because they imagined that they could be severely punished by the gods. They felt anguish when a tempest or an earthquake arose; wanting to appease the so-called anger of the divinities, they had recourse to useless prayers. Instead of searching the true causes of things, people

21. *De rerum natura*, V, 1169–1171. Lucretius (Epicurus) does not deny the existence of divine beings, but in his view they have nothing to do with humans or with the ruling of the universe. What the author criticizes is the way in which humans have interpreted the nature, function, and activity of divine beings: he considers these beliefs totally worthless.

22. *De rerum natura*, V, 1183–1193. In Epicurus' opinion the whole universe, including the harmonious movements of heavenly bodies, is the result of accidental meetings of atoms.

23. *De rerum natura*, V, 1194:

> O genus infelix humanum, talia divis
> cum tribuit facta atque iras adiunxit acerbas!

Humans attributed to gods what was, in fact, the outcome of their own work.

24. *De rerum natura*, V, 1203: "sed mage pacata posse omnia mente tueri." In Epicurean teaching the tranquility of the mind represents the highest degree of happiness.

lived in a mood of unrest without any reason: as a result of their religious practice they became victims of their imagination; they lost their identity and the awareness of their real dignity.[25]

In this survey of Lucretius there is an important view regarding the topic of human relations: man evolved from a prehuman condition to that of a civilized existence and behavior: this evolution is closely connected with the growing openness toward other individuals, first in monagamous marriage and family life, then in friendship with neighboring families, further in political communities governed by laws. The creation of language and the establishment of laws and justice made these larger societies possible. Through his contacts with other people man discovered his identity and dignity.

According to Aristotle man is by nature a social animal: the author does not speak of a prehuman stage, in which men were like animals, without friendship, mutual concern, and reciprocal understanding. It is characteristic of human beings to be endowed with reason and moral sense, and yet all humans are not gifted with these privileges to the same extent. Some individuals are slaves by nature[26]; are they still in a kind of prehuman stage of development? Not exactly, because they are actually endowed with reason, able to communicate with other individuals, but their rational capacity is very limited. Therefore, they constantly need the assistance of others to be directed in their life and conduct.[27] Did not Aristotle realize that slavery is in conflict with the dignity of a human being, a dignity that ought to be respected by all other individuals? The teaching of the Stagirite is to be understood in the framework of Greek society in the fourth century and in the light of the truth value that the

25. *De rerum natura*, V, 1218–1240. Ignorance of the causes is a source of mental disturbance: "Temptat enim dubiam mentem rationis egestas" (V, 1211). According to Lucretius lack of understanding is harmful: people imagine all kinds of dangers threatening their existence. Religious worship is a typical example of this situation: people implore the help of divine beings because they do not understand the real causes of the universe.

26. *Politica*, I, 5, 1255a1–3. In Aristotle's opinion it is beneficial and right for some individuals to be slaves; they need the direction and guidance of other persons. Left to themselves they are unable to develop a responsible course of behavior.

27. *Politica*, I, 5, 1254b20–23. Part of the people are considered to be unable to assume the responsibility for their life; this situation is regarded as a social fact which cannot be put into question. Does this condition fit into the teleological interpretation of the universe? Apparently this question does not bother Aristotle: those who are slaves by nature have to be directed by other people; they have to fulfill in society the function they are able to achieve.

author attributes to prephilosophical opinions. Slavery was considered to be a very ancient institution, which was universally approved; prephilosophical opinions are regarded by Aristotle as almost natural knowledge. He excludes the possibility that these beliefs can be merely false.[28] Philosophical reflection is mostly a critical investigation of such opinions; in the case of slavery also the author critically studies the tradition of his time and the convictions of his contemporaries. In this way he arrives at a philosophical doctrine that considerably restricts this social institution.[29]

In Aristotle's view slavery is a natural subordination: as political society corresponds to a natural inclination of human beings, so slavery conforms to nature, which is always oriented toward the good.[30] However, it would be false to conclude that all those who are effectively slaves are also slaves by nature and are naturally subordinated to other individuals[31]: the author only maintains that at least some humans are slaves by nature, since they are unable to assume the responsibility of their own behavior and life fully. Did Aristotle not attribute this deficiency to a lack of education? Did he not consider the possibility of educating those people and carrying them to a higher level of rationality and responsibility?[32] Apparently the author did not envisage this possibility, probably because the capacity of learning also depends on the degree of rational thinking; if this degree is very low, the capacity of being educated will also be small. According to the Greek Master his teaching on slavery is quite justified and includes nothing exceptional: subordination is found everywhere in nature. Man himself is compounded of body and soul; according to nature the soul commands, whereas the body obeys and is subdued. If the body commands, such an individual will inevitably be corrupted and perverted, as the soul belongs to a

28. G. Verbeke, *Philosophie et conceptions préphilosophiques chez Aristote*, p.424–430.
29. *Politica*, I, 3, 1253b17. Aristotle wants to improve the current attitudes of his time (λαβεῖν βέλτιον τῶν νῦν ὑπολαμβανομένων). He knows that some people oppose slavery and regard it as unjust (1253b20–23): in their opinion, the distinction between free citizens and slaves would originate only from legal rules, not from nature; therefore, it would be compulsory and wrong.
30. *Politica*, I, 5, 1254b16–20. Aristotle believes that the difference among humans is comparable to the one between body and soul, or between men and animals. The capacity of some humans is confined to the use of the body.
31. *Politica*, I, 6, 1255a5–7. According to ancient legal rules whatever is conquered during a war becomes the property of the victor. Thus prisoners of war are reduced to the condition of slaves, whatever their intellectual capacities may be.
32. In Aristotle's view laws are concerned with the education of people for the common good (*Eth. Nic.*, V, 2, 1130b25–26).

higher level than the body. The soul rules over the body with the authority of a master toward his slaves, whereas the intellect governs the emotional movements with the authority of a political ruler or king.[33] According to this statement the difference between a slave and a master is comparable to the one between body and soul. Human soul is gifted with reason, whereas the body is irrational; slaves are put at the level of the body, not at that of emotional movements.[34] The reason is that emotions and passions are in the soul; they are part of it, whereas the body is distinct from the soul. A slave is comparable to the body; he is a tool: the master uses his slaves like animated tools. This analogy cannot be applied to passions, which are irrational movements present within the soul.[35] Man is by definition a rational animal: all other animals, which are not endowed with reason, are naturally subordinated to man. This relation especially obtains in the case of domestic animals, which are superior to wild beasts. Consequently it is a privilege of domestic animals to be subjugated to man[36]; in the same way it is a benefit for slaves to follow the direction of their master. Finally Aristotle mentions in this context the natural subordination of women to men[37]: this opinion corresponds to the social condition of women in the fourth century B.C. and to widespread convictions at that time. The author considers the rational activity of women to be on a lower level, since their behavior is strongly influenced by emotional factors.

33. *Politica*, I, 5, 1254a28–36. What Aristotle wants to show above all is that the subordination of slaves is not against nature; on the contrary, it corresponds to nature.

34. *Politica*, I, 5, 1254b4–10. The body is subdued to the rule of the soul: in Aristotle's view this situation is beneficial for the whole. It would be totally awkward if the soul were submitted to the body: the soul is by nature superior to the body, and this superiority cannot be disregarded. There is in Aristotle a principle of natural subordination: "In all organic nature the lower or less perfect is *subordinated to*, ordered to assist or serve, the higher and more perfect. In the world of nature as well as of art the lower always exists for the higher" (1333a22–23) (T. Tracy, *Physiological Theory and the Doctrine of the Mean*, p.287).

35. *Politica*, I, 4, 1253b32–33. According to Aristotle, ὁ δοῦλος κτῆμά τι ἔμψυχον. A master may possess many inanimate properties or tools: slaves are not on the same level as those, since they are living beings.

36. *Politica*, I, 5, 1254b10–13. It is a privilege of domestic animals to be ruled by man. The same obtains in the case of slaves: far from being harmful, it is a benefit for them to be directed by their master; in this way their well-being is ensured.

37. *Politica*, I, 5, 1254b13–14. A different doctrine has been initiated by the Stoics: in their view men and women are equal. This new teaching was mainly based on metaphysical considerations: a particle of the divine Logos is present in all human beings, including women.

Consequently it is not an exceptional fact in nature that some beings are subordinated to others. But the difficulty in Aristotle's view is to specify the degree of subordination that is required in the case of slaves; should this subordination be a total one? Aristotle's answer is quite formal: if the difference between a slave and his master is comparable to the one that exists between body and soul, or between man and beast, then slavery is fully consistent with nature.[38] One may wonder whether such a situation actually exists. Aristotle believes that it happens: the activity of some individuals is confined to using their body, nothing more. They are capable of implementing instructions given by others, but they are not able to decide their own behavior and way of life: it is a benefit for them to be guided by others.[39]

However, Aristotle recognizes that there are many slaves who do not belong to this category, who were reduced to slavery as a result of war, because they had been captured and became the property of the conquerors. At that time this practice conformed to positive law: the author wonders whether such a ruling is right.[40] It is true that the conqueror is physically and morally superior to the defeated; one may draw the conclusion that the conqueror has the right to reduce the defeated to slavery.[41] The author, however, hesitates to accept this viewpoint: a war may be unjust; in this case the defeated should not be constrained to become slaves. Moreover, it cannot be right to enslave somebody who does not deserve it. Natural slavery is confined to those whose rational capacity is very low.[42]

In Aristotle's view a slave is fully the property of the master, comparable to an animated object.[43] The human dimension is not taken into account: a slave belongs totally to his master, who decides

38. *Politica*, I, 5, 1254b16–20. Dealing with the relationship between a husband and his wife, Aristotle stresses the fact that friendship between the two is not one of equality, but of superiority (καθ᾽ ὑπεροχήν); man is superior to his spouse (*Eth. Nic.*, VIII, 7, 1158b11–13). However, both should remain faithful to each other (*Eth. Nic.*, II, 5, 1107a11–17; V, 2, 1130a29; 1131a6; V, 6, 1134a19–22).

39. A slave participates in reason as he is able to perceive rational instructions and implement them, without properly possessing the rational faculty (*Politica*, I, 5, 1254b22).

40. *Politica*, I, 6, 1255a21–24.

41. *Politica*, I, 6, 1255a7–21.

42. *Politica*, I, 6, 1255a24–31. Aristotle does not yield to some practices and customary uses of his time: he carefully maintains his doctrine on the criterion allowing the conclusion that somebody is a slave by nature.

43. *Politica*, I, 4, 1253b32–33.

how to use him.[44] It is the proper duty of a slave to obey his master, what is regarded as a privilege. If a slave were left to himself, he would behave in an irrational way and would be the first victim of his conduct. This teaching of Aristotle does not mean that a master may use his slaves as he likes; in his relations with slaves a master ought to behave as a virtuous person. If not everything is allowed with respect to slaves, it is not because of their human dignity, but because the master in all circumstances has to live in conformity with moral values. According to Aristotle a slave is a servant in terms of actions[45]; the author speaks of praxis, not of poiesis. The latter is a productive activity, oriented toward the work that is effected; this activity does not contain the end of the work that is achieved; the activity of a mason or a carpenter is oriented toward the result that is produced. Praxis is different: it does not tend toward something that is effected, something that does not coincide with the action; the activity inherently involves its end, and the end coincides with the performance of the act. A moral action does not intend an external result; it finds its end within itself.[46] The subject intends to behave in conformity with moral values, nothing more; he certainly does not pursue some benefit or reward. A virtuous man accomplishes what is good because it is good, with no other goal. When the author mentions praxis in his discussion of slavery, he does not envisage the activity of slaves but that of masters. These masters want to free themselves as much as possible from domestic affairs; therefore, they appoint a superintendent to take care of the material interests of a family. In this way a master is able to dedicate his time and energy to politics and philosophy.[47] As has already

44. *Politica*, I, 4, 1254a11–13: a slave totally belongs to his master (ὅλως ἐκείνου). A part entirely belongs to the whole of which it is a part; the same obtains in the case of slaves, who are like parts of their master.

45. *Politica*, I, 4, 1254a8.

46. *Eth. Nic.*, VI, 5, 1140b7. Aristotle frequently insists on the difference between making (ποίησις) and praxis (πρᾶξις). When the author deals with the acquisition of moral habits, he repeatedly makes a comparison with learning technical skills: these skills are also abiding habits that have been acquired by training. Yet there is also an important difference since technical skills aim at producing some effect that does not coincide with the act, whereas moral actions do not pursue an end that is distinct from the action itself.

47. *Politica*, I, 7, 1255b33–37. Aristotle wants to free masters from taking care of slaves and commanding them in the work they should perform. The ability of using slaves concerns only the daily household: it involves nothing noble or lofty and will not contribute to promoting the perfection and happiness of a master.

been mentioned, manual labor is not highly valued by Aristotle; it is not considered to be a means to attaining the end of life, the full development of man's capacities. Such labor does not lift the level of human life; rather it lowers it: it harms the body and it does not develop the mind. Hence it is preferable to entrust slaves with this kind of work.[48] On the contrary, intellectual activity represents the highest degree of human perfection; political activity also increases the worth of existence, since the laws of a state are necessary in view of the moral life of its members.

Aristotle wonders whether a link of friendship may ever exist between a master and his slave. The answer is shaded: if the condition of a particular slave is not derived from nature but from man-made regulation and from violence, then a relation of friendship is impossible. On the contrary, if somebody is a slave by nature, a community of interest and even a relationship of friendship are possible. In the first case a slave will oppose his master, because he will consider his situation unjust, whereas in the latter he will feel supported and helped by his master.[49] Moreover, Aristotle asks whether a relation of justice exists between a master and his slave: the answer is negative. There is neither justice nor friendship with respect to animals; insofar as a slave is slave, he is property and a tool of his master; from this viewpoint justice and friendship are excluded.[50] But insofar as a slave is a human being, it is possible to have a relationship of friendship with him.

According to I. Kant three fundamental principles govern moral conduct: the second prescribes respect for each human being, for the agent as well as the others, which means respect for oneself and for other individuals.[51] In Kant's view each human being represents an absolute value: it does not conform to the moral idea to use another person as a means; a human being may not be subdued to an end that is different from himself: each person is an end in

48. *Eth. Eud.*, I, 4, 1215a26–32.

49. *Eth. Nic.*, VIII, 11, 1161b3–8; *Politica*, I, 6, 1255b12–15.

50. *Eth. Nic.*, VIII, 11, 1161a32–b3. In Aristotle's view friendship always requires something common to the two individuals who are friends. There is no friendship between a craftsman and his tool, nor between soul and body: insofar as a slave is a tool of his master, no relationship of friendship between them is possible.

51. I. Kant, *Grundlegung zur Metaphysik der Sitten* (ed. K. Vorländer), Hamburg, 1957, p.52: "Handle so, dass du die Menschheit, sowohl in deiner Person als in der Person eines jeden anderen, jederzeit zugleich als Zweck, niemals bloss als Mittel brauchst."

himself, never only a means.[52] This doctrine of Kant's is illustrated by his teaching on the immortality of human soul. Life is not finished at the moment of one's death; it goes on indefinitely: humans have an eternal destiny, a future without any temporal limitation. If everybody possesses such a destiny, an individual constitutes an absolute value. However, the German philosopher acknowledges that theoretical reason is unable to demonstrate the immortality of the soul, as it is unable to prove the existence of God. Theoretical reason is limited in its activity: it applies a priori forms to sensible data. In Kant's view the immortality of the soul is a demand of practical reason, mainly of moral obligation. A moral imperative cannot be absolute if human existence does not indefinitely continue after death: reward and punishment of ethical conduct ought to be unlimited. In each person there is a factor that guarantees an absolute value, namely goodwill, which is present in everybody according to various degrees. Goodwill pursues what is good insofar as it is good; it is not oriented toward any different goal but only toward the good. In all circumstances and situations it intends what is good and endeavors to accomplish it. This orientation is to be regarded as an absolute value, which cannot be subdued to anything else; therefore, one ought to respect each person and promote in everybody the goodwill that leads to moral progress.

Obviously there is quite a difference between Kant's moral principles and Aristotle's teaching on slavery: the absolute value of each human person is not maintained by the Stagirite.[53] And yet what he did regarding slavery constituted important progress: his distinction between slaves by nature and slaves by accidents of war is a decisive one; it means that nobody who is able to assume the responsibility for his life ought to be a slave. Aristotle's doctrine certainly prepared the way for the teaching of the Stoics, stating that nobody could be a slave by nature since everybody participates in Divine Reason.

---

52. I. Kant, *Grundlegung*, p.50.

53. In contemporary society the question of human rights is a very important issue. It is little treated by Aristotle since it was not a problem in the context of Greek culture. This question became more and more crucial within the framework of the absolutist states that developed in modern Western history (Cf. W. Kullmann, *Die politische Philosophie des Aristoteles*, in: *Antike Rechts- und Sozialphilosophie*, ed. O. Gigon and M. W. Fischer, Frankfurt a.M., Bern, New York, Paris, 1988, p.77). Yet Aristotle acknowledges that some natural link and propensity unite all humans (*Eth. Nic.*, VIII, 1, 1155a21–22).

The philosophical study of friendship represents an important part of Aristotle's ethics: the *Nicomachean Ethics* comprises ten books, two of them dedicated to this topic. Why the central position of this issue in a moral treatise? In Greek society friendship was practiced in various ways, and it was carefully studied by philosophers, who endeavored to give it a moral meaning. One of Plato's dialogues, the *Lysis,* is devoted to the same subject; the author tries to disclose the basis of this inclination driving men to establish friendly relations with others.[54] According to Aristotle friendship is a virtue, or at least it cannot be realized without virtue.[55] The author deals with true friendship, which can only exist between virtuous persons. What is the meaning of this rather surprising position? Considering the way in which friendship was practiced in Greek society, one cannot maintain that it always involved virtuous behavior: the love of boys could hardly be regarded as a model of ethical conduct. Aristotle, however, does not intend to write a sociology treatise, although he always wants to start his inquiry from the concrete situation of his time. The author is certainly acquainted with the various forms of friendship in his time, but his main concern is to bring this social phenomenon to a higher level: he endeavors to transform friendship into a stimulating factor in social life, from family to political community. Man is by nature a social being: it is necessary for him to live in a political society ruled by good laws in order to reach the full development of his capacities and true happiness. But there are among men many causes of disagreements, oppositions, conflicts: stable unions and cooperation are not easy. In this context Aristotle attributes to friendship a moral dimension: it makes stable unions possible, and these are indispensable for the development of human life.[56] Marriage and family life are

54. *Lysis,* 212a. In order to disclose the true nature of friendship Socrates turns first to the poets: they are the fathers of wisdom and the guides of the people (214a). Socrates, like Plato, is quite conscious of the deep influence exercised by poets in Greek education. Socrates does not intend to assimilate their teaching uncritically; he rather takes their viewpoint as the start of a truly philosophical and critical investigation.

55. *Eth. Nic.,* VIII, 1, 1155a3–4. Declaring that friendship is a virtue or implies virtue, Aristotle immediately adds that it is quite necessary to human life. It is this second aspect that is immediately explained and justified by the author: man needs friends in order to reach the full development of his life. The moral dimension of friendship is sufficiently clear, as friendship is oriented toward the true self of another individual.

56. According to Aristotle friendship is indispensable for human life: ἀναγκαιότατον εἰς τὸν βίον (*Eth. Nic.,* VIII, 1, 1155a4–5). In all ages of life it is an important benefit (1155a5–16).

based on mutual friendship; small groups of neighboring families are also joined by friendship; as to the large community of a political society, it cannot be held together without friendship.[57] In this way friendship is a virtue: it is not the result of irrational emotions and passions; it is achieved only by balanced, moral individuals.[58] In addition, it makes moral life possible: without a well-ordered political society education and ethical conduct cannot be achieved. Moral behavior is essential in human life: the practice of true friendship is a considerable contribution to the ethical growth of many individuals.

In Aristotle's view friendship is an extension of self-love. All humans are naturally inclined to love themselves: as a philosopher the Stagirite endeavors to specify the object of this love; in his view what is concerned is the true self, the real core of a human being.[59] Self-knowledge is also recommended by Greek religion: man should always be aware of his limits. In Aristotle's ethics the perspective is different: the author does not merely reproduce prephilosophical opinions; he wants to know what is the center of a person, what makes an animal a human being. The author is very cautious in his position; seemingly humanness mainly corresponds to the mind.[60] Undoubtedly the mind is the most noble power of an individual. And yet Aristotle's statement cannot mean that the mind alone constitutes a person; in this case, self-love would coincide with love of one's mind. In Aristotle's view the mind involves and includes other faculties: as a matter of fact, intellectual activity is not possible without sensible experience; even self-knowledge depends upon sense perception. The thesis that was later maintained by Avicenna,

57. Legislators attach more importance to friendship than to justice: friendship favors agreement and concord among members of a political society and avoids oppositions and conflicts, which are mostly harmful to the well-being of the citizens (*Eth. Nic.*, VIII, 1, 1155a21–28). Aristotle strongly recommends faithfulness in marriage: the relationship between a husband and his wife should be regulated in conformity with the ideal of justice (*Eth. Nic.*, VIII, 12, 1162a29–33).

58. *Eth. Nic.*, VIII, 1, 1155a28–31. In this context Aristotle refers to common opinions: people who have many friends are generally considered to be good people.

59. *Eth. Nic.*, IX, 8, 1168b33–35; 1169a11: in Aristotle's teaching a virtuous man ought to be animated by self-love (δεῖ φίλαυτον εἶναι), in the sense that he strives toward the development and perfection of his true self. In Stoic thought οἰκείωσις, or appropriation of the self, is the origin of the whole moral life.

60. *Eth. Nic.*, X, 7, 1178a2; IX, 8, 1169a2–3. Aristotle declares that man is identical with the mind or at least that he mainly coincides with it; in any case, the mind is regarded as the most noble part of a human subject, representing the central principle of a person. The author adds that a moral individual is most firmly attached to this thinking power (μάλιστα τοῦτ' ἀγαπᾷ).

that self-knowledge is possible without sensible experience, would certainly be repudiated by the Stagirite.[61] All intellectual understanding is based on sensible perception; it is achieved by assimilation of an intelligible object, which proceeds from a phantasm. The mind is not an autonomous faculty, operating by itself and independent of the other powers.[62] Moreover, sensitive faculties are related to the bodily organism and cannot exert their activity without it: the body also is required for the activity of the mind. As has been explained, man is a compounded but unitary being: prime matter does not exist in itself and independently. Even the organic structure of the body stems from the soul, and this psychic principle cannot implement its activity without the body. A human being is a unitary compound in which the mind plays a decisive part, as it differentiates man from other animals. In this sense man coincides with his mind: this is the principle of thought, of scientific and philosophical inquiry; the principle also of speech, which is closely related to thought; the principle of deliberation, which governs human action, moral and political conduct. Summarizing, we may conclude that the mind is the real center of each individual; any dualistic interpretation, however, is to be rejected. A moral man loves himself: he chiefly loves his true self, the mind. Friendship is an extension of this love: a virtuous man loves the true self of the others, without excluding the other components of a person.[63] His love is not mainly oriented to the body of the others, for example, of boys: in this case, the heart of the other person is never the object. A virtuous man loves in others what he truly loves in himself: the real core of a human being.

61. *Avicenna Latinus! Liber De anima IV–V*. Édition critique par S. Van Riet, Introduction doctrinale par G. Verbeke, Louvain-Leyden, 1968, p.23*–25*.

62. Intellectual knowledge always derives from sensory data; but not only in its origin but also in its exercise intellectual activity constantly depends on the cooperation of sensitive knowing. In the exercise of theoretical knowing a sensible image must be grasped (*De anima*, III, 8, 432a7–9). This aspect of cognitive activity is important with respect to Aristotle's view of the unity of man, which is manifested in every act of understanding, as it is never merely intellectual but is always combined with sensitive perception. Cf. T. Tracy, *Physiological Theory and the Doctrine of the Mean*, p.262.

63. *Eth. Nic.*, IX, 4, 1166a31: ἔστι γὰρ ὁ φίλος ἄλλος αὐτός; IX, 9, 1169b7; 1170b6; VIII, 12, 1161b28. The Aristotelian expression of the "alter ego" has become almost proverbial, but the original meaning is often disregarded. What Aristotle wants to stress is not primarily the similarity that unites two friends but the fact that real friendship is oriented toward the true self of another individual. A true friend loves within the other what he loves in his own being.

As a virtue friendship is indispensable to realizing the full perfection of human existence: man needs virtuous friends in order to reach happiness, which mainly consists in the development of one's capacities, above all in the performance of intellectual activity. A solitary individual, without friends, without family, without political society, can never attain full actualization of his possibilities and come to happiness. One may ask whether this doctrine does not disagree with another teaching of Aristotle maintaining the self-sufficiency of the wise man. As a matter of fact, a virtuous individual is at the highest level of independence, of autonomy and self-sufficiency: when he devotes himself to intellectual activity, to contemplation, he is able to perform this activity in a more steady way than any other operation, without requiring constantly the cooperation of others. A wise man is also more independent than any other individual because he is not driven by his passions and emotions.[64] In spite of all this, a moral man wants friends; what is the reason? In the first place, because nobody can be wise from childhood; wisdom is not a gratuitous gift of nature.[65] An individual may become wise when he practices virtue during a sufficiently long period of time. In order to reach this level of moral life, everybody needs virtuous friends; he needs above all a political community in which laws embody the ideal of moral behavior.[66] Moreover, if somebody has acquired the virtue of wisdom, he may lose it. In this respect, the teaching of Aristotle differs from the Stoic theory: according to the latter a wise man can never become insane. All irrational movements have been extirpated; the ascendancy of reason can never be threatened. In Aristotle's ethics the situation is different: the wise man has not eradicated his passions; he has only subdued them to the government of the rational faculty. So the

64. *Eth. Nic.*, X, 7, 1177a27–b1. Justice needs some material wealth; otherwise this virtue could not be practiced. Even courage and temperance require some material means; only contemplation can be exercised without external help. A wise man is able to dedicate himself to contemplation without any assistance.

65. In children passions and emotions are present from birth, whereas the activity of reason starts much later (*Politica*, VII, 15, 1334b22–25). Moral life is closely linked to rational insight.

66. Friends are indispensable for all kinds of people: for those who are in the full strength of their life, they are required for virtuous actions (πρὸς τὰς καλὰς πράξεις); VIII, 1, 1155a14–15). Dealing with contemplation, Aristotle states that it is preferable for a wise man to have collaborators (συνεργοὺς ἔχων) (X, 7, 1177a34): man is naturally oriented to meeting other humans and cooperating with them.

presence of passions also remains a threat in the behavior of wise people. In this context it is desirable to have friends and collaborators who help and support even those who have attained the highest level of perfection. An immoral man will never be a friend of a wise individual, since a friend is another self and friendship is an extension of self-love.

The question whether in Aristotle's view sacrifice of life for a friend is possible may be asked: if friendship is an extension of self-love, should we not conclude that an individual can never sacrifice his life for his friend? According to the Stagirite death is the end of human existence: there is no afterlife. Our author provides little information to help solve this problem, yet he states that a son should save the life of his father rather than his own.[67] When the Stagirite attempts to explain sacrifice, he again has recourse to self-love. A person who accomplishes a sacrifice practices self-love: he leaves to the others wealth and honors and many other things that people pursue, and he reserves for himself what is most noble, moral value. In this way even sacrifice is interpreted as a kind of self-love.[68]

Friendship finally plays an important role in the political philosophy of the Stagirite. The author maintains that in political society friendship is equally important as justice: legislators seemingly attribute even more importance to friendship because it secures union and agreement among citizens.[69] Legislators endeavor above all to avoid conflicts and to promote concord, which is regarded as a kind of friendship. When citizens are linked by friendship, they do not need justice, but when they practice justice, they still need friendship. The highest expression of justice seems to be of the same nature as that of friendship. Aristotle is quite conscious of the fact that some link should unite the citizens of a state: this conforms to his philosophy of political society, which in its system of laws embodies a moral doctrine. Such a republic is not founded on the

---

67. *Eth. Nic.*, IX, 2, 1165a1. The statement by Aristotle is rather hesitating and cautious: it is far from being categorical.

68. *Eth. Nic.*, IX, 8, 1169a20–22. Aristotle declares that the mind chooses what is best for its own perfection and that a moral individual obeys the mind (IX, 8, 1169a17–18). The Greek Master remains faithful to his basic perspective: the end of moral conduct is the perfection of the true self.

69. *Eth. Nic.*, VIII, 1, 1155a21–28. As has already been explained, all members of a political community should agree on some basic moral values, which ought to be expressed in laws.

idea of tolerance; it professes some ethical rules, which are expressed in legislation. If moral conceptions are too different among citizens, true friendship will not be realized and there will be a lack of indispensable cohesion.

In moral education friendship plays a decisive role: it is a virtue or at least it is closely linked to virtue. Only virtuous individuals are able to practice real friendship, which is an extension of self-love. What is extended is the love of the true self: man has to love his own true self and also the true self of others. This authentic love is the basis of family life; it is also the foundation of political communities, which are grounded on justice and friendship.

[9]

ANTHROPOLOGICAL
BACKGROUND

Tᴴᴇ ethical works of Aristotle are not treatises of philosophical anthropology, and yet they implicitly contain a concept
of man on which the moral doctrine is founded.[1] As a matter
of fact, what is at issue in the ethical writings is essentially human
happiness or human perfection, the full development of man's capacities. Man is an ambiguous being; he is both in act and in potency;
he naturally tends toward the good and endeavors to actualize his
possibilities.[2] In Aristotle's view moral behavior is the way leading
to happiness, to the full display of man's potency. As any moral
discipline constantly deals with man, his activity, his deliberations,
his choices, his habits, it has to start from a certain idea of a human
being: a series of questions with respect to man is to be answered,
and this view must be implicitly present in an ethical treatise. The
most basic question is concerned with responsibility: is man a responsible being; in other words, is each individual responsible for
his own behavior? What is the meaning of such responsibility? Is
man responsible to a higher authority, the First Substance or Pure
Act? Will individuals' moral conduct be judged by a divine Being

1. J. Verhaeghe, *Het mensbeeld in de Aristotelische Ethiek*, Brussels, 1980. The author
carefully analyzes which concept of man is present in the ethical writings of Aristotle.
This concept has its typical features, selected in view of some moral considerations
and conclusions. According to the author Aristotle did not fully overcome the
duality of moral praxis and intellectual contemplation: these two aspects are rather
juxtaposed than adequately integrated.

2. From the very beginning of the *Nicomachean Ethics (Eth. Nic.)* (I, 1, 1094a1–3)
Aristotle is concerned with the notion of good: instead of clarifying this important
concept and trying to analyze its content, he stresses that everything strives toward
this goal. Man also is present in this universal aspiration: hence moral conduct,
although it is proper to rational beings, is in harmony with the general striving of
cosmic reality.

at the end of their life? Are humans able to take free decisions? If they are, what is the nature of this power? All these questions are related to man: a moral philosopher cannot avoid facing them, at least implicitly.[3]

Aristotle has written a treatise in which he explicitly deals with the nature of man and his activity: it is entitled *On the Soul* (Περὶ ψυχῆς). What is the meaning of this title? Is man only a soul? Certainly not in Aristotle's view, although the author states that the soul, or even the mind, is the core of a human being. Yet his interpretation of the relationship between body and soul is far from being dualistic: soul and body are not two substances linked together; both are components of the same human substance. In Aristotle's view human soul is the first act of a natural body that possesses life in potency, namely an organized body.[4] This definition is phrased in such a way that it excludes any kind of dualism; it is built up with the help of some key notions in the Stagirite's philosophy, for example, potency and act, matter and form. There cannot be any doubt that the soul must be an act: it is the principle of life and of all activities that man performs, from sensible perception to the highest contemplation of the mind. What is important in this definition is that human soul is considered to be the *first* act of a natural body; no other act is prior to the one under consideration.[5] The corresponding principle to this first act must be prime matter, a component that is devoid of any determination in act: so man is composed of soul and prime matter; even the organic structure of the body springs from the psychic constituent. The body possesses life in potency: it will be animated by the soul, and even its disposi-

---

3. The true good of man must be directly related to the proper nature of a human individual. In Aristotle's teaching the specific perfection of man is closely related to the exercise of the highest activity of which a human being is capable, the activity of the mind (*Eth. Nic.*, I, 7, 1098a16–20).

4. *De anima*, II, 1, 412b5–6. Aristotle endeavors to disclose the proper nature of the soul and to show what is common to every soul. After expounding his definition the author immediately adds that it is not necessary to examine whether body and soul are one: unity and being are predicated in many ways, but they primarily belong to act (ἐντελέχεια) (II, 1, 412b6–9). Being the first act, the soul must be the highest principle of unity in living beings.

5. The term used by Aristotle is ἐντελέχεια ἡ πρώτη (412b5). In order to illustrate his viewpoint the author compares the soul to the habit of scientific knowledge, which is always present even if it is not exercised. This comparison is hardly convincing: the soul never stops exercising its activity. Even during sleep the soul continues animating the organism (cf. *De anima*, II, 2, 414a27–28). What Aristotle wants to explain is that the presence of the soul is comparable to that of an abiding habit.

tion to become an animated organism springs from the soul. In this way the unity of man is fully secured.[6]

This unity of body and soul is also important with respect to Aristotle's moral doctrine: his viewpoint is different from Plato's and is much more positive toward the corporeal component and sensible reality. Moral life is not an imitation of transcendent immutable patterns; it is the gradual actualization of man's capacities through virtuous conduct. But why does Aristotle stress the unity of man so much? In his treatise *On the Soul* he carefully studies the various levels of knowledge and their relations with each other. In the field of sensitive perceptions he distinguishes five different activities: seeing, hearing, smelling, tasting, and touching. These various sensations are clearly distinct, but they also possess some common features: the sense faculties are receptive of sensible forms without matter[7]; the sensitive organ, which links together all the different perceptions, is the heart.[8] So there are both unity and diversity. After the study of the five senses Aristotle does not pass immediately to his inquiry on intellectual knowledge: there is an in-between that is constituted by the *sensus communis* and imagination. According to Aristotle the *sensus communis* has a threefold function: it represents an inchoative form of self-knowledge, which is fully realized on the level of intellectual understanding. Somebody who sees or hears or smells a particular object also possesses some awareness of his perceiving.[9] Through the same *sensus communis* man is able to grasp some common sensible objects: they do not belong to a particular sense only but may in fact be seized by several. Such objects are movement, rest, number, shape, and size.[10] Finally the

6. The soul is considered to be the substantial form of a living being: all perfection springs from this formal principle (*De anima*, II, 1, 412b10–17). The term οὐσία properly means beingness: according to Aristotle, the beingness of all beings coincides with their substantial form.

7. *De anima*, II, 12, 424a17–24. In Aristotle's view sensitive faculties are receptive (δεκτικόν): they receive sensible forms without matter. This receptive character is a kind of openness toward the material world: receiving these forms, the senses will assimilate them and establish some cognitive contact with external reality.

8. *De juventute et senectute (De juv. et sen.)*, 3–4, 469a10–33: *De Partibus Animalium (De Part. Anim.)*, II, 1, 647a25–b9; II, 10, 656a30.

9. *De anima*, III, 2, 425b12–25. Aristotle firmly states that there is a sensible awareness of our perceptions: he wonders, however, whether it is the same sense that perceives an object and that is aware of its perceptive activity.

10. *De anima*, III, 1, 425a14–b11. In Aristotle's view common sensible objects can be grasped by various senses, each of which has its own specific object.

sensus communis is at the origin of the unity of sensible knowledge and allows the comparison and distinction of objects perceived by various sensitive faculties.[11] The activity of the *sensus communis* is not yet at the level of thought, but it is more perfect than knowledge achieved by the five senses. The same obtains with regard to imagination: it is not like sense perception, nor is it already thinking activity. Imagination is impossible without sensation, and without imagination there will be no judgment or discursive thinking.[12] According to our author men perform many actions under the impact of imagination; that is the reason why human mind may be obscured by passion or illness or sleep. In any case, humans are strongly influenced by their imagination in what they are doing and undergoing.[13] Both *sensus communis* and imagination prepare the highest degree of man's activity, thinking. Through the illumination of the active intellect sensible images are made intelligible and are assimilated by the receptive intellect.[14] The study of the various levels of knowledge has brought Aristotle to the conviction that man is a unity of body and soul: the roots of intellectual knowledge are in sensible experience.

Is human soul an immortal principle? Plato's answer is certainly positive: in the *Phaedo* he examines the question at great length and expounds various arguments showing that human soul must be immortal. The main argument is based on the fact that man is able to contemplate the transcendent Forms. Such knowledge is only possible if there is a resemblance between the cognitive faculty and

11. *De anima*, III, 2, 426b12–427a16. It must be the same sensitive principle that distinguishes white and sweet: otherwise a knowing subject could not be aware of this distinction.

12. *De anima*, III, 3, 427b14–17. Judgment and discursive thought are on a lower level than contemplation; they are the first steps in intellectual activity and so are closely related to imagination.

13. *De anima*, III, 3, 428b16. In Aristotle's view the activity of imagination may be true or false, whereas sense activity is always or most generally true when the proper object is concerned. So humans acting in conformity with their imagination may easily be misled. According to T. Tracy the central sense power is identical with the faculty of emotion (*Physiological Theory and the Doctrine of the Mean*, p.252). As a matter of fact, the heart is regarded as the principle and source of all sensations (*De Part. An.*, III, 3, 665a11–13; III, 4, 666a12–16).

14. *De anima*, III, 5, 430a14–17; III, 4, 429b29–31. In this very condensed text Aristotle compares the active intellect to light: through the action of light colors in potency are made colors in act. Similarly what is intelligible in potency is made intelligible in act.

the object that is grasped. The transcendent Forms are immaterial, immutable, and eternal; if the soul were mortal, it could never grasp those immutable patterns.[15] Moreover, the soul is principle of life: it does not participate in life; it is essentially life; its very essence is to be source of life. What only participates in life can die: life itself can never die. In this sense man can die, but the principle of life is incorruptible.[16] Human soul more or less belongs to the area of the Ideas: it cannot be put on the level of changing material things; it did not come to be together with the body; it already existed and contemplated the transcendent Forms.[17] Aristotle's perspective is different: human soul must be mortal, because all its activities are in some way linked to the body. They are connected with sensible perception, with the operations of the *sensus communis* and of imagination. The soul cannot continue to exist without exercising at least some activity: if it is unable to implement any operation, it must disappear. This conclusion is not explicitly stated in the anthropological treatise of the Stagirite, but it cannot be avoided. The theory of knowledge inevitably leads to this conclusion.[18]

Man is a mortal being, whose horizon is limited to his life on earth: this statement is contrary not only to the teaching of Plato but also to popular opinions and mythological belief. Consequently the full development of human existence ought to be implemented during man's life on earth, within a short period of time between birth and death. The moral theory of Aristotle may be called an earthly humanism: the perfection of each individual is to be performed within the limits of a temporal existence. Should this teaching be qualified as pessimistic? Certainly not in Aristotle's view: the

15. *Phaedo*, 79c–e: ὡς συγγενὴς οὖσα αὐτοῦ. This doctrine is also used by Plato in a moral perspective: there is a fundamental kinship between human soul and the transcendent Forms. Yet this similarity is not the same in all individuals: through his moral conduct a particular person may reach a higher degree of resemblance with the Ideas than many others; hence he will be able to contemplate the Forms in a more effective and penetrating way.

16. *Phaedo*, 105b–e. By its very nature the soul is a principle of life. It could never become the contrary of what it essentially is; it could never become mortal.

17. The doctrine of reminiscence is closely linked to this viewpoint (*Phaedo*, 76c). Man is able to know what is perfectly equal although he never meets it in sensible reality. This knowledge cannot be derived from sensible experience; it can only be attained in a process of recollection (*Phaedo*, b–c).

18. *De anima*, I, 1, 403a3–27. Human thinking is always linked to some sensible image (*De anima*, III, 7, 431a16; 431b2; 8, 432a13; *De memoria et reminiscentia*, 1, 450a4–13).

whole universe, including man, is oriented toward the good and this natural tendency cannot be in vain.[19] The world exists from eternity and will never pass away: the becoming of the universe is governed by the Supreme Principle, Pure Act. Some beings come to be and die; this evolution is not considered to be evil. In the case of man, Aristotle teaches that human perfection depends upon virtuous behavior and intellectual contemplation; being naturally driven toward the good, man will try to accomplish the full development of his possibilities. Not all individuals are equally virtuous or equally dedicated to intellectual work, but all are responsible for their own degree of perfection: if some people fail and go astray, it is because they indulge in irrational inclinations, in passions and emotions.[20]

Is man a merely physical being, as in Aristotle's view he is mortal? As a matter of fact, man is part of the physical and biological universe: he exists in the same world together with other beings that, like him, are inserted into the evolution of material reality. And yet human behavior is not entirely determined by antecedent factors: man is not merely a thing among other things. In Aristotle's view each individual chooses his own actions after reflexion and deliberation: man's conduct is not simply the result of the circumstances in which it happens to occur; it is, in fact, an autonomous choice of the agent.[21] If man were a merely physical being, he would not be responsible for his behavior: in Aristotle's view each individual is a moral subject, an agent who assumes responsibility for his conduct.[22] Dealing with virtuous life, with contemplation as

19. It is a basic view in Aristotle's philosophy that nature does nothing in vain (*Politica*, I, 2, 1253a9: οὐδὲν γάρ, ὡς φαμέν, μάτην ἡ φύσις ποιεῖ). At the beginning of the *Nicomachean Ethics* (I, 1, 1094a1–2) Aristotle declares that any action and any choice are seemingly striving toward some good. In his further development the author will acknowledge that an intended good may not be a real value: under the influence of emotional forces man may go astray and regard as valuable what is not truly good. Aristotle recognizes that many people are fluctuating and are most influenced by their feelings (*Eth. Nic.*, VII, 10, 1152a25–27; X, 9, 1179b10–16).

20. In Aristotle's opinion moral virtue is practiced by many people (πολύκοινον); some individuals may be naturally incapacitated for moral conduct, but as a general rule humans are able to become virtuous through teaching and dedication (*Eth. Nic.*, I, 9, 1099b18–20).

21. *Eth. Nic.*, III, 3, 1113a4–7. Man not only deliberates about his future actions but also decides to stop deliberating; at that stage he refers the choice to his leading principle, the mind. It is the leading principle (τὸ ἡγούμενον) of a human subject that is responsible for choices.

22. *Eth. Nic.*, III, 3, 1113a9–12; III, 5, 1113b6–7. According to Aristotle a choice is a striving connected with deliberation and oriented toward things that are in our power.

the highest level of human activity, with moral fault and happiness that are effected by ethical action, the Stagirite is firmly convinced of the responsibility of each person. Happiness is not reached by chance or by good fortune; it is truly the fruit of moral conduct. In the light of these considerations man cannot be a merely physical being; he must be metaphysical: he transcends the level of physical reactions that totally depend on previous factors. The essence of a human person transcends the material world, in which all events are determined: autonomous choices require a spiritual principle, which is not conditioned by material causes. The activity of a human subject manifests the nature of its principle: if the activity is autonomous, its source also must be endowed with autonomy.[23] Despite the fact that human soul is considered to be mortal, it is not regarded as a physical and material principle. In this respect our author remains faithful to the teaching of his master Plato, who firmly declares that the soul is spiritual, akin to the transcendent Forms. Aristotle in a sense reaches the same conclusion: if he accepts the soul to be mortal, it is not because it is material but because it cannot operate without the body. A psychic principle that is unable to exert any activity by itself cannot continue to exist after death. All beings are oriented toward the good: this natural propensity is a dynamic one, which is constantly expressed and actualized in the proper activity of the being concerned. If no activity at all proceeds from a particular being, it must inevitably pass away.

Man is a being that is present to itself and to the world: this feature is a basic one in Aristotle's ethics, which is founded on the knowledge an individual possesses of himself. The author does not start from the intuition of moral values; he does not rely on the contemplation of universal Forms existing in a transcendent world. He constructs his ethical ideal on the consideration of a human person with his appropriate faculties and capacities; moral life is regarded as the full development of a person.[24] This evolution is

23. *De Part. Anim.*, I, 1, 641b8. In Aristotle's view human soul does not entirely belong to the physical world: one could hardly maintain that the process leading to the creation of universal concepts is merely physical. In fact, sensible images are radically transformed by the active intellect, which is eternal and separate.

24. *Eth. Nic.*, I, 7, 1097b24–28. It is quite obvious that εὐδαιμονία is a fundamental notion in Aristotle's ethical inquiry: it was a very ancient traditional notion and it has been radically transformed. In his opinion everybody agrees that eudemony is the highest value and coincides with what is most valuable (τὸ ἄριστον), but it is to be more adequately specified. Starting this investigation Aristotle immediately

only potentially present at the beginning of an existence: it ought to be achieved by each individual by means of his activity. Man gradually makes himself into what he wants to be: everyone is the author of his own happiness and perfection.[25] As a being in the world man is dependent upon other humans and also upon material things; he is particularly dependent upon political society and its laws, which incorporate a moral view of life.[26] In Aristotle's ethics man is considered especially as a being that is integrated into the universal dynamism of nature toward the good: man is inserted into a movement that extends far beyond the frontiers of his existence. Striving toward the good, man is not an exception in the universe; on the contrary, he takes part in a universal orientation that drives all beings toward supreme perfection.[27] Does everything in the universe participate in moral life? Not in Aristotle's view; man's inclination toward the good is not the same as that existing in other beings: man is conscious of his natural tendency and its object; he questions the nature of the goal to which he is spontaneously moved.[28] Inanimate things, plants, and irrational animals experience this impulse passively and ask no questions about the nature of the end; only man questions this issue. He wants to understand what the good really is and how he may reach this goal. Since this value has a human dimension and implies in fact the full development of man's existence, each individual has to reflect upon himself and to ask what kind of being he is and how he differs from other things in the world. Aristotle is convinced that the good of man must be

---

wonders what is the proper activity of a human being (τὸ ἔργον τοῦ ἀνθρώπου). A flute player, a sculptor, and any craftsman have their own appropriate activity and in performing this activity they achieve what is valuable. Each craftsman has been trained for a particular function. Hence the encompassing question: what is the proper function of a human being?

25. *Eth. Nic.*, I, 7, 1097b28–33. People who have been trained in technical skills have their proper function to perform; this also obtains with respect to the various organs: eyes, hands, feet all have their own function.

26. *Eth. Nic.*, I, 2, 1094b7–10. What is good for an individual will also be valuable for a community, yet the good of a political society is higher and more important than that of an individual.

27. *Eth. Nic.*, I, 1, 1094a2–3. Universal teleology is indeed a fundamental aspect of Aristotle's ethics: man could never reach his full development without conforming to the universal striving of nature.

28. *Eth. Nic.*, III, 5, 1113b3–7. A tendency toward the good is present in man without his choice: as to deliberation, it is concerned with the means leading to the proper end of human life. Choices are related to those actions that are considered to be means leading to happiness, namely virtuous actions.

appropriate to his essence; therefore, he analyzes the nature of humans and reaches the conclusion that their proper characteristic resides in reason.[29] This faculty is present only in man; it is not found in other beings. Hence the author draws the conclusion that perfect and constant activity of reason represents the highest degree of human perfection and of happiness.[30]

How does Aristotle reach this conclusion? In his view happiness can only be found in the performance of an activity, since act is always more perfect than potency.[31] As to the kind of activity required, the author believes that happiness cannot reside in operations of an inferior level but in the most noble activity man is able to undertake: the activity of the mind. The author concludes that human perfection and happiness consist in intellectual speculation, performed in a constant and capable way. Such speculative activity must proceed from an abiding habit or capacity, which has been acquired by frequently repeated former acts. Without this previous preparation an individual will never be able to exercise intellectual activity in a way that ensures man's highest perfection.[32] In Aristotle's teaching there is a close connection between happiness and leisure (σχολή): seemingly eudemony consists in enjoying leisure, as laboring people pursue some rest and as those who make war intend peace.[33] In this context leisure does not mean absence of activity; it refers to an activity that is entirely self-sufficient: political engagement always seeks something beyond the action itself, either power or honors, whereas intellectual contemplation does not search for an aim beyond the exercise of the act. In this sense intellectual contemplation is regarded as leisure: its perfection does not depend on whether or not it reaches a goal that is distinct from the act. Therefore, to exercise intellectual contemplation in a constant and capable way is highly enjoyable, it is self-sufficient, and it is true leisure, as it does not pursue anything else.[34] The

29. *Eth. Nic.*, I, 7, 1098a7–11. Of course, the performance of an activity may be more or less perfect; it depends upon the capacity and the training of the agent.

30. *Eth. Nic.*, I, 7, 1098a16–18.

31. *Eth. Nic.*, I, 7, 1098a3–7. In Aristotle's view the activity of the mind is the highest achievement of human beings, although it is not independent of the bodily organism.

32. *Eth. Nic.*, II, 1, 1103a31–33; I, 9, 1100a4–9.

33. *Eth. Nic.*, X, 7, 1177b4–6.

34. *Eth. Nic.*, X, 7, 1177b6–26. In Aristotle's view not only is intellectual contemplation a privileged activity of leisure, but so is tasting music: therefore, music belongs to the education program (*Politica*, VIII, 3, 1338a13–24).

permanent intuition of truth may be the result of many efforts, but
when this level of activity has been reached it is exerted permanently
in an atmosphere of rest and tranquility: repose is more enjoyable
than motion.[35]

At first glance this teaching seems to be unrealistic and abstract,
the outcome of a merely formal analysis.[36] Man is not only mind;
there are many other matters in which he is involved: in addition to
intellectual activity there are passionate drives, emotional impulses,
concerns with daily life in a family or a political society, labor that
is implemented in order to provide what is necessary for one's
subsistence and that of a family. One may wonder whether Aristotle
has actually overlooked all those important aspects of human life.
This is hardly likely; the author founded his ethical theory on
prephilosophical views in Greek culture, on his experience of life
and his knowledge of human nature[37]: he did not rely on abstract
considerations. In order to understand Aristotle's position, it is
indispensable to keep in mind that the author is dealing with the
highest ideal of human life, without specifying how many individuals effectively attain this goal. Quite obviously the contemplative
ideal will only be reached by a small group of highly talented
people[38]: it is not unimportant, however, that at least some outstanding individuals dedicate themselves to this speculative activity,
the search for truth, because their intuitions and the example of
their life are also beneficial to other people. In Plato's opinion those
who contemplate the transcendent Forms are to be invested with
the responsibility of ruling the city; in this way all members of the

35. *Eth. Nic.*, VII, 14, 1154b26–28.
36. Aristotle himself is conscious of the fact that contemplative life is beyond
human capability (*Eth. Nic.*, X, 7, 1177b26–27).
37. Aristotle is quite conscious of the fact that some other conditions are relevant
to happiness, but they are not essential: in this context the author mentions wealth
and pleasure (*Eth. Nic.*, I, 8, 1099a31–b8). Pleasure is considered to be a kind of
complementary goal (*Eth. Nic.*, X, 4, 1174b31–33). It must be recognized, however,
that pleasures and pains play a central part in Aristotle's ethics: moral virtue is mainly
concerned with pleasures and pains (*Eth. Nic.*, II, 3, 1104b8ff; 1105a10–13; *Eth. Eud.*,
II, 4, 1221b33–39). It is considered as a kind of impassibility or tranquility with regard
to pleasures and pains, whereas vicious conduct is the opposite (*Eth. Eud.*, II, 4,
1222a3–5). As to material wealth, the author strongly emphasizes that too much is
not needed, only what is necessary for food and health (*Eth. Nic.*, X, 8, 1178b33–
1179a9).
38. *Eth. Nic.*, X, 7, 1177b26–31. In this respect, the presence of friends is beneficial
(IX, 9, 1170a5–6).

community gain some profit from their wisdom.[39] The Stoics had to face the same problem: they were conscious of the fact that their ideal of wisdom was only realized by very few people.[40] In his ethics Aristotle apparently endeavors to show to which supreme level of perfection a man may lift himself by his activity: in this respect there is no envy of any divine being, but there is also neither help nor support from a higher power.[41] Everybody is responsible for his life: a man has to actualize his possibilities within the framework of a political community in friendship and cooperation with other individuals.

Stating that the highest degree of human perfection resides in intellectual contemplation, Aristotle does not want to overlook or disregard the other aspects of moral behavior.[42] This most noble activity implies the presence of moral virtue: if passions and emotions are not ruled by reason, the full display of this faculty will constantly be hampered. It remains true that reason distinguishes man from other animals: the proper dignity of human beings consists primarily in rational activity, but this activity cannot be separated from the substantial unity of a person: it is closely linked to the presence of courage, justice, temperance. In other words, it depends on the moral attitude of an individual as a whole.[43] It would be quite contrary to his unitary concept of man if Aristotle maintained that contemplative activity is independent of the other aspects of moral behavior. A man who

39. *Respublica (Respubl.)*, VI, 484a–485a. In Plato's opinion philosophers cannot at once devote themselves to the ruling of the state and to contemplation. They should fulfill both duties but successively: at one time they will dedicate themselves to contemplation and at another to political action (VII, 540a–b).

40. Seneca, *Epistolae ad Lucilium (Epist.)*, 42, 1. "Nam ille alter fortasse tamquam phoenix semel anno quingentesimo nascitur." A similar viewpoint is repeatedly formulated by Seneca (*De constantia sapientis*, 7, 1). Of course, if wise men are so exceptional, the question may be asked whether the history of the world could be a masterpiece of Divine Reason, as is taught by the Stoics.

41. *Eth. Nic.*, X, 7, 1177b34.

42. One may ask whether in Aristotle's view contemplation is an incentive to moral action, as it is in Plato. The answer cannot be merely negative: inasmuch as the object of contemplation is the highest good, this intuition must contribute to man's ethical progress. In this regard J. Verhaeghe overstresses the difference between Plato and Aristotle (*Het mensbeeld in de Aristotelische ethiek*, p.188).

43. J. R. Moncho Pascual, *La Unidad de la vida moral según Aristoteles*, Valencia, 1972, p.269–336 ("Las relaciones entre la acción y la contemplación"). According to the author the whole of moral practice is teleologically subordinated to the activity of reason: "De donde se infiere que toda la praxis, toda la moralidad, se subordina teleológicamente a la actividad del lógos; en ella encuentran su fin y sentido. Así se afirma repetidas veces en el *Protreptico*" (p.293). Yet ethical action does not lose its proper and specific worth.

devotes the best of his life to intellectual speculation must be a person whose reason is not disturbed by irrational movements and inclinations. In Aristotle's view the highest symbol of human perfection is not an athlete or a powerful politician; it is a person who dedicates his life and energy to philosophical inquiry. Expounding this viewpoint in his ethical writings, the author certainly kept in mind the examples of Socrates and Plato; he also relied on his own experience. His whole life was devoted to the discovery of truth; in his view everybody could contribute to the disclosure of truth.[44] In many cases this contribution is rather limited; in the case of Aristotle, it was considerable: from his stay with Plato in the Academy until his death he was always eager to discover new areas of research. From the study of heavenly bodies to the investigation of plants and animals, he never stopped inquiring into the universe in which human existence develops. In a sense the highest ethical ideal, as it is described in Aristotle's writings, is embodied and concretized in the life of the Greek Master.

Referring to the supreme level of human activity, the author states that intellectual speculation should be assiduous and ought to be performed with capability.[45] What is the meaning of this important qualification? All human knowledge starts from experience and observation: in our knowledge of the world the first step and starting point is an accurate observation of facts.[46] Being the son of a physician, Aristotle had a special interest in biological and physiological phenomena. Many of them are expounded in his treatises; they are the result of observation made by him and his collaborators. When he left Athens after the death of Plato and spent some years in the Near East, he used this opportunity to study the flora and fauna of the countries he visited.[47] As far as observation

44. *Eth. Eud.*, I, 6, 1216b30–31. Aristotle does not accept the Platonic doctrine of reminiscence: his statement cannot be understood in this context. In his *Politics* Aristotle favors a limited democracy: the opinions of the majority of the people have more value than those of a single individual. Hence among political deviations democracy is regarded as the least bad (*Eth. Nic.*, VIII, 10, 1160b20).

45. *Eth. Nic.*, I, 7, 1098a7–12. With respect to intellectual activity, it is very important that it be performed with capacity (κατὰ τὴν ἀρετήν); otherwise instead of revealing truth, it would lead to error and falsity.

46. *Eth. Eud.*, I, 6, 1216b26–28.

47. J. Düring, *Aristoteles*, p.51. Presumably during his stay in the Near East Aristotle met his most faithful collaborator, Theophrastus: after all the discussions in the Academy on the Theory of Ideas, he then devoted himself mostly to empirical research.

is concerned, it provides a body of material that is to be submitted to further investigation. When the material has been carefully gathered, man knows only what happens in the world, which phenomena occur around him; his eagerness for knowledge is not yet satisfied. He wants to clarify these phenomena; he attempts to understand them. Hence the question: what does it mean "to clarify, to explain"? In Aristotle's view it means that we not only know facts or phenomena but also understand why they occur; in other words, we know the "why" or the cause of what we have noticed.[48] A phenomenon becomes clearer, it is clarified, when its cause is uncovered. According to Aristotle what happens in the world, the becoming of things, is a constant transition from potency to act: things are in potency in certain respects; they are able to be transformed, although they cannot actualize their potency by themselves. In order to become what they not yet are, they are to be moved by some external thing, which is the cause of the transformation. In this view things are constantly influenced by each other; they are changed by each other according to their respective potency: hence the importance of the notion of cause. Aristotle is convinced that we should clarify the phenomena in the world with the help of the concept of cause and that we are able to grasp causal impacts from one thing to another.[49] This opinion is largely based on his philosophical theory of potency and act: a potency can never be brought to actualization without the causal influence of an act. To explain the world means to show the cause or the act that originates the actualization of a particular potency. So a man who has carefully observed some facts ought to go a step further: he has to disclose the causes of what he has noticed. Such knowledge represents a higher level of understanding, because it shows why a particular phenomenon takes place.

Aristotle carefully examined the notion of causality. His predeces-

48. *Metaphysica*, (*Metaph.*), I, 1, 981a28–b6. In Aristotle's view the knowledge of causes is not only an addition or a complement to the knowledge of facts; it is an understanding of a different kind: it belongs to a higher level of clarification. A phenomenon is more adequately known when its cause has been disclosed.

49. *Physica*, (*Phys.*), III, 1, 201a9–15; 19–25. In the material world things are both active and passive, as they are at once in potency and in act. Insofar as they are in potency they are more than what they are at a particular moment. Studying the constant movement of the sensible world, Aristotle proposes an explanation that is founded on the potential nature of things and on external causal influence. The relation between the two factors is reciprocal: causal influence is possible because things are in potency, and things are in potency because they are able to be actualized by some causal action.

sors had already dealt with the same issue; they also wanted to explain the universe and they endeavored to discover a unifying principle of the cosmic diversity. They wanted to reduce the variety of the universe to some basic *archè*. Aristotle took them to task because they were only concerned with the material cause of the cosmos; they proposed either water or air or fire as the principle of everything.[50] This criticism, however, is not adequate: it has been suggested as a consequence of the distinction of four kinds of causality, but this distinction was introduced by Aristotle; it was not known to his predecessors. According to our author there are indeed four kinds of causality: the material and formal causes are internal, belonging to the structure of a particular being, whereas the efficient and final causes are external.[51] One may ask whether matter and form are to be called causes, since they are the components of beings. In Aristotle's view they are causes because the existence of a sensible reality depends upon them: without a material and a formal constituent a sensible thing can never come to be. Scientific knowledge means something more than collecting facts: one has to disclose the causes of what he observes.

With regard to the knowledge of causes Aristotle introduces a further distinction: some causes are immediate factors related to a particular event, whereas others are more distant, or even ultimate. Immediate causes are directly linked to a phenomenon that in some way depends upon them. Wanting to explain the constant becoming and evolution of the world, man will look first at the most proximate cause of an event.[52] This cause will refer to a more fundamental

50. *Metaph.*, I, 3, 983b6–18. According to Aristotle's interpretation the most ancient Greek philosophers were only concerned with disclosing the basic material cause of the universe: they wanted to know from what matter the world had been made. In other words, they were looking for the material component of the cosmos, without asking further questions.

51. *Metaph.*, I, 3, 983a24–b3; *Phys.*, II, 3, 194b16–195b30. The four causes of Aristotle represent various ways in which a potency may be actualized. To the active influence of a particular cause corresponds the potency of a subject; thus there are constant interactions among beings according to their potency and their active powers. Moral education develops in the same world in which all these interactions occur: it is made possible through some natural dispositions, but there is also an active influence of some beings upon others. In this context Aristotle refers to teaching and training. Education also is a transition from potency to act.

52. *Analytica Posteriora (Anal. Post.)*, II, 18, 99b7–14. Regarding a particular phenomenon several causes may be taken into consideration: some of them will be nearer, others further away from the fact that is explored. In Aristotle's view the determining factor that is nearest to the phenomenon should be regarded as its cause.

causality. This proceeding, however, cannot be repeated indefinitely; there must be an ultimate cause of the universe, to which all other causes are related. This ultimate cause is Pure Act, which is at the origin of all actualizations that constantly take place in the cosmos.[53] It is the duty of metaphysics to demonstrate the existence and to disclose the proper nature of this ultimate principle. The disclosure of the first principle, which is the most intelligible reality, is also the most scientific degree of knowing of which man is capable; this knowledge represents the highest level of truth, since it refers to the most knowable object.[54] When the ultimate cause is attained, it is impossible to proceed further: this cause does not depend on anything else; it is Pure Act and consequently immutable. As a final cause it is the source of all becoming: whatever is actualized tends to this supreme perfection.

Everybody desires knowledge and truth[55]: man not only wants to observe phenomena but to explain them, to grasp their causes. Hence man is a scientific being: he constantly asks why such and such phenomena occur. Science is a creation of humans; it results from their concern with the clarification of what they observe. Man is even a metaphysical being: he wants a full explanation of everything; he endeavors to disclose the ultimate causes of whatever exists.[56] He possesses the wonderful capacity of being amazed: philosophy is born as a result of this amazement.[57] With regard to the highest degree of happiness the question may be asked whether Aristotle in the *Eudemian Ethics* maintained the same intellectualist position as in the *Nicomachean Ethics*. Referring to the final part of the former treatise, one may conclude that the supreme norm of

53. *Metaph.*, I, 2, 982b7–10. The author is quite convinced that a series of causes cannot be unlimited: there must be some first causes or first principles, at least if causes are subordinated to each other.

54. *Metaph.*, XII, 7, 1073a3–13. Aristotle maintains that the first cause of the universe is an eternal, immutable, and suprasensible substance; moreover, it cannot have any quantity; it must be without parts and indivisible; finally it is impassible; it cannot change from one quality to another, as it does not move from one place to another.

55. *Metaph.*, I, 1, 980a20. Desire for knowledge belongs to the very structure of human beings; it is part of their natural capacities. This statement is made by Aristotle on the basis of experience: humans spontaneously strive toward more knowledge, toward more and more adequate understanding.

56. *Metaph.*, I, 1, 982b7–10. Man is indeed a metaphysical being since he is not fully satisfied with grasping the approximate causes of things. He wants something more, namely the knowledge of the ultimate causes and principles.

57. *Metaph.*, I, 2, 982b12.

human behavior is linked to the contemplation of God, since the pursuit of natural goods will only be justified if it contributes to this ultimate end.[58] Yet a careful analysis of the texts shows that in the *Eudemian Ethics* the position of the author is less spiritual and intellectual: there are in this work no passages where man is mainly reduced to the mind; this kind of rather abstract psychological doctrine is no longer present.[59] Hence happiness and human perfection are regarded as a synthesis or combination of particular virtues working together; this synthesis is called complete virtue or *kalokagathia*.[60] True, this complete virtue also includes contemplation, but human perfection is no longer reduced to this highest activity. If this interpretation is right—and it is seriously supported by several indications in the treatise[61]—this doctrine represents a more mature position in the philosophical evolution of the Greek Master.[62]

But man is not only eager for truth; he is not only in search of knowledge: he is also a loving being, wanting to love and to be loved. According to the ancient Delphic maxim man has to know himself and should always be conscious of his limits. In ancient Greek culture there is no corresponding maxim stating that man should love himself: in a sense everybody loves himself; self-love is a natural and spontaneous inclination of all animals. And yet in Aristotelian ethics self-love, as well as self-knowledge, plays a central part: as a matter of fact, man is a complex being, including various aspects and components. He is compounded of body and soul, and within the soul are not only the mind but lower cognitive powers and irrational movements or tendencies. In Aristotle's view all these factors belong to the same unitary being; nevertheless the question what exactly man should love within himself must be asked. Aristotle's answer to this question could only be that man ought to love his true self, that which represents the core of his being as a person, and

---

58. *Eth. Eud.*, VIII, 3, 1249b16–21.

59. J. D. Monan, *Moral Knowledge and Its Methodology in Aristotle*, p.132: "Here in the EE [*Eth. Eud.*], we have a convincing indication that the psychological horizon of the EE has broadened beyond the narrow identification of man with his *nous*." This viewpoint "has been supplanted in the EE by a more integral conception of man."

60. *Eth. Eud.*, II, 1, 1219a38–39; VIII, 3, 1248b8–20; VIII, 3, 1249a16.

61. G. Verbeke, *L'idéal de la perfection humaine chez Aristote et l'évolution de sa noétique*, in: *Fontes Ambrosiani*, XXV, 1951, p.95.

62. J. D. Monan, *Moral Knowledge and Its Methodology in Aristotle*, p.133.

that is mainly the mind.[63] To love the true self means to endeavor to achieve the complete development of human capacities, particularly the intellectual powers. Aristotle states that friendship is an extension of self-love: in his view friendship is a virtue, or at least it always includes virtue. What we love in the other individual corresponds to what we love in ourselves, and what we love in ourselves is decisive for our whole moral attitude. An individual who tries to improve and develop his true self will be an authentic moral person.[64]

In Aristotle's view self-love is a natural propensity, but it is also a duty, a moral achievement: the moral writings of our author try to show how the perfection of the true self may be attained; he is further convinced that this perfection coincides with happiness. Self-love is not the same as egoism, striving for the satisfaction of sensible desires and aspirations: irrational inclinations should not be extinguished, but they should be ruled and dominated by the rational faculty.[65] Self-love is not confined to the concerns of a particular individual; it is open to other persons. In this sense friendship is an extension of self-love and is the foundation of social life.[66] In fact, there is a close connection between self-knowledge and self-love: in the light of Plato's and Aristotle's philosophy man has to disclose his true self; he has to uncover what he really is. If this is the basis and source of moral life, everybody must be able to discern what he actually is.[67] In Aristotle's view this knowledge is accessible to everybody; every man is able to grasp the proper nature of humans as compared to other animals. Hence every individual can realize that the true self does not coincide with irrational powers and tendencies, which are found also in other animals: reason,

63. Aristotle makes a clear distinction between two kinds of self-love: many people endeavor to attain plenty of wealth, honors, and bodily pleasures; they want to satisfy their desires, their passions, the tendencies of their irrational soul. The self-love of those individuals is rightly blamed (*Eth. Nic.*, IX, 8, 1168b15–23). There is, however, another kind of self-love, which consists in the pursuit of virtue and moral nobility (*Eth. Nic.*, IX, 8, 1168b25–31). J. R. Moncho Pascual writes: "Philautia es sinónimo de virtud; porque el fenómeno que ella expresa, la amistad o armonía entre las potencias del alma, es una característica fundamental de la virtud, de módo que sólo el virtuoso puede ser φίλαυτος" (*La Unidad de la vida moral*, p.294).

64. *Eth. Nic.*, IX, 8, 1168b28–34. Since moral life is intended to achieve the full development of a person, self-love plays an important part in ethical behavior.

65. *Eth. Nic.*, IX, 8, 1168a28–b5. True friendship starts from self-love; the final end that is pursued is true perfection of the self.

66. *Eth. Nic.*, IX, 8, 1168b5–6.

67. *Eth. Nic.*, IX, 8, 1169a2–8. A moral individual may be characterized by self-love: more than anybody else he possesses self-love, which is far from being egoistic.

language, moral sense, and friendship are characteristics of human beings. It is easy for everyone to discover what distinguishes him from other animals and to understand that in these proper features the real self of man must consist.[68]

Like all other beings man tends toward the good: from a moral perspective he has to strive toward the highest perfection of the self. In this respect there is a correspondence between Aristotle's ethical thought and the Stoic notion of *oikeiosis*, which essentially means consciousness of and attachment to the self: these features belong to the natural equipment of all living beings, which spontaneously are aware of what they are and try to protect and preserve themselves.[69] The question arises, however, whether this natural inclination can be the origin of moral behavior. According to the Stoics the true self of man is only reason (logos): human soul is considered to be a particle of the Divine Logos. Hence it is the duty of each individual to become what he really is: he has to suppress all irrational movements and inclinations totally; the wise man is freed of all passions.[70] It is a difficult task to achieve the Stoic *oikeiosis* fully; the spontaneous self-awareness and self-concern is only a starting point. If it remained at the level of a natural tendency, it would be devoid of any ethical relevance. On the contrary, if this natural inclination is consciously and freely assumed by a subject, if it becomes the origin of a freely accepted moral choice and constantly pursued development, then *oikeiosis* coincides with the moral activity of a person. Through his ethical behavior a man "belongs" more and more to himself: he better and better knows his true self and he constantly acts accordingly.[71] What at the beginning was

---

68. *Eth. Nic.*, IX, 8, 1169a11–15. Through his ethical conduct a moral man, loving himself, also helps and supports other people (καὶ τοὺς ἄλλους ὠφελήσει). In Aristotle's view self-love is by no means opposed to love of other people.

69. G. Verbeke, *L'humanisme stoïcien* (Volume in honour of Prof. Evanghelos Moutsopoulos) (in press). The doctrine of *oikeiosis* did not start with Chrysippus, as was maintained by F. Dirlmeier; it is also present in the teaching of Zeno, the founder of the School (Porphyrius, *De abstinentia*, III, 19 (SVF I, 197); Diog. Laert., VII, 87; Cicero, *De finibus*, IV, 45).

70. The Stoic notion of impassibility should be understood in connection with the concept of passion (πάθος). A wise man ought to be impassible, because passion is essentially contrary to reason. Passions cannot be educated; they ought to be suppressed.

71. The fundamental tendency of living beings is not toward pleasure, but toward self-conservation and self-development (Diog. Laert., VII, 86–87). According to Panaetius, even the love of other humans springs from this basic orientation: man is naturally attached to himself and inclined to friendship with others (Cicero, *De officiis*, I, 4, 12–14).

only a natural propensity gradually becomes the expression of an ethical attitude.

The teaching of Aristotle on this subject is perhaps less formal and explicit, but it is certainly present in his writings, although it is less radical than the Stoic position. Man is by nature a moral animal: all human beings are able to know and to love their true self. In this regard man is different from other animals, which are not gifted with reason. On the level of sensible knowledge the latter have only an inchoative awareness of their operations: as has already been explained, the *sensus communis* to some extent grasps the activities of the various senses.[72] The same obtains with respect to self-love: an animal is naturally inclined to the conservation and development of its own substance. In the case of humans, however, the situation is different: a natural disposition will gradually evolve to a conscious and freely adopted attitude.[73] Of course, an individual may go astray: he may ignore his true self and indulge in irrational impulses; instead of appreciating the worth of reason, he may cling to his passions and corporeal pleasures. Such behavior is immoral in Aristotle's view: it cannot lead to the full perfection of the self; it cannot ensure happiness. People who indulge in these inclinations must be deeply unhappy and tragically imperfect.[74] They are missing the goal of their life, to which they are naturally oriented: the good of the authentic self.

Finally one of the characteristic features of man consists in his cultural activity, which is also important from an ethical viewpoint: the way in which Aristotle describes this cultural activity eloquently illustrates the philosophical anthropology that is the basis of his moral teaching. In a sense man is the author of his own world: other animals live in an environment provided by nature. They use things which they happen to find, but they do not introduce inventions that radically transform their environment. Man is a

72. *De anima*, III, 2, 425b12–25.
73. *Rhetorica (Rhet.)*, I, 11, 1371b18–26. Self-love is used by Aristotle as a basis to justify private property: this property may contribute considerably to the moral development of a person (*Politica*, II, 5, 1263a41–b14).
74. *Eth. Nic.*, IX, 8, 1169a15–18. In Aristotle's view there is a chasm between the real behavior of an immoral individual and the acts he should perform; there is no coherence in the conduct of such people. As to a moral person, he does what he ought to do: he implements what the mind suggests and what is most beneficial for his development.

creator of culture, constantly making new discoveries that profoundly change his way of life: he creates all kinds of artistic, technical, scientific, and social innovations, which are a common patrimony of mankind and elevate the level of human life beyond that of irrational animals. These animals live in conformity with their inborn equipment, which remains roughly the same in the course of time; irrational animals are, as it were, locked up within the frontiers of their natural structure. In Aristotle's view mankind started from a very low and primitive level of civilization[75]: the first stage in the evolution was not a kind of a paradise, an ideal utopia in which all humans were equal and perfectly happy. The history of civilization is not one of uninterrupted degeneration and decline but one of gradual progress and improvement. Primitive men lived in poor conditions: they had to devote all their time to provide what was strictly necessary to stay alive; they were only concerned with food and protection against the dangers of their everyday existence; their life was frequently threatened by wild animals and by the inclemency of the weather. The attention of humans was totally concentrated on the most urgent needs of survival.[76] The second stage is characterized by the discovery of technical skills, which are related to the production of tools intended to improve the conditions of life: masons build houses, carpenters make furniture, shoemakers provide shoes; in this way man gradually increases his comfort and becomes more able to adapt his way of life to human dignity.[77] In the third period people proceed to the organization of political society: this stage is particularly important with respect to moral education, which in Aristotle's view is only possible in a

75. Philoponus, *In Nicomachi Isagogen (In Nicom. Isagogen)*, I, 1 (Aristotelis Fragmenta selecta, ed. W. D. Ross, Oxonii, 1955, *De philosophia*, fr. 8). In the first stage of civilization the term wisdom (σοφία) had a primitive meaning: it was not understood as an inquiry into the first causes and principles of the universe; the meaning was related to the satisfaction of the most urgent and immediate needs of humans. A wise man was an individual who had considerably contributed to the survival of the people.

76. Philoponus, *In Nicom. Isagogen*, I, 1 (*De philosophia*, fr. 8). When man is much concerned with the needs of daily life, he cannot dedicate himself to the search for truth and speculation.

77. Philoponus, *In Nicom. Isagogen*, I, 1 (*De philosophia*, fr. 8). Aristotle emphasizes the fact that at this stage the works of craftsmen transcend the immediate necessities of life: μέχρις τοῦ καλοῦ καὶ ἀστείου προϊούσας. Moreover, the great number of discoveries made at this time oriented the minds of the people toward God (εἰς θεὸν τὰς τούτων ἐπινοίας ἀνέφερον).

political community and under the direction of compulsory laws. Such constraint is indispensable, especially for young people.[78] In the fourth stage man proceeds to the study of nature: he endeavors to extend his knowledge of the universe; he investigates the heavenly bodies and the material world in which life develops. Physics is a science; it is at once an empirical and a philosophical study. Aristotle does not introduce a distinction between the two aspects. A physicist carefully observes the phenomena of the sensible world and tries to discover their causes.[79] And yet the study of nature does not represent the final stage of cultural development: after this study comes metaphysics or first philosophy, which deals with the supreme causes of the universe. Metaphysics examines the totality of all existing beings and attempts to disclose the ultimate causes. This discipline constitutes the highest activity of which man is capable: there is no more noble knowing; the science of metaphysics is the highest degree of human culture. Man cannot proceed beyond this stage; he has to stop at this level.[80] This evolution shows again that human perfection is achieved in exercising the highest intellectual activity.

Aristotle opposes moral intellectualism, as it was vindicated by Socrates, yet the anthropological background of his ethical ideal is undoubtedly intellectualist. Reason has to rule over the body and the passions: a moral man is a balanced person, not dominated by irrational movements but equipped with firm and abiding ethical habits. As to the highest ideal of ethical perfection, it is attained by those who dedicate their life to the search for truth, who, like Aristotle, never stop undertaking new investigations in order to disclose the universe, not only in its immediate causes but in its ultimate explanation. On the basis of self-knowledge and self-love man is spontaneously oriented toward the full development of his being; in this way he participates in the universal love of the cosmos toward the Supreme Perfection.

78. Philoponus, *In Nicom. Isagogen*, I, 1 (*De philosophia*, fr. 8).
79. Philoponus, *In Nicom. Isagogen*, I, 1 (*De philosophia*, fr. 8). Aristotle's physics intends to provide a full explanation of sensible reality: the discipline not only deals with the immediate causes but endeavors also to disclose more fundamental principles. Yet physics does not coincide with metaphysics as it does not investigate being as being.
80. Philoponus, *In Nicom. Isagogen*, I, 1 (*De philosophia*, fr. 8). The highest level of study deals with divine beings, which are beyond the world (ὑπερκόσμια) and totally unchangeable (ἀμετάβλητα παντελῶς).

[10]

MORAL EDUCATION AND METAPHYSICS

ARISTOTLE introduced into Greek thought a notion of God very different from the one accepted in popular belief, yet he was not a complete innovator; in this respect he had some remarkable predecessors. Heraclitus of Ephesus had already maintained the view that the divine being is Logos (Reason), a principle of order, harmony, and proportion: this power is present everywhere, and it constantly shapes an orderly cosmos out of conflicting forces. Through the Logos the opposing powers in the world, which are the origin of a permanent movement, are brought together to a balanced whole.[1] This doctrine is far removed from popular opinions, which accept a great number of divine beings, hardly different from humans except that they are immortal; it was commonly believed in Greek religion that the gods were not indifferent to human affairs; they had their favored worshippers and frequently interfered in events on earth. This kind of religion is radically transformed by the teaching of Heraclitus.

Socrates also was in profound disagreement with his contemporaries about religious matters: he was a deeply religious man, and yet one of the charges against him was that he did not recognize the gods of the city.[2] In a sense this allegation was true: Socrates

---

1. Diels, *Vorsokratiker (Vors.),* Heraclitus, B53.

2. *Apologia,* 24b: θεοὺς οὓς ἡ πόλις νομίζει οὐ νομίζοντα, ἕτερα δὲ δαιμόνια καινά. There can be some doubt about the precise meaning of νομίζω: it may refer to practical worship or to intellectual acceptance. In any case, the charge indicates some disagreement between Socrates and the political society to which he belongs: Socrates does not agree with his fellow-citizens on some religious matters. Everybody had to conform to the religion of the city: it was regarded as harmful if an individual withdrew from the official cult.

did not unreservedly accept the Greek mythological tradition; from a philosophical viewpoint he certainly repudiated this belief. Whether he also refused to participate in the religious ceremonies of his country is less certain. He wanted his whole life and activity to be an act of worship of God: his religious conviction was monotheistic and strongly emphasized divine providence.[3] Socrates believed that God was concerned with man: wrongdoing could not remain unpunished, whereas moral behavior must be rewarded. His religious attitude was a very noble one: he dedicated his whole life to the search for truth and the worship of God.[4] In Plato's philosophy also there is no room for traditional religious belief: there is no polytheism, but belief in one supreme divine principle, which probably coincides with the highest Idea or transcendent Form, the Good.[5] Everything imitates the perfect exemplars and participates in them, so everything partakes in the divine goodness and perfection: when the Demiurge in the *Timaeus* creates the worldsoul he constantly contemplates the transcendent Forms in order to make his work as perfect as possible.[6] Everything is subordinated to the Idea of the Good: everything in the world is penetrated by divine goodness. As to man, he ought to become more and more what he already is, a true image of the divine; man should make himself more and more similar to the divine.[7]

Being dissatisfied with mythological tradition Aristotle endeavors to justify his acceptance of a divine being: this attitude is new; the author wants to rationalize his religious conviction. Nobody ever

3. *Apologia*, 28d–29a; 29c–e: even at the cost of his life Socrates wants to pursue his divine mission. If the Athenians agree to discharge him provided he ceases to continue the activity among his fellow-citizens, he will immediately refuse his liberation; 41c–d.

4. *Apologia*, 30e–31a. Socrates describes his activity as one of full dedication to the city: he never ceases awakening his fellows, he endeavors to persuade them, he also blames them when necessary. He considers himself to be entrusted with a divine call and he believes that it will be difficult to find somebody else to do the same work.

5. *Respublica (Respubl.)*, VI, 508c–509c. The Idea of the Good is comparable to the sun: to whatever is known, it provides not only the possibility of being known but also its being and subsistence, whereas the Good itself is beyond being.

6. *Timaeus*, 28c–29a. The Demiurge, when he made the visible world, created it after the eternal pattern. This teaching follows from the fact that the cosmos is full of beauty and that the Demiurge is good.

7. *Theaetetus*, 176b. Man has to withdraw from this world of evil and imperfection: he ought to become more and more similar to God (ὁμοίωσις θεῷ κατὰ τὸ δυνατόν). This process of assimilation involves justice and holiness together with wisdom.

tried to demonstrate the existence of Apollo or Zeus: these divinities, like mythology as a whole, are linked to a more primitive stage of human interpretation of the universe. Our author attempts to demythologize the religious tradition of his time and to build a kind of rational religion. Like his immediate predecessors he strongly opposes polytheism: in his view there is only one Divine Substance, which is the ultimate final cause of whatever occurs in the universe; everything in the world is oriented toward that supreme perfection.[8] In Aristotle's view it makes no sense to maintain a multiplicity of divine beings: there is one world and the ultimate cause of it must be unique; it cannot be subordinated to another principle, nor can it share its power with another substance equally perfect, since in this case it cannot be Pure Act, without any potency.[9] Aristotle also opposes the frequent interference of gods with human affairs; in his opinion the Divine Substance must be immutable and cannot be involved in the perpetual movement and becoming of the universe. It must be of a different kind from sensible reality and cannot undergo any impact proceeding from what happens on earth[10]: the Divine Substance is not considered to be a kind of administrator of the universe or of human society: in this interpretation, it is immediately involved in the history of the world and this is incompatible with divine perfection.[11] Pure Act is not regarded as the maker of the world: the Stagirite does not ask the most basic philosophical question, namely that of the world's existence or being. The universe has always existed, and its existence is not put into question. Aristotle's Divine Substance has almost no relation to mythological belief; it is the outcome of a truly metaphysical reflection.

8. *Metaphysica (Metaph.)*, XII, 7, 1073a3–5. In Aristotle's view there must be a principle whose substance is Pure Act (XII, 6, 1071b19–20): only such a cause is able to secure the perpetual movement of the world. If that principle were not Pure Act, it would involve potency, and whatever is in potency may not be actualized.

9. *Metaph.*, XII, 8, 1074a35–38. There is only one first principle of movement: it is Pure Act and is not compounded of matter and form. If it included a material component, it would involve some potential aspect.

10. *Metaph.*, XII, 6, 1071b3–11. In Aristotle's view there must be an unmoved eternal substance: if all things were perishable, the whole world would be corruptible; this conclusion could not be accepted since movement and time never started and will never end.

11. *Metaph.*, XII, 9, 1074b33–35. The perfection of a cognitive act depends upon the object that is contemplated: when the object is very lofty, the knowing act will attain the same level. Hence the object of divine knowledge must be the cognitive act itself, which coincides with the Divine Substance.

Let us look more closely at the Aristotelian argument. The starting point is the experience of continuous change that occurs in the
sensible world: the ceaseless movement of the heavenly bodies, the
coming to be and passing away of living beings, the alternation of
seasons, the local, qualitative, and quantitative changes that constantly take place in sensible things. In Aristotle's view these changes
are not an illusion; the author does not agree with the teaching of
Eleatic philosophers claiming that real change is impossible because
things can never become what they are not.[12] According to the
Stagirite change is real; it belongs to the very nature of the sensible
world. In order to explain this instability, the author has recourse
to the notion of potency. Things are more than what they are at a
particular moment: they are in potency to what they are not but
may become. Of course, this potency is not unlimited: it is confined
within the structure of each being; every being has its specific
nature and can never evolve beyond the frontiers of this natural
endowment. Moreover, potency in Aristotle is a passive capacity:
things cannot by themselves bring about their changes and development; they are stimulated by other beings, which possess in act
what they cause. In the sensible world things constantly act upon
each other and produce changes according to the proper capacities
of the beings involved.[13] The notion of potency is an intermediary
between being and nonbeing: against Parmenides Aristotle maintains that beings may have the possibility of becoming what they
are not at a particular time.

Hence the question whether this process of interaction may be
pursued indefinitely, without arriving at a first cause that is not
present in this concatenation. In other words, is it possible that the
world is composed of beings that are all potential to some extent?

12. Diels, *Vors.*, Parmenides, B6: with respect to being, one can only declare and
think that it is; in other words, there cannot be a multiplicity of beings or change.
In both cases a contradiction is implied: if there are many beings, one of them *is not*
the other; so one declares of being that it is not. If there is change, a being becomes
what it *is not*. The same objection obtains. Consequently being is immutable and
one.

13. G. Verbeke, *The Meaning of Potency in Aristotle*, p.59–61. In Stoic philosophy
the notion of seminal reason is more active and dynamic than the Aristotelian
potency: the potency of a particular being is limited; it depends upon its essential
structure. Yet each potency can only be actualized from without. A seminal reason
already contains from the beginning all the elements of its future evolution. In a
sense there is nothing new: what is displayed in the course of time was already there.

According to Aristotle it is necessary to accept a first cause that is Pure Act[14]: all subordinated causes are dependent upon superior causes in the very exercise of their activity. If all causes were subordinate and dependent, their activity could never be adequately explained: the whole of subordinate and dependent causes must be of the same nature as its components. Consequently it refers to something different, to a first cause that does not depend on a superior principle: this cause, being without potency, is at the origin of the becoming taking place in the universe.[15]

The first cause represents the highest degree of perfection, as there is no potential aspect in it: it is not inserted into the continuous development of the universe; it is unchangeable and independent of any other being. And yet it is the final end to which all other beings strive, not only humans but irrational animals, plants, and inanimate things. The whole universe is animated by an internal dynamism that orients it toward the supreme good, and yet this goal will never be attained[16]; the changeable things of the world will always remain mutable and imperfect; man also will remain part of the universal evolution and will never reach the level of Pure Act. Nevertheless, this dynamism is not in vain, since things can attain a limited perfection corresponding to their proper structure. The striving toward the good is always present in the universe, and so the world never passes away; it is not disaggregated but goes on existing without end. According to Aristotle the first principle moves the universe, not, however, as an efficient, but as a final cause: the author declares that Pure Act is an object of love.[17]

14. *Metaph.*, XII, 6, 1071b17–26: ἐνδέχεται γὰρ τὸ δυνάμει ὂν μὴ εἶναι. A fundamental question asked by Aristotle is whether potency is prior to act: beings constantly pass from potency to act. Yet in an Aristotelian perspective this transition is only possible through the causal influence of an act. Moreover, what is in potency may not be actualized. Hence from an ontological viewpoint act must be prior to potency.

15. *Metaph.*, XII, 7, 1072a23–26. The first cause moves without being moved: if it were moved, it would be dependent and could not be Pure Act. Hence it moves not as an efficient cause but as a final one.

16. *Metaph.*, XII, 7, 1072b3: κινεῖ δὲ ὡς ἐρώμενον. The first principle moves as an object of love. The term used is not φιλούμενον: friendship is something different, as a friend is another self.

17. *Metaph.*, XII, 7, 1072a26–28. In this context Aristotle uses the term βουλητόν, which indicates a spontaneous tendency toward the good. Its meaning is different from what is chosen after a careful consideration and deliberation. The first goodness and beauty are objects of a spontaneous striving.

Everything in the cosmos tends toward this final goal, and this aspiration is like a universal love: in the case of man, this love is a conscious and freely accepted inclination. Moral conduct concretely fulfills the dynamic orientation toward the good: if man becomes more perfect as a result of his virtuous conduct, he moves nearer to Pure Act and enhances his resemblance to the Divine Substance. On the contrary, when his behavior is not in conformity with ethical standards, he inevitably moves further away from the supreme perfection. In this sense conscious love of the Divine Substance is an incentive to moral conduct. The question as to whether Pure Act is also a moral being may arise; the answer depends, of course, upon the meaning attributed to "moral being." Obviously there is in God no internal conflict between reason and passions: in the case of humans, ethical conduct is mainly concerned with establishing a harmonious relation between thought and irrational movements. Such a conflict does not occur in Pure Act: it would be incompatible with divine simplicity.[18] The first substance is not a compounded being; it is purely spiritual: like the transcendent Ideas of Plato, Pure Act is simple and immutable. A compounded being depends upon the elements that enter into its structure, whereas the Divine Substance is entirely independent. Nevertheless Pure Act represents the supreme good: consequently it must be the ideal of moral life, a permanent and perfect intellectual contemplation. In God this contemplation is never hampered by irrational forces and propensities: it is perfect in all respects.[19]

But what is the object of such contemplation? It certainly cannot be the world: Pure Act does not know the cosmos; at least it does not grasp it directly. Since it does not produce the world, it is not the creator of the universe.[20] What is the origin of the world? Aristotle maintains that the universe has existed always; it is not the

18. *Metaph.*, XII, 7, 1072b28–35. The First Substance is simple, uncompounded, and in act: if it were compounded, it could not be the first principle; unity is prior to any form of multiplicity. The first principle is good and desirable by itself (δι' αὐτὸ αἱρετόν): again if it were desirable as a result of something else, it could not be the highest cause.

19. *Metaph.*, XII, 9, 1074b33–35. God contemplates himself as he represents the most perfect object that may be known. In the case of Pure Act self-knowledge constitutes the highest level of activity.

20. According to Aquinas, God knows the world without any kind of passivity: being the creative cause of whatever exists, God is conscious of the object of his activity without needing impressions proceeding from created reality.

work of a creator, who originated the various kinds of beings. In Plato's philosophy sensible things are in their existence dependent upon transcendent Forms, and ultimately upon the highest Form, the Idea of the Good. In the *Timaeus* the Demiurge is presented as a craftsman who, contemplating the transcendent Forms, shapes the world as an imitation of these perfect patterns.[21] In Plato's view the Idea of the Good is the source of all lower beings, and of sensible things. Apparently Aristotle did not formulate this most fundamental metaphysical question, which refers to the very existence of things. In Greek prephilosophical thought there are various kinds of cosmogonies; they deal with the coming to be of the world and are the result of a spontaneous extrapolation. The world is compounded by beings that come to be and pass away: it was a widespread popular belief that the cosmos also had come to be and had been produced by some higher powers.[22] Quite understandably Aristotle repudiates this mythological belief on philosophical grounds: if the universe had come to be, time also would have a beginning; it would have started together with the universe. This phenomenon, however, is impossible: how could time ever start? If it started, what was there before it began?[23] In speaking of a "before" we imply the existence of time; if one accepts a beginning of time, he inevitably enters into contradiction. The present instant is always located between a before and an after: the envisaged first moment implies a before. So there is no beginning of time as there is no coming to be of the universe.[24] Of course, the metaphysical question

21. *Timaeus*, 28c–29a; 29d–30c. The Demiurge made the world as perfect as possible: criticizing an ancient religious tradition, Plato states that the Demiurge, being good, is never moved by any kind of jealousy.

22. Hesiod, *Theogony*, 116–122. According to Hesiod the first thing that came to be was open space (χάος) as a kind of all-embracing receptacle. Then follow successively Earth and Eros: the latter is called the most beautiful among immortal gods, yet it curbs the mind and thoughtful decisions in the hearts of divinities and humans.

23. *Metaph.*, XII, 6, 1071b6–10. Aristotle teaches that movement can never start: if it started, there ought to be a first movement. Yet this so-called first movement could not be the first: it could not come to be without a preceding movement or change, and so on, indefinitely.

24. *Physica*, VIII, 1, 251a10–28. Time could never have come to be: if one supposes that there was a beginning of time, he has to explain how the situation was "before" that beginning. This question already implies the existence of time. According to the metaphysical doctrine of Thomas Aquinas, the question itself ought to be repudiated: if time has been created by God, there is no "before" with respect to the beginning of time, since divine creation is beyond time. Cf. *In octo libros Physicorum*

still remains: how should one explain the very existence of the universe? If the world does not depend upon a cause, it must exist by itself. This conclusion, however, is impossible: things are constantly in movement; there is a continuous transition from potency to act; things come to be and pass away. Even if this process never started, it must be explained by referring to a higher cause, which is the origin not only of movement but also of being. A whole of potential beings cannot exist by itself; it cannot be self-sufficient.[25] In his inquiry Aristotle confines himself to the level of becoming; he does not properly deal with the more basic question of existence.

In any case, the Divine Substance does not originate the universe and does not know it: if it grasped it, it would be dependent upon material reality. The Supreme Act would be compelled to observe the world, to encounter it and receive impressions supplying information about things. That is clearly impossible: Pure Act is not passive; it is not in potency toward the world. Besides, the perfection of a cognitive act is related to the dignity of the object that is known, since knowing is regarded as a process of assimilation. If the object known belongs to the level of material things, the degree of perfection of the act will be low; on the contrary, if the object is very noble, the knowing act will also belong to a higher level. Hence we have to conclude that the First Substance does not contemplate the universe: Aristotle's God is not providence; he is not directly concerned with the world or with humans.[26] Is this attitude one of indifference? In Aristotle's view it is not: it would be indifference if the First Substance knew the world and men without being concerned with them. In fact, Pure Act could not be informed of the vicissitudes of human life, since it is not the creative principle of the universe. Being, however, the final cause of man and world,

---

Aristotelis expositio, VIII, 1.2, n.987: "Ostensum est autem supra quod productio totius esse a causa prima essendi, non est motus, sive ponatur quod haec rerum emanatio sit ab aeterno, sive non."

25. Aristotle strongly emphasizes the priority of act to potency: what is potential cannot by itself pass to act (*Metaph.,* XII, 6, 1071b23–26). In a sense, however, potency is prior to act: each movement is a transition from potency to act. But from an ontological viewpoint act must be prior to potency.

26. *Metaph.,* VII, 9, 1074b21–33. According to Aristotle divine contemplation is constantly oriented toward the most divine and noble object. Hence divine knowledge is not directed to the sensible world: this material reality is not created by the First Substance; so the Divine Act cannot know it without being passive.

it must have some indirect knowledge of them, insofar as it is present to itself.[27]

In dealing with the self-knowledge of the Divine Substance, Aristotle uses a very condensed expression: God thinks his own thinking (νόησις νοήσεως).[28] He stresses the fact that divine knowing is purely intellectual and spiritual. As to the object of knowledge, it is an act, namely the act of thinking. As the envisaged substance is Pure Act, it must be immutable. This characteristic is also present in divine knowledge: the object, namely thinking, remains the same. But thinking also must have an object: how can the object of thinking ever be the act of thinking? Moreover, the act of thinking implies a subject: there is always someone who thinks. In Aristotle's view the Divine Substance thinks its own pure actuality and is always present to itself.[29] What the author has in mind is the purely actual character of divine thinking without intending to deny that thinking implies a subject as well as an object. Knowing itself, the first principle cannot ignore that it is the final cause of the universe. In this way the Divine Substance must possess at least some indirect knowledge of the universe. The self-knowledge of God implies to some extent the knowledge of the world. This issue, however, remains unspecified: it is not settled by a formal teaching; it can only be regarded as an implicit doctrine. Does the First Substance love itself? The author declares that it moves the universe as an object of love.[30] The world loves the first principle, as all things love the good: we may suppose that the Divine Substance, knowing

27. *Metaph.*, XII, 7, 1072b3. According to Aristotle thinking is not a movement; it is rather a coming to rest (ἠρέμησις) or a halting (ἐπίστασις) (*De Anima*, I, 3, 407a32–34).

28. *Metaph.*, XII, 9, 1074b34–35. Aristotle clearly wants to avoid any passivity or imperfection in divine knowledge: this knowledge is reduced to self-consciousness; it is not the contemplation of something else but the awareness of an act that remains identical to itself.

29. *Metaph.*, XII, 9, 1075a3–5. Aristotle refers only to the act of thinking without mentioning an object or a subject. Of course, in Pure Act there is no multiplicity: the act of knowing coincides with its subject and its object. In other words, the act of knowing is not really distinct from the subject that knows and the object that is known. With regard to the Divine Substance Aristotle tries to avoid any kind of composition.

30. ὡς ἐρώμενον (*Metaph.*, XII, 7, 1072b3). God moves the world as a final cause. Does he move himself? Certainly not, since he is an unmoved and immutable mover. God is not the final cause of himself. Yet he constantly contemplates himself, and in this sense he always wills his own perfection: divine thinking must be penetrated by willing.

itself, also loves its own perfection. When Aristotle wonders whether friendship between God and man is possible, he replies that the level of perfection is very different: friendship based on resemblance between the two friends is in this case not possible, and yet the author does not exclude such a relationship, which he calls a friendship according to some superiority, one of the friends being notably more perfect than the other.[31]

Since the First Substance of Aristotle does not directly cognize the world or human individuals, quite understandably the author declares in the *Eudemian Ethics* that God is not a ruler issuing commandments: practical wisdom commands in view of the divine being that is the final cause of the universe.[32] Moral life is a conscious and free striving toward the highest good that coincides with Pure Act. In Kant's moral philosophy God is the foundation of an unconditional ethical obligation, which derives from the divine will: it is the duty of man to fulfill the will of God; if he does not, he will be punished.[33] This perspective is not present in Aristotle's ethics: a duty imposed on man by a divine ruler does not make sense if God does not directly know each human individual; how could he ever reward or punish anybody? The ethical doctrine of our author is not concentrated on the idea of an obligation imposed upon man by a higher being: what is at the heart of his teaching is the notion of goodness. Like all beings in the universe, man naturally tends toward the good; if he consciously and voluntarily assumes this spontaneous orientation, he will be a moral individual.[34] Will man

31. *Eudemian Ethics (Eth. Eud.)*, VII, 4, 1239a17–19. People want to be friends with others who are superior to them: in this case, they gain both friendship and superiority. In Aristotle's view a friend is another self: to have a noble friend is to lift oneself to the level of the other.

32. *Eth. Eud.*, VIII, 3, 1249b14–16. Aristotle stresses the fact that the Divine Substance is not in need of anything. In his view, if God issued commandments, it would mean that he needs something that he intends to get with the help of others. According to the Stagirite moral wisdom commands in view of contemplation.

33. E. Kant, *Critique de la Raison pratique*, trad. F. Picavet, Introduction de F. Alquié, Paris, 1943, p. VI. According to Alquié, Kant opposed the Pietist movement: "Ce que le piétisme attribuait à Dieu, Kant l'attribue à notre raison et à notre liberté. Cherchant en l'homme seul le principe de la moralité, il explique par la dualité humaine ce que le piétisme considérait comme la marque d'une radicale transcendence." This interpretation is too radical: in Kant's ethical treatise the idea of God still plays an important part: God guarantees the synthesis of virtue and happiness.

34. In Aristotle's view moral action consists not only in doing what is good but in accomplishing it because it is good (*Eth. Nic.*, VI, 5, 1140b6–7). The intention of

be punished if his conduct is not in conformity with the ideal of ethical life? In a sense yes; but the punishment will not be inflicted by some higher power; it will result from the conduct itself. If a man does not behave morally, he will never attain happiness, which coincides with true human perfection. He will be a victim of his own weakness. A remuneration after death is clearly excluded, since human soul is not considered to be immortal. There is a kind of immanent justice according to which each individual earns the fruits of his behavior: unlike Plato, Aristotle does not mention a final trial or a divine judge. Each individual history has its own course, leading to the outcome to which it is oriented, perfection and happiness or imperfection and unhappiness. The main concern of Aristotle is to show that man is the author of his own destiny: it is not settled by fate nor by any higher power, not even by the Divine Substance. Are there no moral commandments in Aristotle's view? There certainly are, but they do not spring from a divine ruler, they are formulated by man himself, since they are the laws of political society. In a democratic community all free citizens are involved in formulating and approving laws, which are the embodiment of a moral ideal.[35] As has been explained before, these rules have to be compulsory, particularly with respect to young people: they are an indispensable condition of moral education.[36] Moral commandments are necessary, but man himself is the author of his ethical rules. Of course, those who do not behave in conformity with the laws will be punished by the authority.[37] Does God sanction

---

the agent is one of the components of a moral action. After Aristotle the importance of the intention was especially emphasized by the Stoic philosophers. A human agent could not and should not change the cosmos or the course of history: his possibilities are reduced to the internal acceptance or refusal of the events of life and the history of the world. In this framework the internal attitude of an agent is a primordial factor in moral behavior.

35. *Eth. Nic.*, X, 9, 1180a1–5. In Aristotle's opinion laws are indispensable not only for young people but for everybody: the author is quite conscious of the fact that the great majority of humans more readily obey constraint than reason; they are more deeply influenced by the threat of punishment than by the radiation of the good. Not all constitutions are equally adapted to various kinds of populations: the choice of a particular constitution cannot be made without taking into account the kind of population for which it is intended (*Politica*, IV, 2, 1289b17–20).

36. *Eth. Nic.*, X, 9, 1180a21–22. According to Aristotle, laws are rational rules that spring from practical wisdom and moral insight.

37. *Eth. Nic.*, X, 9, 1180a5–12. Aristotle is severe toward those who do not behave in conformity with legal prescriptions: immoral people who constantly are in search of pleasure should be chastised like irrational animals; as to those who are incorrigible, they should be totally excluded.

the authority of the state? Not in Aristotle's view: each political community is the result of a human initiative; people come together and live together for their well-being; the laws play an important part in such a community, indicating the way in which its members should live in order to reach their goal. If people do not conform to the rules, they will be punished twice: first by the responsible authority and also by the immanent justice implied in all ethical ruling.

According to Plato the supreme norm of moral conduct is a transcendent and immutable Form, the Idea of the Good, which represents the highest level in the hierarchy of Forms: this Idea is far beyond the instability of the sensible world; it is not inserted into the continuous becoming and change of material beings, and yet it is regarded as the norm of all ethical behaving. The Idea of the Good does not participate in any higher form; all other forms are subordinated to this supreme level of perfection and participate in it. The highest Good dominates the transcendent realm of forms and also dominates the sensible world, which is only a shadowy reflection of its perfection. Man, too, has to behave in conformity with this supreme norm: through his moral conduct he will come closer and closer to this ideal; he will gradually become more similar to the highest good.[38] In Plato's thought the Idea of the Good probably represents a philosophical interpretation of the Supreme Being, rather than the Demiurge, it most likely coincides with God. In this ethical teaching God occupies a central position: moral conduct is an imitation of the Supreme Good and a participation in its perfection. Of course, sensible reality, too, participates in the perfection of the transcendent Forms, but in the case of man this participation is of a special character distinguished from that of other beings. In a sense man consciously and freely determines his degree of imitation and participation. Man is able to raise himself

38. This moral teaching should be interpreted within the framework of his meta-physical doctrine: the sensible world participates in the transcendent perfection of the ideal Forms. It is an imitation of these immutable patterns; it has something in common (κοινωνία) with the paradigms of the higher world. The Demiurge made the sensible world as perfect as possible: when he created it, he contemplated the eternal Forms. In the field of moral conduct the same central notions are present: a moral man is one who contemplates the Ideas of justice, of courage, of temperance, of wisdom and tries to imitate them, to participate in their perfection, and to be more and more akin to them. Moral life becomes a conscious and deliberate imitation of transcendent exemplars.

to the contemplation of the Forms: in view of this goal he has to submit his irrational propensities to the ruling of the mind.[39] Some similarity between the knowing subject and the cognized object is always required: if an individual becomes more similar to the higher Forms, he will be able to grasp them better, and seizing them more adequately he will enhance his degree of resemblance to them. In Plato's view, as in Aristotle's, God does not issue any commandments: the goal of human life is to become as akin as possible to the divine perfection. And yet there is a noticeable difference between the two teachings: in Aristotle's philosophy Pure Act is the final cause of the universe, not its efficient principle, whereas in Plato's doctrine God is the inexhaustible source and origin of all perfection.[40] The notion of participation is quite central in this regard: the goodness of man is a participation in the divine goodness; God communicates his perfection to human beings, who by their moral behavior endeavor to become more and more similar to him. This notion of participation is not present in Aristotle's doctrine.

As we already know, the Stagirite does not agree with Plato on this subject: generally speaking, he repudiates the whole theory of transcendent Forms, which in his view are a useless duplication of sensible reality. The higher Forms correspond to what exists in the sensible world, but they are more perfect: on both levels the same beings occur; their degree of perfection, however, is different.[41] Plato wanted to explain how it is possible to know something that is more perfect than what is found in sensible reality, for example, a perfect triangle. Therefore, he invented the world of Ideas, which

39. *Phaedrus*, 247b–248b. According to this mythical narrative human souls dominated by irrational impulses and forces are unable to lift themselves to the contemplation of true reality; as long as they remain in this condition, they cannot obtain access to the plane of truth (τὸ ἀληθείας πεδίον).

40. *Respubl.*, VI, 509a–b. In Plato's view the Good is beyond being as it is the principle and source of all being. This doctrine probably stems from a fundamental insight, present also in Aristotle: all beings strive toward the good. Hence one may be tempted to conclude that the good is beyond being, since it is an object of desire in all beings. In the teaching of Plotinus, the Good coincides with the One; on the level of the Intellect, the second hypostasis, there is already some multiplicity. So the Good is considered to be the highest principle of whatever exists. This doctrine represents a basic ontological optimism.

41. *Metaph.*, I, 9, 990a34–b8. The intention of Plato is certainly not merely to add some beings to those he wants to explain: in his view the imperfect realities of the sensible world cannot exist without being dependent on some higher beings.

are perfect patterns of what exists in our material world. Aristotle did not need these transcendent Forms: in his view man is able to understand intelligible objects through the activity of a creative principle, which transforms sensible data into thinkable objects.[42] With respect to moral behavior, Aristotle firmly opposes Plato's view that a transcendent Idea can be the norm of ethical conduct; in his opinion the Idea of the Good cannot be put into practice, nor can it be conquered: it is neither πρακτόν nor κτητόν.[43] As a matter of fact, all Ideas belong to a higher level, not to the field of human action; the Idea of the Good is not realized by moral conduct, nor is it ever acquired by an individual. This Idea always remains at the transcendent level to which it belongs: the good that man has in view is one that he is able to achieve by means of his ethical activity. The Supreme Goodness is far from concrete human preoccupations and concerns. Can this Idea of the Good ever help somebody to discover what is truly valuable in the concrete circumstances of life? Aristotle's answer is negative: all sciences endeavor to attain some good, something beneficial, and they all are indifferent to this transcendent norm, because it cannot be helpful in searching for what is truly valuable in a particular situation. Man constantly moves from one situation to another and cannot refrain from acting in a certain way: the contemplation of an ideal Form, however, is unable to contribute in any manner to a justified decision.[44]

Moreover, if the Idea of the good is considered to be the only

---

42. *De anima*, III, 5, 430a14–17. How could sensible objects become intelligible? The answer of Aristotle refers to the active intellect (ποιητικόν). In Plato's teaching sensible objects are not made intelligible: through recollection man is able to grasp intelligible notions.

43. *Eth. Eud.*, I, 8, 1218a38–b8; *Eth. Nic.*, I, 6, 1097a33–35. Aristotle's criticism is a fundamental one: ethical philosophy deals with human behavior as a way leading to happiness. The ideal Forms of Plato are unchangeable: they cannot be realized by human action. Plato would certainly agree with Aristotle's viewpoint: in his opinion the Ideas are only patterns, models that man should contemplate in order to be guided and helped in his conduct. The Idea of the Good cannot be achieved by human action, yet man has to know it in relation to his own behavior.

44. *Eth. Eud.*, I, 8, 1217b26–1218a1. In order to be able to discover what is truly good man cannot be helped by contemplating an immutable Idea: what he needs is practical wisdom, which is to be gradually acquired on the basis of experience and moral behavior. Cf. G. Verbeke, *La critique des Idées dans l'Ethique Eudémienne*, in: *Untersuchungen zur Eudemischen Ethik*, herausg. P. Moraux und Dieter Harlfinger, Berlin, 1971, p.146–148.

good that is in and by itself, then this Form must be totally empty; it cannot possess any concrete content. In this context the author tries to uncover the proper meaning of the supreme Form proposed by Plato: this notion is very general and cannot guide an agent in his search for what is valuable in particular circumstances. On the contrary, if one believes that there are many things that are good in themselves, such as honor, practical wisdom, and pleasure, then all these things must have something in common. Whereas the definitions of these goods are different, they do not coincide, so the notion of the good is not univocal.[45] Hence the study of this idea cannot be achieved by one single science; there is no common factor or element that may be found in all concrete values. The concept of good possesses a variety of meanings; it may be stated in as many ways as the notion of being: instead of being univocal, it is analogous.[46] According to Plato moral behavior is essentially an imitation of transcendent paradigms. Although Aristotle rejects the Theory of Ideas, he does not repudiate the notion of imitation in his ethical doctrine. In his *Poetics* the author states: "Imitation is natural to man from childhood, one of his advantages over the lower animals being this, that he is the most imitative creature in the world, and learns at first by imitation. And it is also natural for all to delight in works of imitation."[47] In this context the Stagirite mainly deals with poetry, painting, and sculpture, but there is no doubt that imitation also plays a considerable role in moral education. However, the exemplar is not a transcendent Form, such as justice or courage, but a concrete person, the *spoudaios,* who embodies in his life the ideal of ethical behavior. In his definition of virtue Aristotle refers to the judgment of a moral person: virtue always aims at the mean with

45. *Eth. Eud.*, I, 8, 1218a2–15. In Plato's view the transcendent Forms are unchangeable, so the Idea of the Good never changes nor passes away: it always remains what it is. Aristotle criticizes this viewpoint: what is white only one day is not less white than what has the same quality for several days. What is eternally good is not more good than what possesses this quality for a limited time. The criticism of Aristotle is not to the point: the Idea is essentially good and is supratemporal; it is not part of the becoming of sensible reality.

46. *Eth. Eud.*, I, 8, 1217b27–36. According to Plato, there is only one Idea of the Good; it is the highest principle and the source of whatever exists. Aristotle rejects this teaching because the notion of the good is not univocal.

47. *Poetica*, 4, 1448b5–9. Aristotle, *Rhetoric*, transl. by W. Rhys Roberts; *Poetics*, transl. by I. Bywater, New York, 1954, p.226–227; cf. *Rhetorica (Rhet.)*, I, 11, 1371b4–10.

respect to us; this mean is to be settled by reason and more specifically in the way in which a wise man would determine it.[48] The
spoudaios is a kind of concrete norm in ethical conduct: his moral
judgments are right.[49] Yet there may be a difficulty: if the judgment
of a wise man is considered to be a norm of moral behavior, is there
not a danger of relativism and subjectivism? As the circumstances
of life constantly change and are always complex, a person may pay
more attention to one aspect rather than to another and so come to
his own insight, which may differ from that of somebody else. In
Aristotle's teaching, however, there is in the first place an objective
analysis of man's nature leading to the conclusion that the highest
perfection of a human being consists in an enduring and capable
intellectual contemplation.[50] Moreover, moral education is secured
by the laws of a political community: these laws are not merely the
work of an individual; they are regarded as the expression of the
ethical sense of a society. They are constantly adapted and improved:
insofar as these laws are the result of an agreement among the
people of a political group, their objectivity and truth value are
guaranteed.[51] In this way the danger of subjectivism is avoided: the
judgment of a wise man will conform to the structure of human
nature as well as to the moral insights of a political community. In
any case, each agent has to discover in the various circumstances of
life what is truly good in view of the development of his being. The
basis of this reflection should be an adequate knowledge of human
nature: man ought to know himself in order to be able to discern
what is really beneficial for his perfection. Humans are complex
beings, having various components and powers. With respect to
moral behavior, it is necessary not only to know which are these
constituents but also to realize their relative function and value. In
Aristotle's view man is a unitary being, but the mind is much more
important than the body; it represents the proper worth of a human
individual.[52] An adequate valuation of the various components of a

48. *Eth. Nic.*, II, 6, 1106b36–1107a2.
49. *Eth. Nic.*, III, 4, 1113a25–33.
50. *Eth. Nic.*, I, 7, 1097b22–1098a20.
51. *Eth. Nic.*, X, 9, 1180a34–1180b3.
52. *Eth. Nic.*, X, 7, 1178a2–3. The interpretation of R.-A. Gauthier concerning the
anthropological view present in the Aristotelian ethics is too radical; Aristotle never
declares in an unqualified way, "L'homme, c'est l'esprit." (Cf. *La morale d'Aristote*,
Paris, 1958, p.17–45).

human person is decisive in view of moral activity: if intellectual contemplation is considered to be the highest level of moral perfection, this doctrine quite obviously is based on a particular theory of man. This general concept, however, is to be embodied into concrete moral judgments that guide an agent in the various situations of life. These assessments are far from being infallible: it is not at all easy for an agent to formulate right judgments in the changing and complex circumstances of life.[53] Instead of discerning the truly good, man may easily go astray and be diverted by what appears to be valuable without being really good. A man who does not dominate his irrational impulses and who has little experience of moral practice will hardly be able to elaborate right ethical judgments.[54] Aristotle attaches much importance to the virtue of prudence or practical wisdom; it is an intellectual virtue, but it is closely connected with moral behavior: it guides man in his decisions and choices. The result of moral behavior is that irrational propensities are subdued to reason and do not disturb the normal activity of the mind. On the other hand, practice also is necessary: as in the case of a craftsman, experience of moral conduct promotes right intuitions in the changing situations of life.[55] A merely theoretical knowledge of man is not sufficient for guiding our ethical conduct: something more is required, namely practice and experience of moral life.

In Aristotle's teaching ethical action should not be justified from without but finds its justification within itself: a moral agent achieves what is good because it is good. No further justification is required, and if there were any, it would even jeopardize the ethical quality of the action.[56] According to Kant a moral individual accomplishes his duty because it is his duty, not to gain any reward or to avoid punishment. Aristotle also distinguishes moral action from

---

53. *Eth. Nic.*, II, 2, 1104a5–10. A moral judgment concerning concrete situations of life cannot be fully accurate; the degree of *akribeia* is rather low. The highest degree of scientific knowledge is related to what is immutable, uncompounded, and necessary.

54. *Eth. Nic.*, VI, 12, 1144a34–36. Dealing with concrete conduct in various circumstances of life, a moral judgment will easily deviate under the influence of passions and emotions.

55. *Eth. Nic.*, VI, 11, 1143b11–14.

56. *Eth. Nic.*, II, 4, 1105a32: προαιρούμενος δι' αὐτά. In Aristotle's perspective a good action cannot be chosen because it is commanded by God, since the Divine Substance does not issue commandments.

technical activity: the latter is oriented toward some external arte-
fact, a house or clothes. This activity does not find its meaning
within itself: what is really intended is the product. The Stagirite
distinguishes making (ποίησις) and acting (πρᾶξις) and states that
in the field of moral behavior good action is the end (εὐπραξία
τέλος).[57] This statement means that there is no further goal: what
the moral agent intends is behaving well. He does not pursue a
reward, he does not search for honor as an outcome of his conduct,
he does not endeavor to fulfill the will of God. A virtuous agent
does not utilize his moral conduct to attain some other goal; it is a
requirement of truly ethical behavior that the subject only intends
to behave well. A virtuous individual intends his own perfection or
happiness: in Aristotle's view a truly moral action springs from a
firm and abiding disposition; it should proceed from a virtuous
habit.[58] The reason is quite obvious: a moral individual is one who
through his constant efforts has acquired enduring ethical habits.
Virtue as a steady disposition contributes to the moral quality of an
action: ethical virtues are connected with each other; the presence
of one virtue implies to some extent the presence of the others. If
a particular action proceeds from an abiding habit, it means that
the whole past of the agent is involved, since he has acquired this
disposition through former conduct; and since one particular virtue
is not an independent entity, but is linked to other similar dispositions, an action that, for example, proceeds from the virtue of
temperance, refers to an agent who in all respects has acquired a
moral attitude. From an ethical viewpoint the conduct of such an
individual will be more perfect than an action springing from an
agent who does not have enduring moral dispositions.

  Aristotle acknowledges that it is not easy to attain the ideal of
moral life; it is really difficult to be a virtuous man[59]: to acquire the

  57. *Eth. Nic.*, II, 4, 1105b5–10; VI, 5, 1140b6–7. In the case of moral actions what
matters is not some practical result but the accomplishment of the action itself.
  58. *Eth. Nic.*, II, 4, 1105a32–33. A moral habit is the result of many previous actions;
it is the expression of an enduring attitude of a person. If an individual acts according
to an abiding disposition, his action will more properly belong to him, because it is
the outcome of many previous decisions (*Rhet.*, I, 10, 1369b16–20; I, 11, 1370a6–7).
  59. *Eth. Nic.*, II, 9, 1109a24. It is not easy to be a moral individual because the
conflict between reason and irrational forces is constantly present in man. Being
threatened and influenced by those irrational impulses, man cannot easily discover
or perform what is right: virtue always aims at the mean between two extremes. In
this respect, there is the twofold difficulty of disclosing it and of accomplishing it.

various virtuous habits demands constant effort and endeavor, since everybody bears within himself an internal conflict between reason and passions. These passions always remain irrational impulses, which may oppose the ruling of reason; they may also considerably contribute to a dynamic evolution of human existence.[60] To submit the passions to the rational faculty and to effect an internal and permanent balance are heavy tasks. Aristotle does not ask where this internal conflict comes from: Why is man not naturally balanced? Why is internal harmony the result of a moral struggle? In Christian teaching this lack of balance and harmony is attributed to former faults: everybody is the outcome of a past that he did not freely choose; each generation receives from the previous ones a weight of faults that have been committed. In Aristotle's ethics this question is not formulated: the author starts from the evidence of the conflict present in all humans and attempts to find a solution. Nevertheless, the attitude of the Greek Master is rather optimistic: he believes that many humans participate in moral behavior that may be practiced by all those who are capable of virtuous activity.[61] This teaching is to be understood in the light of Aristotle's teleological doctrine: everything in the universe naturally strives toward the good; on the other hand, nature achieves its goal in the majority of cases; hence we may conclude that the majority of humans participate in moral life. Some activities, however, are not taken into account when the development of moral life is at issue, for example, the exercise of vulgar arts. What the author has in mind is the performance of activities intending only to earn some success: individuals who are engaged in these arts are moved only by ambition.[62] As to manual labor, it cannot promote the perfection of a person: such work is harmful to the body and does not favor the development of the mind.[63] Finally, the author also excludes small commerce: it happens

60. *Eth. Nic.*, I, 13, 1102b23–25. According to Aristotle, the conflict between reason and irrational tendencies exists within the soul. The degree of this opposition is different from one individual to another, according to their level of moral conduct. Moral life is a constant attempt to submit irrational impulses to the guidance of reason.

61. *Eth. Nic.*, I, 9, 1099b18–20. In a sense this viewpoint is optimistic: as a matter of fact, it fits into the framework of Aristotle's universal teleology.

62. *Eth. Eud.*, I, 4, 1215a29–30.

63. *Eth. Eud.*, I, 4, 1215a30–31. In this context Aristotle is dealing with various kinds of life and their relation to happiness. The author believes that a life devoted to manual labor cannot contribute to happiness. This doctrine is coherent with

that farmers and craftsmen bring their wares to the market without immediately finding a buyer; then they have recourse to an interme- diary who promises to sell the goods. Such small commerce is not approved by our author, who regards it as an immoral search for profit.[64] Plato also is very negative regarding commerce, which he considers to be a source of evils.

In his inquiry about the most perfect moral behavior Aristotle mainly deals with three ways of life: philosophical life, which is dedicated to the search for knowledge and truth; political life, which is devoted to the rule of the state; and hedonistic life, which is concerned with the pursuit of pleasure.[65] In the framework of his humanism the author proposes a way of life that is a mixture of the three forms: in this perspective an individual will dedicate himself to contemplation; he will endeavor to practice moral virtue and will also enjoy the pleasure that accompanies the exercise of all these activities. In this way an agent will fully actualize his potentialities and come closer to the perfection of Pure Act.

Which is now the role played by the Divine Being in this ethical theory? The most important factor is that God is considered to be the final cause of the universe and of humans; being Pure Act, God represents the highest level of perfection; he is the supreme good. Each individual is naturally oriented to this highest ideal: the ten- dency toward the perfect good is not an acquired habit; it belongs to the nature of a human being. In the case of humans, this tendency is conscious and freely accepted: although the distance between God and man is very considerable, some kind of friendship between the two is still possible. Man is naturally inclined to the love of God, and the First Substance, knowing itself, must possess some indirect awareness of the beings tending to its perfection.[66] In Aristotle's

---

Aristotle's concept of man: the main component of a human being is the mind; manual labor as such does not promote or favor the development of intellectual activity.

64. *Eth. Eud.*, I, 4, 1215a31–32.

65. *Eth. Eud.*, I, 4, 1215b1–5.

66. θεοφιλέστατος (*Eth. Nic.*, X, 8, 1179a22–24; a30). The term is puzzling: if God does not have any knowledge of the world, how can a man be called especially dear to God? By dedicating himself to intellectual speculation an individual comes as close as possible to the divine perfection. Moreover, knowing himself, God must know that he is the final end to which everything in the universe strives and tends: divine knowledge would be imperfect if the Divine Substance did not realize it was the ultimate end of everything, including human beings.

view the love of God is the very basis of moral life; it must be acknowledged that man will never join the divine perfection and his love will never be fully satisfied. Nevertheless this great love will not remain useless: it will provide him with a limited perfection derived from his moral conduct. If man acts morally, he does not pursue any reward: he accomplishes what is good without any other goal. The performance of what is good finds its reward in itself as it guarantees man's happiness: nothing else is to be sought. In Aristotle's teaching human perfection is viewed and described according to the divine pattern: what is suggested is, of course, not self-contemplation but a constant and competent exercise of intellective activity. In this respect the object of intellectual intuition is important: knowledge of the ultimate cause of the universe will be the highest intellectual activity.[67] Metaphysical understanding is not only scientific knowledge; it constitutes the highest degree of philosophical understanding. Contemplation of God is the most perfect knowing of which man is capable: an individual who dedicates himself to this intuition is in a special way a friend of God (θεοφιλέστατος). In this sense God is truly present in Aristotle's ethics: he is present as an object of natural and conscious love; he is present also as a pattern of human perfection and as an object of metaphysical contemplation.[68]

Aristotle's ethical doctrine represents an earthly humanism in which the notion of God still occupies a central position as the ultimate model of human perfection.

67. *Eth. Eud.*, VIII, 3, 1249b16–23. Whatever favors the contemplation of God is regarded as the most valuable in life; on the contrary, whatever hampers this activity is considered to be evil. In this way the supreme criterion for evaluating human actions or choices is their contribution to the contemplation of the divine perfection.

68. In the context of the *Eudemian Ethics* Aristotle mentions not only the contemplation of God but the worship of the Divine Being (*Eth. Eud.*, VIII, 3, 1249b20).

[11]

ETHICS AND LOGIC

THE subject treated in this chapter is closely connected with the general issue of our research, namely moral education. The goal of such education is quite obvious: it is to prepare people to behave morally in the various circumstances of life and so to secure their true perfection and happiness. In this perspective education implies two aspects, an intellectual one and a practical: the first requirement in view of ethical conduct concerns knowledge; the agent has to know what is truly good in the changing situations of life. As has been already expounded, there are two kinds of ethical knowledge: the first one is general and deals with the perfection of all human beings, with what is really good for all humans. This kind of understanding is found in a treatise of moral philosophy, for example the *Nicomachean Ethics* of Aristotle: in this writing the author largely relies on the Greek cultural tradition, critically analyzed and transformed in the light of his own philosophical teaching.[1] This reflection is mainly based on a concept of man, as it results from Aristotle's own investigation: the author stresses the natural orientation of man toward the good. This tendency, however, is not a distinctive feature of human beings; it belongs to everything in the universe.[2] What is proper to man is the way in which this orientation is actualized: as shown previously, in the case of human

---

1. At the beginning of his *Nicomachean Ethics* (*Eth. Nic.*) Aristotle mentions three ways of life that are to be taken into account in a study of human happiness: some people believe that happiness actually depends upon pleasure; others are convinced that it is linked to political activity and power; still others are persuaded that it is derived from philosophical speculation. These opinions are found in Greek society at the time of the Stagirite (I, 5, 1095b14–1096a10): the author knows that there is no agreement on this subject. A philosophical inquiry into the matter is necessary.

2. *Eth. Nic.*, I, 1, 1094a2–3: Aristotle's universal teleology is the basis of his moral teaching.

beings the tendency is at once conscious and freely accepted.[3] This basic approach qualifies the nature of moral education in Aristotle: it is not something imposed from without, it is not a constraint nor a compulsion urged upon man, it is rather the development of a natural craving or aspiration. Everybody wants to lead a moral life, to attain his full perfection and happiness. If some compulsion is approved by our author, it is intended to make people conscious of what they really want.[4] Aristotle's ethical investigation is a constant effort to disclose the true nature of human happiness. In his view this goal can only be reached through the practice of the moral virtues and particularly through the full development of the mind, in other words, through contemplation.

In addition to this general reflection there is also practical wisdom, which is concerned with the changing conditions of life in which man has to make choices and to act. This kind of ethical knowledge is rather different from the former: it is directly concerned with a particular way of behaving in concrete circumstances.[5] It is not sufficient to know the goal of human existence, if one wants to disclose what is to be done in a given situation: this is the result of a deliberation, not simply a conclusion from some universal principles. Of course, a choice or a decision may be expressed in the form of a practical syllogism: this, however, is only a synthetic way of formulating a process of deliberation.[6] A decision is rather the outcome of a reflection in which many factors are to be assessed in order to come to a global intuition and appreciation. Since it is impossible to enumerate and valuate all possible factors involved,

3. In Aristotle's view man does not deliberate about the ends but only about possible means leading to the ends (*Eth. Nic.*, III, 3, 1112b11–15). Man naturally tends toward the good; there is no matter of deliberation in this respect. Yet the kind of good intended by a concrete individual depends upon his moral conduct (*Eth. Nic.*, III, 5, 1114a31–b5).

4. It has already been explained that laws of a political community ought to be compulsory: they are a kind of reason proceeding from practical wisdom and intellectual insight (*Eth. Nic.*, X, 9, 1180a21–22).

5. *Eth. Nic.*, II, 2, 1104a3–10. Cf. T. Tracy, *Physiological Theory and the Doctrine of the Mean in Plato and Aristotle*, p.223: "Consequently Aristotle's discussion in these works is directed toward the practical guidance of human action rather than toward a profound scientific analysis of it, i.e. he is speaking πρακτικῶς rather than φυσικῶς."

6. *Eth. Nic.*, VII, 3, 1146b35–1147a10. In this context Aristotle speaks of practical syllogisms in order to explain that in some cases man does what he knows to be wrong: the author does not maintain that man deliberates proceeding in a syllogistic way.

the agent has to rely on his moral experience and practice.[7] If he has moral virtues, his insights will not be misled through emotional impulses: Aristotle believes that ethical intuitions of virtuous individuals will normally be right.[8] With regard to moral education, it is of primary importance to enable people to elaborate right ethical judgments in the changing situations of life.

In the context of moral education, however, knowledge is not sufficient: there is not always a correspondence between knowing and doing. It is extremely important to know what is right and what is wrong, not only in general but in view of particular actions. Nevertheless a disagreement may occur between some kinds of knowing and human conduct: somebody may realize in general or in a habitual way that a concrete action is wrong and yet perform it.[9] For this reason education requires some practical training: through it abiding virtuous habits are acquired and right moral intuitions are developed. For this indispensable training Aristotle mainly relies on the laws of a political society: in his view laws are the expression of a moral ideal. They are not the work of one author or of a society at a particular period: they are to be constantly revised and improved in the course of time; thus they are the work of many previous generations. They have to secure the moral education of young people; they also have to guarantee the ethical behavior of all members of a political community.[10] Laws should be compulsory, but Aristotle is convinced that after some practice and experience of moral conduct people will freely make their conduct conform to the regulations of the laws.

7. *Eth. Nic.*, VI, 8, 1142a14–15; VI, 11, 1143b13–14: Practical wisdom springs from experience related to various ways of behaving and their consequences. The link between particular ways of behaving and their results cannot be disclosed on theoretical grounds: in Aristotle's opinion they are gradually uncovered in the experience of daily life. Young people cannot possess this experience as it requires a long period of time (VI, 8, 1142a15–16: πλῆθος γὰρ χρόνου).

8. *Eth. Nic.*, VI, 12, 1144a34–36. It is impossible to possess moral wisdom without being a virtuous person.

9. *Eth. Nic.*, VII, 3, 1147a10–18. Those who act under the impact of passions are comparable to people who are asleep, or drunk, or mentally ill: they are prevented from using the knowledge they possess. In Aristotle's view if somebody knows a particular act to be wrong, he cannot accomplish it unless this knowledge be concealed in some way.

10. Moral education is to be achieved in a political community: in this respect Aristotle does not mention the responsibility of parents or that of schoolteachers (*Politica*, VIII, 1, 1337a11–32). The unity of a political community is secured by the fact that all the members participate in the same ethical values expressed in laws.

In Plato's view laws ought to be introduced by some comment explaining their meaning and making them agreeable: the author wants to persuade all citizens and to show that the legal regulations intend to promote their true benefit.[11] According to Aristotle, too, education involves some rhetorical element: it is not merely a question of compulsion but also of persuasion. In a political society rhetoric plays a considerable part: laws should be formulated, they ought to be accepted, and finally they are to be kept. In all these stages rhetoric may be influential and play a decisive role in the moral education of the people.[12] In Aristotle's opinion there is a close connection between rhetoric and ethics, as there is one between rhetoric and dialectic: the author considers rhetoric an offshoot of dialectic and also of moral studies.[13] It stems from dialectic since persuasive arguments do not belong to the area of scientific knowledge; it is linked to ethics and politics because persuasion plays a central role in a democratic society, in which important decisions are to be taken by the citizens.[14] Whether it be in matters of legislation or in forensic affairs the art of persuasion is of primary relevance. According to our author there are three modes of persuasion employing spoken words. The first factor is related to the personal character of the speaker: the speech ought to be delivered in such a way that it appears to be credible; this is regarded as the most effective means of persuasion. Another factor is the state of mind of those who listen: the audience should be put into an emotional condition that favors agreement with the orator. The final factor is the argument itself, which should be built and developed in such a manner that it induces the audience to accept the viewpoint of the speaker.[15] The method of rhetoric is clearly different from the one used in demonstrative science: Aristotle elaborates two

---

11. *Leges*, IV, 719e–723e. Laws should not simply be imposed by force; it is desirable that they include a preface in which their meaning is explained. Plato endeavors to persuade people of the utility of legal prescriptions: in this way laws are presented in the same way as musical compositions or discourses, which also are preceded by an exordium.

12. *Eth. Nic.*, I, 2, 1094a28–b7; X, 9, 1181a14–19; *Rhetorica* (*Rhet.*), I, 2, 1356a25: rhetoric is considered to be a ramification of dialectics and moral philosophy. It is connected with moral philosophy because it deals with human characters, with virtues and emotions. All these factors are important in a process of persuasion.

13. *Rhet.*, I, 2, 1356a25–27.

14. *Rhet.*, I, 2, 1357a30–33; I, 4, 1359b8–18.

15. *Rhet.*, I, 2, 1356a1–13.

means of persuasion. The first proceeds from particular examples: by showing some concrete cases, which represent a particular way of behaving, the audience may be persuaded that the conduct under consideration leads to the proposed consequences. With the help of examples someone may show that Dionysius' wanting a guard indicates an inclination to tyranny. This arguing is far from being demonstrative: it is based on a similarity of conduct: by comparing the conduct of Dionysius to that of some tyrants, one might convincingly show that he wants tyrannical power.[16] Another way of proceeding is based on enthymemes: in this method of argument some deductions are drawn from probabilities and indications; such an indication may be fever, which shows that somebody is ill, or a woman's producing milk, indicating that she has given birth to a child.[17]

As I have mentioned already, Aristotle also points to some factor related to the character of people involved in the process. First of all, the character of the speaker is an important element in an attempt to persuade: if the speaker is apprehended as a reliable person, his arguing will be much more convincing than that of an individual who can hardly be trusted.[18] What is at stake is not only the reasoning itself but the whole personality of the speaker. Moreover, it is not a matter of indifference in this respect whether an orator is gifted with practical wisdom or not: in Aristotle's view moral insight results from ethical behavior and experience. People will listen more eagerly to somebody who has proved to possess right intuitions and good experience than to somebody whose moral conduct is not reliable.[19] The attitude of the audience is also an important factor in the

16. *Analytica Posteriora (Anal. Post.)*, I, 1, 71a9–11; *Rhet.*, I, 2, 1356b2–18. According to Aristotle, the use of examples is a kind of rhetorical induction: it starts from particular cases and tries to formulate some general conclusions. Of course, what is at issue is by no means a complete enumeration: a conclusion is drawn from a limited number of examples.

17. *Rhet.*, I, 2, 1357a34–b25. If somebody states that learned people are just, because Socrates was learned and just, he may easily be refuted. The question is whether Socrates was just because he was learned. On the contrary, if somebody declares that an individual is ill because he has fever, he cannot be refuted: in this case, the indication is a τεκμήριον.

18. *Rhet.*, I, 2, 1356a4–13. Aristotle stresses the fact that the way of speaking should persuade the audience that the individual concerned is a reliable person. The impression of being reliable ought to be produced by the speaker himself: it should not be based on some other information but result διὰ τοῦ λόγου.

19. *Eth. Nic.*, VI, 5, 1140a25–31. A wise man is able to deliberate rightly: in this respect, a distinction is made between particular goals and the end of life; in this latter case, what is at issue is the full development and perfection of human life.

process of persuasion: on some occasions an orator will arouse emotions in order to convince people. Emotions, such as pity, or love, or envy, or hatred, have a strong influence on human conduct. Here again rhetoric is not only concerned with developing rational arguments: intending to persuade people, it also uses the power of emotions.[20]

From all these considerations it follows that moral education is a complex process, involving many aspects. It requires an adequate knowledge of human individuals, which discloses the true perfection and happiness of man. It further involves practical wisdom and ethical training, which are the origin of enduring moral habits. This development is only possible in a political community with good laws. Such laws ought to be compulsive, but at the same time people should be prepared to accept and to conform to them readily. In this respect, rhetorical argument has a vital function. In the light of these factors we have to study the relationship between ethics and logic.[21]

Aristotle is considered to be the discoverer of logic: in the evolution of ancient thought he was the first who composed treatises on this matter, which have been translated and explained in university teaching up to the present day. Aristotle's logic has deeply influenced Western science: the author was very much concerned with shaping a pattern of scientific thought clearly distinguished from common opinions and prescientific beliefs. In ancient philosophy there are mainly two systems of logic, the Aristotelian and the Stoic: the latter is founded on an empiricist theory of knowledge; according to the Stoics there is no passage from empirical data to universal notions. There is no process of abstraction, which can be the origin of universal knowledge, but only a passage from concrete experience to its verbal expression (*lekton*).[22] In this perspective one

20. *Rhet.*, I, 2, 1356a14–19. In Aristotle's view opinions and convictions depend not only on intellectual insights but very often on emotional dispositions. A speaker may appeal to such emotions in order to reach the goal he pursues, namely to persuade people of a particular viewpoint.

21. In his rhetorical treatise Aristotle mentions various kinds of laws. Some of them are particular; they have been settled by a political community and are applied to its members. These laws are normally written but may also be unwritten. Next to these particular rules the author also refers to a universal law, which is the law of nature: it was in the name of this universal law that Antigone buried her brother Polyneices (*Rhet.*, I, 13, 1373b4–13).

22. G. Verbeke, *La philosophie du signe chez les Stoïciens*, in: *Les Stoïciens et leur logique*, Paris, 1978, p.401–424. In Stoic philosophy human soul is a particle of the

reaches the level of intellectual knowing when the object of sensible experience is translated into speech: in the development of knowledge the transition from mere experience to verbal expression is considered to be a decisive step. Language is a privilege of man and is closely connected with reason; if a sensation is expressed in language, it is transformed and lifted to a truly human level. It is no longer a merely sensitive contact with the world: it is introduced into a rational elaboration, by which the subject is able to clarify it for himself and for other people. So language and thinking are intimately related.[23] Stoic logic cannot be based on universal concepts; it is a logic of propositions. The argument is founded on relations between propositions; for example, in the case of a hypothetical sentence, it is possible to build an argument by affirming the antecedent proposition or denying the consequence; in the first case the consequence will be affirmed in the conclusion; in the second the antecedent will be denied.[24] One should not forget, however, that according to the Stoic theory it is possible to go beyond empirical data and to grasp objects that are not sensible, such as the soul and God. This doctrine is maintained since some sensible things may be a sign of an object that is not perceivable. And yet according to the Stoics whatever is active is corporeal, including the soul and God; these objects, however, are not perceivable. As to time, space, the void, and the expressible, they are considered to be incorporeal, but they are not active.[25]

Aristotelian logic is not empiricist: the author recognizes much importance in sensible experience, which is always the starting point of the cognitive process, even when self-knowledge is concerned.

Divine Logos, present everywhere: this logos, however, does not create universal notions out of sensible experience. Sensible images are made expressible, so human language directly refers to the concrete images of the senses.

23. G. Verbeke, *La philosophie du signe*, p.404. In the context of Stoic thought language plays an important part: words are signs; they refer to something else, even to something that is not perceptible. The meaning of words is not conventional but natural.

24. G. Verbeke, *La philosophie du signe*, p.405–407. The Stoic way of arguing is closely connected with their view on the coherence of the universe: all parts of the cosmos are linked to each other; they are like parts of a living organism. Through this universal coherence, divination is possible.

25. G. Verbeke, *La philosophie du signe*, p.409–410. Since the whole cosmos is permeated by the Divine Logos, everything in the world is meaningful; it is penetrated by meaning. So one part of the world may refer to some other part; it may also refer to something that is not perceivable.

As a matter of fact, the data of sensible perception are radically transformed under the impact of the active intellect: they are made immaterial, intelligible, and universal.[26] The whole logic of our author is grounded on universal concepts: in order to know whether a predicate may be attributed to a subject, Aristotle compares the two terms to a third one, which is called the *medium term:* by means of this comparison the author is able to determine the relation that is sought. The medium term occurs twice in the premises and is not present in the conclusion; it is further required that the medium term be understood at least once in a universal way. When this term can be understood in two distinct ways, the clarification of the relation between the extreme terms is not secured.[27] Moreover, it is necessary in Aristotle's logic that a distinction be made between essential characteristics and nonessential features; among these latter a further distinction should be introduced between proper characteristics, which are invariably linked to the essence, and features that are merely accidental. In this way Aristotle is able to build his logic on the distinction between universal and necessary predicates and the category of contingent and accidental attributes.[28]

But how did Aristotle arrive at the discovery of this discipline? Talking of scientific discoveries, the author states that the first step is always the most important: this step decisively determines any further development that is closely related to the initial intuition. After the first step it is not difficult to disclose the solution of other problems and to initiate further progress.[29] In the case of rhetoric and other arts, it was not necessary to discover everything, since these disciplines had already attained considerable progress in the

26. *De anima*, III, 5, 430a15–17. There is a close connection between Aristotle's logic and his theory of knowledge: in this respect, the most important aspect is related to the capacity of the mind to form intelligible objects.

27. *Analytica Priora (Anal. Priora)*, I, 1, 24b27; I, 4, 25b31–34. The concept of the Aristotelian syllogism is quite clear in the first figure, which is immediately based on the *dictum de omni* and the *dictum de nullo*. As to the notion of universal, cf. *Anal. Post.*, I, 4, 73b26–74a4.

28. *Topica*, I, 5, 101b37–102b26. Aristotle's logic is clearly based on his interpretation of real things: in this respect the structure of sentences, involving a subject and different kinds of predicates, is fundamental.

29. *Sophistici Elenchi (Soph. El.)*, I, 34, 183b22–26. At the beginning the starting point of a new discovery does not produce fast progress. Yet it is more profitable than the later development. This starting point is also especially difficult: although it be very powerful and influential, it is very small and not easily grasped. After an initial discovery it becomes much easier to make progress.

past; the most important discoveries had already been made.[30] With respect to logic, however, nothing had been achieved before Aristotle. In the work of Plato some fruitful intuitions that could stimulate the evolution of logic are present, but the Greek thinker never elaborated a systematic treatise on this matter.[31] As to the teaching of rhetoric, the masters did not handle questions of logic. They simply composed discourses in which arguments pro and contra a particular thesis were expounded; the students had to learn by heart the texts prepared by the teacher. According to this method, Aristotle remarks, the process of learning was fast but not adequate. Since it was confined to an exercise of memory, it was not a real education of the mind. Learning should not be reduced to assimilating a body of knowledge; it ought to be primarily a training of the intellect.[32] In the field of rhetoric many ancient works were available, but concerning argumentation there was nothing; everything had to be invented. The author declares that he spent much of his time in exhausting inquiries on logic. He asks everybody to be grateful for what has been found and benevolent with regard to omissions and deficiencies.[33]

Aristotle does not use the term *logic;* when he employs the adjective *logikos,* he actually refers to dialectic, which studies the doctrine of probable argumentations. The term *logic* is found in the writings of Cicero, but here again it means dialectic. Alexander of Aphrodisias is the first who uses the term in the sense of the discipline discovered by Aristotle.[34] As to the Stagirite himself, he has recourse to the term *analytics.* As a matter of fact, analysis plays an important part in logic: the arguments are divided into the various figures of

---

30. *Soph. El.,* I, 34, 183b26–34.

31. *Soph. El.,* I, 34, 183b34–36: ἀλλ' οὐδὲν παντελῶς ὑπῆρχεν. This statement is very radical: what the author has in mind is a systematic treatment of logical questions. In this respect Aristotle did not have any predecessor.

32. *Soph. El.,* I, 34, 183b36–184a8.

33. *Soph. El.,* I, 34, 184a8–b8. Aristotle is convinced that the study of logic is very important, although it is not a part of philosophy. It is important in itself as a study of scientific thought; it is important also with respect to philosophy since it is an indispensable instrument.

34. The term *logic* refers to the Greek term λόγος, which in its original meaning differs from νοῦς; it is rather connected with reasoning, arguing, demonstrating. Among the logical treatises of Aristotle, one deals with the various kinds of predicates, another studies sentences and statements, a third examines the nature of syllogisms, a fourth investigates the specific character of scientific knowledge, a fifth is concerned with dialectical reasoning, and the last with sophistical refutations.

syllogism, whereas syllogisms are composed of several propositions, which in their turn are reduced to some terms. Hence decomposition or analysis fulfills a central function in the study of logic: by showing the constituents of speech and argument the author endeavors to clarify the structure of scientific thought.[35]

In Aristotle's view logic is not an autonomous science among other scientific disciplines; it is rather regarded as a kind of general culture, which everybody wanting to engage in scientific research ought to possess. This discipline allows one to discern for which statements arguments should be demanded and which kinds of arguments are required.[36] For this reason the whole of Aristotle's logical writings are called *organon,* which means instrument. Logic is not a part of philosophy; it is an instrument used by philosophers for making their investigations.

The origin of logic is connected with the usual method of debating: a dialectical syllogism implies the presence of two people, one who asks questions and another who replies. The one who formulates questions knows which goal he intends to reach. He already has in mind the conclusion he wants to reach, and the questions he asks are selected in order to bring his interlocutor to the intended conclusion. As to the premises, they express some considerations that are offered to the interlocutor in view of obtaining his agreement. In fact, the questioner does not start from the premises in order to reach the conclusion: the starting point is rather the conclusion, and from there the debate moves to the premises. The person who replies also knows the conclusion from the beginning, but the questioner proceeds in such a way that the interlocutor, in accepting some premises, is constrained to agree with the conclusion.[37] This way of arguing may be expressed in the form of a syllogism, which perfectly corresponds to its Aristotelian definition.

35. Aristotle does not offer a specific definition of logic. In his view this discipline studies syllogistic arguing, which proceeds from some propositions to show necessary consequences (*Topica,* I, 1, 100a25; *Anal. Priora,* I, 1, 24b18). Logic clearly differs from grammar, psychology, and metaphysics.

36. Instead of being a science, logic is a technical skill: it provides the capacity of reasoning or arguing.

37. Aristotle makes a distinction between a philosophical investigation and a dialectical debate: in this latter case questions are asked in order to lead the respondent to agree to the conclusion (*Topica,* VIII, 1, 155b10–16); cf. P. Moraux, *La joute dialectique d'après le huitième livre des Topiques,* in: *Aristotle on Dialectic: The Topics,* ed. G. E. L. Owen, Oxford, 1968, p.277–311; p.284: "Toutes les questions qu'a

Hence the premises are not sentences incidentally formulated; they are carefully chosen in view of supporting the conclusion. They ought to be convincing and to lead to the intended consequence. The original object of logic is dialectical syllogism or syllogism as it is developed in conversation. In its original form logic was the science that studies a way of arguing embodied in a dialogue in which some people try to persuade others. Logic actually refers to a period when spoken language was more important than written texts; the discovery of logic is linked to living speech and discussion, in which one of the speakers tries to convince the other.[38] In fact, logic examines the components of any discussion: categories, propositions, various forms of arguing, ultimately the structure of science. With regard to the relation between ethics and logic, it is indispensable to know the Aristotelian theory of science: only when the precise nature of scientific knowledge has been uncovered will it be possible to specify which kind of knowledge is actually involved in moral thinking.

In his inquiry on science, Aristotle starts from the topic as it was expounded in the *Meno* of Plato: one of the questions in this dialogue is whether a real increase of human knowledge is possible[39]; everybody will agree that there is a development or evolution of knowledge; at one stage of life an individual may know much more than he knew at a previous period. The problem, however, is not solved thus far, for the nature of this development is to be determined: is there an addition to some former patrimony of knowledge, or is the development rather the organic growth of an initial germ? Or is this development rather the manifestation and actualization of some hidden and sleeping knowledge, which everybody possesses and bears within himself from the very beginning of his existence? In Plato's view there is no real growth of human knowledge: what

---

posées le premier partenaire n'avaient qu'un but: faire admettre par l'autre, sans qu'il soupçonne où on le mène, les prémisses d'un raisonnement d'où découle nécessairement comme conclusion la thèse du questionneur."

38. E. Kapp, *Greek Foundations of Traditional Logic*, New York, 1943. The author convincingly shows how the origin of logic is linked to the practice of discussion and debate.

39. In the framework of the *Meno* the development of human knowledge is treated in connection with the teaching of virtue. The basic issue of the dialogue is the nature of virtue and the possibility of teaching it (*Meno*, 70a). If virtue is a science, it must be possible to teach it: for one who wants to know whether virtue may be taught, it is indispensable to examine its true nature.

man discovers in the course of time is not truly new, because it was not really ignored before he grasped it.[40] When the slave of the *Meno* gradually discovers the right answers to Socrates' questions, he does not add new knowledge to what he already knew; in Plato's view what happened in this dialogue was a process of recollection. Through Socrates' questioning the slave proceeds step by step to the "discovery" of what he already knew.[41] But what is the origin of this inborn knowledge? Since human soul is immortal, it must exist from eternity; it never came to be. Before it was joined to the body, it lived in the world of Ideas and was able to contemplate them directly. But when the soul was united with the body, the knowledge of the transcendent Forms was not annihilated; it remained in the mind as a hidden and unconscious treasure of learning. Through his personal efforts and endeavor, man could, however, recall what he had known formerly.[42] Quite obviously Aristotle does not agree on this doctrine: he decidedly repudiates Plato's teaching on the transcendent Forms; he also rejects the immortality of human soul. Consequently man does not know everything from the beginning of his life, not even in a seminal way: in the course of time a real growth of knowledge is achieved and new knowledge is added to the old. But how is this acquisition of new knowledge possible? In Aristotle's view knowing is an act of a living being; it is a vital or biological process: the object of knowledge is integrated into the organic unity of what has been already assimilated, as in a process of nutrition the new elements must be integrated by the knowing subject. They enter, as it were, into the substance of the knower, into the living organic unity of what the mind already knows.[43]

According to Aristotle there are two ways in which knowledge may develop: from particular objects to universal insights or from universal concepts to particular cases.[44] In Aristotle's logic the induc-

40. According to the *Phaedo* learning is recollection or recalling (*Phaedo*, 72e).
41. *Meno*, 84b–d. The knowledge that the slave bears within his mind is regarded as truly scientific: ἀκριβῶς ἐπιστήσεται περὶ τούτων.
42. *Meno*, 85d–86b.
43. *Anal. Post.*, I, 1, 71a1–11. According to Aristotle any development of knowledge is achieved on the basis of what a subject already knows: new elements of knowledge are integrated into the patrimony that is already present.
44. *Anal. Post.*, I, 18, 81a39–b1. In Aristotle's view all knowledge is derived from demonstration or from induction. In the latter case it proceeds from sensible experience and supplies the principles of demonstration. In this way all knowledge stems from the senses.

tive process is not mainly related to the passage from particular sensible objects to universal intuitions; it rather starts from a full enumeration of species and so arrives at the knowledge of the corresponding genus.[45] What is envisaged by our author is perfect or complete induction: when all species are known, the transition to the generic notion can present no difficulty. In our author's opinion induction is not a proper form of argumentation; it is rather the immediate intuition of a universal notion on the basis of its particular occurrences.[46] In this context Aristotle does not have to face the problem often discussed in modern science of how it is possible to make a transition from the observation of particular facts to the formulation of universal laws. The validity of universal laws, as it has been treated by David Hume, is not examined by Aristotle; modern notions, such as verification or falsification, are not present in his writings. It was not necessary to handle this issue, since induction in his view means essentially the intuition of a universal from its particular instances.[47]

In the deductive process there is a transition from a universal insight to its particular cases. An objection may be raised that all concrete instances are contained within the corresponding universal notion: hence the question whether a transition from a universal concept to its particular instances constitutes an increase of knowledge. In Aristotle's view real progress is achieved in this passage: if someone knows a universal notion, he only potentially grasps the particular instances included in it. So there is a transition from a potential knowing to an actual one and from an intuition that implicitly includes all particular instances to an explicit grasping of these concrete cases. This viewpoint of Aristotle's is clearly based on his interpretation of the universal. Let us take an example in geometry: the sum of the angles in a triangle is equal to the sum of two right angles. One could explain this thesis in a limiting way: the sentence would refer only to those triangles that have been

45. *Anal. Priora*, II, 23, 68b18–29.

46. If the enumeration of the particular instances is not complete, the argument can only produce some belief in a general principle: this principle cannot be regarded as demonstrated (*Aristotle's Prior and Posterior Analytics*, ed. by W. D. Ross, Oxford, 1949. Introduction, p.50).

47. As to rhetorical induction, it has already been treated: it starts from a limited number of examples and tries to persuade an audience that some general rule may be drawn from them.

observed and studied by the person who formulated the theory. In this interpretation a universal is not truly universal: it includes a limited number of cases that have been observed. Aristotle does not understand a universal in this way: in his view the universal includes all triangles, without any exception, not only those that have been examined by a particular subject. But how is it possible to know an object that we have never met or investigated? Quite obviously the Aristotelian view of the universal is founded on the distinction between necessary and accidental characteristics. Human mind possesses the capacity to make this distinction: it is not always easy; it is generally the result of an accurate inquiry and comparative study.[48] Not all necessary features belong to the same level: some are more fundamental than others. Essential features are more basic than properties: the latter are not constituents of the essence, but they necessarily derive from the essential structure. Hence if somebody knows the necessary characteristics of a thing, he knows at once all the instances belonging to the same category. In an Aristotelian syllogism the transition from a universal notion to a particular instance is grounded on the conviction that all beings belonging to one and the same species possess the same essential structure.[49]

It would be erroneous to believe that in Aristotle's theory science is a mainly deductive process: such an interpretation would contradict the author's theory of knowledge. If all intellectual knowledge, even self-consciousness, is founded on sensible experience, scientific insights cannot be deduced from a priori principles. Scientific research must start from immediate data of sensible experience: these data are in a sense intelligible, since in the case of humans sensitive knowing is already permeated by reason. In other words, sensitive knowing is not merely sensitive: a human person is a unity of body and soul, of sensitive and intellective knowledge. So what is given in sensible experience is both clear and obscure: it appears as an irrefutable fact, a certainty, but at the same time it raises many

48. G. Verbeke, *La notion de propriété dans les Topiques,* in: *Aristotle on Dialectic: The Topics,* p.257–276.

49. According to W. D. Ross, there are in Aristotle various levels of scientific knowledge: a science that knows not only facts but also their causes is superior to one that provides merely a collection of facts. When an object is more abstract, the science that deals with it will be on a higher level. Finally among pure sciences a discipline that studies simple entities will be superior to one that investigates complex objects (*Aristotle's Prior and Posterior Analytics,* ed. W. D. Ross. Introduction, p.74).

questions and is a source of problems that require further clarification. What is immediately knowable for us is not what is most knowable in itself: the explanation that is wanted will be found at a higher level of intelligibility.[50] Aristotle is convinced that the building of scientific knowledge is grounded on the immediate intuition of some primary principles, which do not need any further justification. Yet the knowledge of these principles is not merely inborn: it is acquired from experience by means of an inductive process.[51] In this way the author remains faithful to the central idea of his theory of knowledge, which emphasizes the primordial importance of sensible experience.

After these more general considerations on Aristotle's logic we should now face the main question: which kind of knowledge is involved in the author's ethics, is it a truly philosophical and scientific treatment? Scientific knowledge always includes a process of clarification and of rational justification: a scientific discipline is always concerned with the "why" or cause of some observed facts.

It is quite clear that ethical inquiry cannot be located at the level of first philosophy or metaphysics: in Aristotle's view this discipline represents the highest degree of scientific understanding, as it deals with the first cause of the universe.[52] Starting from the endless becoming of sensible reality, it proceeds to a principle that is perfectly intelligible, Pure Act, immaterial and immutable. Although the first cause does not produce the cosmos, it contributes to making it intelligible: without Pure Act the continuous changing of the world cannot be adequately explained.[53] The study of the first principle is reserved to metaphysics, precisely because this discipline endeavors to disclose the supreme cause of whatever occurs in the cosmos.

50. G. Verbeke, *Démarches de la réflexion métaphysique chez Aristote*, in: *Aristote et les Problèmes de méthode*, Louvain-Paris, 1961, p.122–129.

51. *Anal. Post.*, II, 19, 100b3–5. According to Aristotle, universals are present in particular realities in the same way as the intelligible is present in the sensible and the genus in the species. A sensible image may become a universal object: of course, this transformation is only possible under the influence of the active intellect. Yet the process would be impossible if in some way the intelligible were not present in the sensible.

52. *Metaphysica (Metaph.)*, I, 2, 982b7–10.

53. *Physica (Phys.)*, VIII, 5, 256a8–13. Any change is a transition from potency to act: a being can only pass to an act that it already possesses in potency; in other words, the change of a particular thing always remains within certain boundaries, namely the limits of a concrete potency.

After metaphysics comes physics, dealing with the things of the material world, inanimate beings, plants, and animals. It is well known that the author incorporates into physics what we call natural sciences, which are not considered to be separate and independent disciplines: they are an integral part of philosophy. The physics of the Stagirite studies the composition and evolution of material beings and of the heavenly bodies. Investigating the becoming of physical things, the author is not only concerned with the immediate causes of natural phenomena; he attempts to disclose the first cause of all change, the unmoved mover.[54] Yet the physical inquiry is not the highest level of scientific knowledge, because the proper object of this discipline is the material world. Is man also included in physical reality? In a sense yes: the bodily organism certainly belongs to the same level as the organic structure of other animals. Yet Aristotle could not accept that intellectual understanding and free choice are merely physical operations. Although he does not consider human soul immortal, he believes that it transcends physical reality.[55] This viewpoint has a considerable impact on the elaboration of Aristotle's ethical doctrine.

All things of the physical world are included in a process of becoming, but the species remain the same; they are invariable. In this way there is at least some stable element in the ceaseless stream of change. In the field of human conduct the instability is even greater; each action is a unique event, since it is connected with constantly changing circumstances. Each agent has to apply the rules of moral conduct to the particular situations of his life.[56] A concrete moral judgment is extremely complex, since it has to take into account the variable circumstances and is all the time influenced by internal and external factors. The most immediate danger derives from the passions, irrational movements, which are not always sufficiently controlled by reason. If these impulses are not submitted

54. G. Verbeke, *La structure logique de la preuve du Premier Moteur chez Aristote*, in: *Revue philosophique de Louvain*, 46(1948), p.137–160.

55. *De Partibus Animalium (De Part. Anim.)*, I, 1, 641b9. Human soul does not belong to the level of physical reality since it is at the origin of free choices and of universal concepts. In this sense the activity of the soul transcends the material world.

56. The study of human conduct cannot reach a high level of scientific accuracy: it does not deal with an object that is necessary and immutable. On the contrary, each human action has its own physiognomy and is related to the variable circumstances in which it occurs (*Eth. Nic.*, II, 2, 1103a34–1104a5).

to the rational faculty, moral judgment will inevitably be distorted.[57] A moral action is always performed in a particular context: as far as concrete ethical judgments are concerned, they belong to the area of practical wisdom. They are extremely important, but their scientific character is rather limited; science is primarily concerned with what is universal, necessary, and unchangeable.

Nevertheless in his ethical treatise Aristotle attempts to present an ideal of moral life, which is not arbitrary but corresponds to a scientific justification. The object of the inquiry is the true human good, or what is beneficial to the development of man in the various conditions of his life.[58] The author endeavors to show in which manner humans may reach the ultimate goal of their life, how they may attain happiness and actualization of the potencies they bear within themselves. Humans naturally tend toward the good, but it remains always possible to be misled under the influence of irrational impulses, particularly when concrete moral judgments are to be elaborated. What Aristotle aims at is a general treatment of the matter, so he does not deal directly with particular cases but with the human good in general: what is truly good for all human beings.[59] In this respect the author comes to the conclusion that the way leading to happiness is virtuous conduct and that the highest degree of perfection is represented by intellectual or contemplative activity, achieved with capacity and perseverance.[60] This teaching constitutes the essential part of the ethical treatise: the author investigates the general conditions of moral behavior, the way in which virtues are acquired, deliberation and choice; then he examines the various virtues. He further deals with the question of how moral faults are possible. Finally, having studied friendship as an important constituent of moral conduct, he passes to the description of contemplative life.[61] This

57. *Eth. Nic.*, VI, 12, 1144a34–36.

58. Concerning the nature of the truly good there is no agreement between philosophers and ordinary people (*Eth. Nic.*, I, 4, 1095a20–22). Yet Aristotle does not disregard common opinions about this matter: in his ethical treatises he often appeals to Greek tradition and widespread beliefs without accepting them uncritically.

59. As usual, Aristotle starts his inquiry from what is immediately knowable for us (*Eth. Nic.*, I, 4, 1095b3–4). This starting point corresponds to what is given in daily experience: on the basis of a critical analysis the author then tries to attain what is most intelligible in itself.

60. *Eth. Nic.*, I, 7, 1098a16–20.

61. *Eth. Nic.*, X, 7, 1177a12–22. Aristotle's interpretation of happiness is closely linked to his notion of the mind as the center of a human individual.

treatise by Aristotle has been for centuries the pattern of moral philosophy as it was handled in university teaching, especially after the Latin translation of the *Ethics* in the twelfth and thirteenth centuries.

How does Aristotle proceed to justify his moral doctrine? Quite obviously his method is not deductive: the author does not ground his ethics on some first principles known a priori from which particular applications would be deduced. Such a theory would not be in conformity with the author's interpretation of human knowledge, in which special emphasis is put on sensible experience.[62] In the light of this general teaching we must accept that moral insight also is based on experience and develops gradually in connection with moral conduct, not only of each individual but also of society.[63] An essential doctrine of Aristotle's ethics is related to virtue as a mean between two possible extremes, what is too much or too little. According to our author all excesses derive from irrational movements: reason is a factor of measure and balance, whereas passions drive man to unbalanced behavior. This view is present throughout the ethical treatise: a virtuous person acts according to reason and carefully avoids all excesses; his behavior is characterized by harmony and stability.[64] The doctrine regarding the value of the mean has not been invented by Aristotle; it is notably more ancient and dates back to the beginning of Greek thought. The maxim "Nothing too much" is, in fact, the expression of some ancient wisdom urging man to avoid extreme attitudes and to live a balanced existence. In ancient times this rule was connected with religious beliefs about the envy of the gods toward man. The ethical teaching of Aristotle is deeply influenced by prephilosophical opinions present in Greek culture: such opinions are found in literature, mainly in epical and tragical literature; in popular beliefs and religious convictions; in maxims and proverbs; and in various kinds of sayings about life and

---

62. *Eth. Eud.*, I, 6, 1216b3–5. At the beginning of this chapter the author states that he wants to convince by means of rational arguments (διὰ τῶν λόγων) and use observed facts (τοῖς φαινομένοις) as evidence and illustration.

63. *Eth. Nic.*, I, 4, 1095b4–9. A moral man easily grasps the real good of man; he needs no rational justification (οὐδὲν προσδεήσει τοῦ διότι).

64. *Eth. Nic.*, II, 6, 1106a36–b2. Cf. T. Tracy, *Physiological Theory and the Doctrine of the Mean*, Chicago, 1969, p.237: "There Aristotle distinguishes the mean between excess and deficiency as: 1) *absolute* or objective, and this is one and the same for all men, and 2) *relative to us*, which is neither too much nor too little, yet is *not* one and the same for all."

happiness. In his moral treatise Aristotle largely relies on the ethical pattern of his culture and time. Some commentators even maintained that Aristotle confined himself to describing and reproducing the moral ideal of his society.[65] It is true that the author frequently uses prephilosophical opinions, particularly in his ethical works, but these opinions are assimilated in a critical way and are assessed in the light of his philosophical theories.

Prephilosophical views used by Aristotle in his ethical writings are primarily those connected with language.[66] This context does not only include the original meaning of words: linguistic elements mostly date back to a prephilosophical stage of human thought; they originate from people who wanted to communicate with each other in view of the necessities of daily life. In connection with life in society there is a tradition of value language, to which Aristotle frequently appeals: some actions are praised; others are blamed. This way of speaking represents a pattern of judgment and assessment that is common to a cultural group and is transmitted from one generation to another. If such value judgments are very ancient, universally accepted, and permanently present in a cultural tradition, they are regarded by the Stagirite as an important source of truth and insight. The background of this theory is again a teleological interpretation of nature: in Aristotle's teaching nature always strives to the good and does nothing in vain. If a great number of humans permanently agree with each other on important views concerning man's behavior, these opinions ought to be taken seriously; they can hardly be erroneous. For if they were false, the whole doctrine of universal teleology should be questioned: an enduring general misunderstanding by mankind of important matters is incompatible with the natural tendency of all things toward the good. So common opinions in moral matters cannot be overlooked: they are the expression of a common experience, which should not be repudiated. They

65. Cf. J. Burnet, *The Ethics of Aristotle*, London, 1900. Introduction, p. XLIV: "From all this it follows that the starting-point of Politics cannot be anything more than a general truth. . . . And it will be absolutely impossible to lay down universal rules of action."

66. J. D. Monan, *Moral Knowledge and its Methodology in Aristotle*, Oxford, 1968, p.98: "The everyday use of a value-language, therefore, served Aristotle as an unreflected source of truth for the formulation of definitions of good human actions"; p.104: "In defining the moral virtues Aristotle obviously chose the linguistic crystallization of moral experience as object of his reflection."

are to be critically analyzed and assessed in a positive perspective, as a source of moral thinking. In this context there is no metaphysics of value, but there is a philosophical foundation for the worth attributed to common opinions and language.[67]

Finally Aristotle's ethics implies a philosophical anthropology that does not fully agree with the teaching of the *De Anima* on the subject. In this work the author firmly stresses the unity of each human individual: since one of the components is totally undetermined, all specifications spring from the formal constituent, the soul; any kind of psychological dualism is discarded. The anthropology of the ethics is decidedly spiritualistic[68]; the author emphasizes the conflict between reason and passions: moral conduct is mainly reduced to the subordination of the passions to reason. All virtues represent an aspect of this subordination: ethical life is dominated by an ideal of conduct fully conforming to the commandments of reason. The highest ideal of man is understanding, a life that is totally dedicated to contemplation. The doctrine of friendship and its position in ethics also depend upon an implicit concept of man: a friend is another self, and the self is essentially the mind. Hence friendship is a kind of virtue: man must exert constant effort to achieve it.

The ethics of Aristotle is a real philosophical discipline in which the human good or well-being is studied in a rational way: in the author's opinion this good coincides with the actualization of man's capacities and happiness. In order to discover the object of his inquiry, the Stagirite largely relies on the tradition of Greek culture, on popular opinions universally accepted, and on the experience of moral behavior. But the traditional elements are not passively adopted: they are critically judged and adapted to the philosophical anthropology of the author. In this way the ethical teaching of Aristotle relies both on the tradition of Greek culture and on a coherent philosophical system. As to the question whether this

67. J. D. Monan, *Moral Knowledge and Its Methodology in Aristotle*, p.101: "At this precise point, unfortunately, Aristotle's methodology reveals its limits, in the sense that it manifests no fully developed roots, nor indeed does it grow to maturity in any fully developed metaphysic of value."

68. In his essay *La morale d'Aristote*, as I have already mentioned, R. A. Gauthier stresses the spiritualistic character of Aristotle's ethics. In my opinion the author goes too far; what Aristotle says about the mind's being the center of each human individual is more shaded and qualified than it is expounded by Gauthier (p.17–45).

moral research corresponds to the scientific pattern of Aristotle's logic, the reply ought to be specific: it is necessary to make a distinction between general knowledge, as it is expounded in the ethical treatises, and a concrete judgment that is related to a particular action.[69] The first knowledge is not the result of a deductive process; it is a critical reflection on prephilosophical opinions in the light of Aristotle's metaphysical and anthropological doctrine; this knowledge is considered to be scientific, but is represents a lower degree of science than metaphysics or physics, since the object is very complicated and unstable. As to the moral valuation of particular acts, it is still less scientific: this appreciation is mainly the result of ethical experience and practice; it requires of the agent a good deal of practical wisdom and intuition.

In the light of these considerations, moral education is quite indispensable, although man is by nature an ethical being. Moreover, this education involves two aspects, which are closely linked to each other, teaching and training. Knowing what is good is not sufficient for doing it; on the other hand, it is necessary to behave morally in order to grasp what is truly good. This is the paradox that Aristotle endeavors to face and to solve in his ethical teaching.

69. *Eth. Nic.*, II, 2, 1103b34–1104a11. Aristotle compares a moral agent to a physician or a ship pilot: both have to take into account the changing circumstances in which they happen to be. Every act is singular and cannot be performed according to unchangeable rules.

CONCLUSION

A RISTOTLE's doctrine on moral education deeply influenced the Western world: it was already assimilated by early Christian writers in a period when Platonism and Stoicism were the prevailing philosophical trends. At the end of the fourth century some elements of Aristotle's teaching were incorporated by Nemesius of Emesa in his famous treatise *De natura hominis,* which was translated into Latin in the Middle Ages by Alfanus of Salerno and by Burgundio of Pisa. Important issues of Aristotle's ethical doctrine were also present in the *De fide orthodoxa* of John Damascene. As to the ethical writings of Aristotle, they were gradually translated into Latin and in the first part of the thirteenth century Robert Grosseteste elaborated a full translation of not only the *Nicomachean Ethics* but also of several Greek commentaries on this work. Some of these commentaries had been written by Christians, whereas others were composed by non-Christians, such as Aspasius. The Latin versions were broadly used in university teaching and a large number of medieval commentaries on these texts have been preserved. True, this ethical teaching of the Stagirite was adapted to the Christian message: it was regarded as compatible with religious belief. This adaptation was not a formal criticism of the Greek Master; it was rather a flexible interpretation in accordance with Christian theology.

In this way some basic Aristotelian ideas were assimilated by Western thought and became gradually part of its tradition. Let us briefly point to some of these fundamental notions:

(i) Man is considered to be by nature a moral animal. Ethical behavior, far from being a kind of compulsion or constraint imposed from without, corresponds to the true nature of human beings: it is the only way that guarantees their full development and real perfection. In recent times some authors have tried to show that ethical efforts derive from a hypocritical and inauthentic attitude characteristic of individuals who want to be different from what they actually are. In Aristotle's view moral education is an attempt to make people more fully what they already are, as they are endowed with rational insight, able to understand and elucidate ethical values.

(ii) Despite their natural disposition, all humans need an appropriate moral education. All are gifted with reason and speech, they possess a kind of natural understanding of ethical values, and yet they badly want moral education, since they are the theatre of a permanent conflict. In his internal world man experiences a constant struggle between rational understanding and irrational propensities and emotions. In Aristotle's opinion these inclinations should not be suppressed or eradicated, but they ought to be ruled and governed by reason. Passions may be a source of excesses and uncontrolled attitudes, whereas reason is a principle of balance and harmony. Aristotle adopts in his ethics the ancient Greek maxim "Nothing too much." A moral man is regarded as a balanced individual; he is not a prey of irrational impulses. The mean is located between two extremes; it preserves man from excessive positions.

(iii) Moral education implies not only learning but also training. It certainly includes some intellectual preparation: moral knowledge is not inborn; it must be acquired, for it is indispensable. It is quite necessary to know what is right and good in order to implement it. Such knowledge is both general and particular: everybody needs to grasp what is right in the changeable circumstances of life. But it is not enough to know what is good: man does not automatically perform what he realizes to be right. He ought to be trained by achieving right actions, so that he may gradually acquire abiding habits in the various fields of moral behavior. One becomes a moral person in the same way as people become skillful craftsmen.

(iv) In Aristotle's view there are no moral commandments issued by a divine being. Yet the ethical teaching of the Stagirite is not atheistic. The author maintains the existence of a Divine Substance, Pure Act, who is not regarded, however, as providence: the Divine Being is not directly concerned with the world. Nevertheless Aristotle declares that some moral constraint is necessary: in terms of ethical education, laws in a political society should be compulsory, particularly with regard to young people, who are quite unable to discover independently what is right in the complex situations of life, since they lack moral experience and practice. Therefore, a particular way of behaving ought to be imposed upon them in a compulsory way; when they will have more experience and more ethical practice, they will realize that the imposed conduct was the right one and will become able to judge by themselves.

(v) A moral man is endowed with practical wisdom, which enables him to formulate right ethical judgments in the most variable situations of life. This ability is not innate; it must be acquired. It is not merely a matter of learning; in this area there is a close connection between knowledge and practice. Only a moral individual is able to discover what is right in the changing conditions of life, since he will not be misled by passions and emotions. If irrational impulses are ruled by reason, ethical judgment will not be subverted. Practical wisdom is an intellectual virtue, but it is also the outcome of previous virtuous conduct.

(vi) Man is also by nature a political being: in this respect language plays an important part. Through articulate language humans are able to clarify basic ethical notions, such as justice; this clarification implies that such notions are analyzed, the various components are disclosed, definitions are elaborated. Other animals may also utter some sounds, but they are not gifted with articulate language: they can only indicate something to other animals, but they are unable to clarify moral insights. Man is also able to communicate his intuitions to his fellows: in this way it is possible to reach a common agreement on fundamental ethical issues to be expressed in appropriate laws. Aristotle believes that outside a political community moral education is impossible.

(vii) In Aristotle's view the whole universe tends toward the good; it ultimately strives toward the Supreme Good, which is Pure Act. In the case of man, this tendency is not merely spontaneous and instinctive: it is conscious and free; it develops into a personal choice. Insofar as he endeavors to attain the good, man is not an exception in the universe: what is proper to humans is the way in which they achieve this universal movement. Moral education is an attempt to lift a spontaneous inclination to the level of a deliberate and personal choice, constantly carried out in the concrete circumstances of life. Each individual is responsible for his destiny, which is a limited participation in true perfection and happiness.

(viii) A moral theory is far from being the result of an arbitrary choice; it is not a kind of personal option based on emotional factors and subjective preferences. In Aristotle's opinion an ethical treatise is part of a philosophical system, along with the philosophy of being, the theory of knowledge, philosophical anthropology, and the philosophical study of the physical universe. Although an ethical inquiry has its own characteristics and method, it is a truly philosophical investigation, intimately connected with other philosophical disciplines. Since it deals with the perfection of man and true happiness, it cannot be elaborated without appealing to some anthropological and metaphysical viewpoints. According to the Stagirite's theory of science, the study of ethics is on a lower level than metaphysics and physics: its object is far from being uncompounded, immutable, and necessary. On the contrary, it deals with human behavior in complex and changing circumstances and tries to discover what is beneficial to the full development of man's capacities. As the end that is pursued is human perfection and happiness, ethical teaching is not the most scientific, but it is the most relevant of all philosophical disciplines.

All these ideas have been largely incorporated into Western thought. Aristotle was deeply concerned with moral education: in our time his insights may still contribute to the ethical formation of responsible persons. Everybody needs this balanced and stable moral equipment.

INDEX

N